Safety and Disaster Management

Published by
Saurabh Publishing House

SAFETY AND DISASTER MANAGEMENT

Prof. O.P. Dutta

Publishing House
4735/22, Prakash Deep Building,
Ansari Road, Daryaganj,
New Delhi-110002

Published by :
SAURABH PUBLISHING HOUSE

Distributed by :
LOTUS PRESS PUBLISHERS & DISTRIBUTORS
Unit No. 220, Second Floor, 4735/22, Prakash Deep Building,
Ansari Road, Daryaganj, New Delhi - 110002
Ph : 011-23280047, 32903912, 098118-38000
E-mail : lotus_press@sify.com

Saurabh Publishing is an imprint of
Lotus Press Publishers & Distributors

Safety and Disaster Management

ISBN : 978-93-83045-08-2 (H/B)

Printed at : Bharat Offset Works, Delhi

Preface

A natural disaster is any natural phenomenon which causes such widespread human material or environmental losses that the stricken community cannot recover without external assistance Examples include earthquakes, cyclones, storms, floods, drought, bush forest fire, avalanches etc. At regular but unpredictable intervals, people around the world are affected by natural hazards. These may be caused by climate (*e.g.*, drought, flood, cyclone) geology (*e.g.*, earthquake, volcano, tidal wave, landslide) the environment (*e.g.*, pollution, deforestation, desertification, pest infestation) or combinations of these. Hazards become disasters when people's homes and livelihoods are destroyed. Poverty, population pressures and environmental degradation mean that increasing numbers of people are vulnerable to natural hazards. Increasing population and urbanisation is increasing the world's exposure to natural hazards, especially in coastal areas (with greater exposure to floods, cyclones and tidal waves). Although worldwide disaster occurrence seems to follow an upward trend, some of their impacts on societies (victims and economic damages) have not increased as preparedness has improved.

A natural disaster is the effect of a natural hazard (*e.g.*, flood, tornado, volcano eruption, earthquake, or landslide) that affects the environment and leads to financial, environmental and human losses. The resulting loss depends on the capacity of the population to support or resist the disaster and their resilience. This understanding is concentrated in the formulation: "disasters occur when hazards meet vulnerability." A natural hazard will hence never result in a natural disaster in areas without vulnerability, *e.g.*, strong earthquakes in uninhabited areas. The term natural has consequently been disputed because the events simply are not hazards or disasters without human involvement. With the tropical climate and unstable landforms, coupled with high population density, poverty, illiteracy and lack of adequate infrastructure, India is one of the most vulnerable developing countries to suffer very often from various natural disasters, namely drought, flood, cyclone, earthquake, landslide, forest fire, hail storm, locust, volcanic eruption, etc. Which strike causing a devastating impact on human life, economy and environment?

This book deals with the topics of—*Introduction to Disaster and Its Types; Disaster and Risk Management Programme; Earthquakes and Seismology Designs; Disaster Preparedness and Management; Disaster Management and Global Development; Social Responsibility and Disaster Management; Earthquake Resistance Buildings; Disaster Prevention and Management; Emergency Management and Prepardness; Disaster Management and Policy Framework; Building Assessment and Strengthening; Risk Transfer Mechanisms; National Disaster Management Framework; Coalition Activities and Disaster;* etc.

I hope that students and those in the education field will find it useful for academic and competitive examinations. I owe a deep sense of gratitude to my publisher for materializing my present endeavour.

Prof. O.P. Dutta

Contents

1

Introduction to Disaster and Its Types

A disaster is the product of a hazard such as earthquake, flood or windstorm coinciding with a vulnerable situation which might include communities, cities or villages. There are two main components in this definition: hazard and vulnerability. Without vulnerability or hazard there is no disaster. A disaster occurs when hazards and vulnerability meet. See the figure along with underlying issues under each.

There are several important characteristics that make Disasters different from Accidents. The loss of a sole income earner in a car crash may be a disaster to a family, but only an accident to the community. Variables such as Causes, Frequency, Duration of the Impact, Speed of Onset, Scope of the Impact, Destructive Potential, Human Vulnerability etc., determine the difference.

Vulnerability

Vulnerability is defined as "The extent to which a community, structure, service, or geographic area is likely to be damaged or disrupted by the impact of particular hazard, on account of their nature, construction and proximity to hazardous terrain or a disaster prone area."

Now take *for example,* a house built from cane and thatch and the other a brick building. The house built from cane and thatch that can be blown in a tropical cyclone are more vulnerable to the wind than a brick building. A badly constructed brick building is more likely to disintegrate with the violent ground shaking of an earthquake than cane or thatch hut and is more vulnerable to earthquake hazard.

Social and economic conditions also determine the vulnerability of a society to an extent. It has been observed that human losses in disasters in developing countries like India tend to be high when compared to developed countries where material losses pre-dominate.

Risk

Risk is a measure of the expected losses (deaths, injuries, property, economic activity etc.) due to a hazard of a particular magnitude occurring in a given area over a specific time period.

The figure on the right illustrates essentially the four factors essentially hazards, location, exposure and vulnerability which contribute to risk.

They are: Hazards (physical effects generated in the naturally occurring event), Location of the hazards relative to the community at risk, Exposure (the value and importance of the various types of structures and lifeline systems such as watersupply, communication network, transportation network etc., in the community serving the population and Vulnerability of the exposed structures and systems to the hazards expected to affect them during their useful life. Risk reduction can take place in two ways:

Preparedness

This protective process embraces measures which enable Governments, communities and individuals to respond rapidly to disaster situations to cope with them effectively. Preparedness includes the formulation of viable emergency plans, the development of warning systems, the maintenance of inventories and the training of personnel. It may also embrace search and rescue measures as well as evacuation plans for areas that may be at risk from a recurring disaster.

Preparedness therefore, encompasses those measures taken before a disaster event which are aimed at minimising loss of life, disruption of critical services and damage when the disaster occurs. All preparedness planning needs to be supported by appropriate legislation with clear allocation of responsibilities and budgetary provisions.

Mitigation

Mitigation embraces all measures taken to reduce both the effect of the hazard itself and the vulnerable conditions to it in order to reduce the scale of a future disaster. Therefore, mitigation activities can be focused on the hazard itself or the elements exposed to the threat.

Examples of mitigation measures which are hazard specific include modifying the occurrence of the hazard, *e.g.,* water management in drought prone areas, avoiding the hazard by siting people away from the hazard and by strengthening structures to reduce damage when a hazard occurs. In addition to these physical measures, mitigation should also be aimed at reducing the physical, economic and social vulnerability to threats and the underlying causes for this vulnerability.

Disaster Management Cycle

Disaster management can be defined as the body of policy and administrative decisions and operational activities which pertain to the various stages of a disaster at all levels. Broadly disaster management can be divided into pre-disaster and post-disaster contexts. There are three key stages of activity that are taken up within disaster management. They are:

(i) ***Before a Disaster Strikes (pre-disaster).*** Activities taken to reduce human and property losses caused by the hazard and ensure that these losses are also minimized when the disaster strikes. Risk reduction activities are taken under this stage and they are termed as mitigation and preparedness activities.

(ii) ***During a Disaster (disaster occurrence).*** Activities taken to ensure that the needs and provisions of victims are met and suffering is minimized. Activities taken under this stage are called as emergency response activities

(iii) ***After a Disaster (post-disaster).*** Activities taken to achieve early recovery and does not expose the earlier vulnerable conditions. Activities taken under this stage are called as response and recovery activities.

Personal and Community Awareness

As Indians we need to be aware of likely hazards and potential hazards, how, when and where they are likely to occur and the problems which may result of an event. With 60% of the land mass susceptible to seismic hazard damage (Moderate, High and Very High Zone); 40 million hectares (8%) of landmass prone to floods; 8000 Km long coastline with two cyclone seasons; 68% of the total area vulnerable to drought; Hilly regions vulnerable to avalanches/landslides/Hailstorms/ cloudbursts; other Human caused hazards it is important most of all, we should be aware of how to cope with their effects. During the time of a disaster there will be delay before outside help arrives. At first, self-help is essential and depends on a prepared community - that is a community which has:

- An alert, informed and actively aware population.
- An active and involved local Government.

- Preparedness and Response Plan.
- Agreed, co-ordinated arrangements for response, preparedness and mitigation measures.

The Indian sub-continent lies upon the Indian Plate. This plate is moving northward at about 5 centimetres per year and in doing so, collides with the Eurasian Plate. Upon the Eurasian Plate lie the Tibet plateau and Central Asia. Due to this collision, the Himalayas are thrust higher and very many earthquakes are generated in the process. This is the cause of earthquakes from the Himalayas to the Arakan Yoma.

An Earthquake - is a series of underground shock waves and movements on the earth's surface caused by natural processes writhing the earths crust.

Onset Type and Warning

Earthquake is a sudden onset hazard. They occur at any time of year, day or night, with sudden impact and without any warning sign. Extensive research has been conducted in recent decades but there is no accepted method of earthquake prediction as on date.

Elements at Risk

Several key factors that contribute to vulnerability of human populations to earthquakes:

- Location of settlements in an earthquake prone area, especially on soft ground, on area prone to landslides or along fault lines.
- Non-engineered buildings constructed by earth, rubble, buildings with heavy roofs (more vulnerable than light weight structures), poor quality and maintenance of buildings Weak or flexible storey intending for parking purposes.
- Dense collection of weak buildings with high occupancy.

EARTHQUAKES HAZARDS AND DISASTERS

The same process, results in earthquakes in the Andaman and Nicobar Islands. Sometimes earthquakes of different magnitudes occur within the Indian Plate, in the peninsula and in adjoining parts of the Arabian Sea or the Bay of Bengal. These arise due to localized systems of forces in the crust sometimes associated with ancient geological structures such as in the Rann of Kachchh. All earthquakes in peninsula India falls within this category.

Hazard Zones

As per the latest seismic zoning map of India the country is divided into four Seismic Zones. Zone V marked in red shows the area of Very High Risk Zone, Zone IV marked in orange shows the area of High Risk Zone. Zone III marked in yellow shows the region of Moderate Risk Zone and Zone II marked in blue shows the region of Low risk Zone. Zone V is the most vulnerable to earthquakes, where historically some of the country's most powerful shock has occurred.

Geographically this zone includes the Andaman and Nicobar Islands, all of North-Eastern India, parts of north-western Bihar, eastern sections of Uttaranchal, the Kangra Valley in Himachal Pradesh, near the Srinagar area in Jammu and Kashmir and the Rann of Kutchh in Gujarat. Earthquakes with magnitudes in excess of 7.0 have occurred in these areas and have had intensities higher than IX.

Much of India lies in Zone III, where a maximum intensity of VII can be expected. New Delhi lies in Zone IV whereas Mumbai and Chennai lie in Zone III. All states and UTs across the country have experienced earthquakes.

Measuring the Size of an Earthquake - MSK 64 Intensity Scale

Intensity is a qualitative measure of the actual shaking at a location during an earthquake and is notated in a roman capital numeral. The MSK (Medvedev, Sponheuer and Karnik) scale is more convenient for application in field and is widely used in India.

The zoning criterion of the map is based on likely intensity. The scale range from I (least perceptive) to XII (most severe). The intensity scales are bas ed on three features of shaking - perception by people, performance of buildings and changes to natural surroundings. The seismic zoning map broadly classifies India into zones where one can expect earthquake shaking of the more or less the same maximum intensity. The shaking intensity associated with different zones is shown in the table below:

Frightening

(i) Felt by most indoors and outdoors. Many people in buildings are frightened and run outdoors. A few persons loose their balance. Domestic animals rum out of their stalls. In many instances, dishes and glassware may break and books fall down, pictures move and unstable objects overturn. Heavy furniture may possibly move and small steeple bells may ring.

(ii) Cracks up to widths of 1cm possible in wet ground; in mountains occasional landslips: change in flow of springs and in level of well water are observed.

Damage of Buildings

(i) Most people are frightened and run outdoors. Many find it difficult to stand. The vibration is noticed by persons driving motor cars. Large bells ring.

(ii) Waves are formed on water and is made turbid by mud stirred up. Water levels in wells change and the flow of springs changes. Some times dry springs have their flow resorted and existing springs stop flowing. In isolated instances parts of sand and gravelly banks slip off.

Destruction of Buildings

(i) Fright and panic; also persons driving motor cars are disturbed, Here and there branches of trees break off. Even heavy furniture moves and partly overturns. Hanging lamps are damaged in part.

(ii) Small landslips in hollows and on banked roads on steep slopes; cracks in ground up to widths of several centimeters. Water in lakes becomes turbid. New reservoirs come into existence. Dry wells refill and existing

General Damage of Buildings

(i) General panic; considerable damage to furniture. Animals run to and fro in confusion and cry.

(ii) On flat land overflow of water, sand and mud is often observed. Ground cracks to widths of up to 10 cm, on slopes and river banks more than 10 cm. Further more, a large number of slight cracks in ground; falls of rock, many land slides and earth flows; large waves in water. Dry wells renew their flow and existing wells dry up.

Typical Effects

Physical Damage. Damage or loss of buildings and service structures. Fires, floods due to dam failures, landslides could occur.

Casualties. Often high, near to the epicenter and in places where the population density is high (say, multistoried buildings) and structures are not resistant to earthquake forces.

Public Health. Multiple fracture injuries, moderately and severely injured is the most widespread problem, breakdown in sanitary conditions and large number of casualties could lead to epidemics.

Water Supply. Severe problems due to failure of the water supply distribution network and storage reservoirs. Fire hydrants supply lines if vulnerable could hamper fire service operations.

Transport Network. Severely affected due to failure of roads and bridges, railway tracks, failure of airport runways and related infrastructure.

Electricity and Communication. All links affected. Transmission towers, transponders, transformers collapse.

Main Mitigation Strategies

Engineered structures (designed and built) to withstand ground shaking. Architectural and engineering inputs put together to improve building design and construction practice. Analyze soil type before construction and do not build structures on soft soil. To accommodate on weak soils adopt safety measures in design. **Note:** Buildings built on soft soils are more likely to get damaged even if the earthquake is not particularly strong in magnitude. Similar problem persists in the alluvial plains and conditions across the river banks. Heavy damages are concentrated when ground is soft.

- Follow Indian Standard Codes for construction of buildings.
- Enforcement of the Byelaws including Land use control and restriction on density and heights of buildings
- Public awareness, sensitization and training programmes for Architects, Builders, Contractors, Designers, Engineers, Financiers, Government functionaries, House owners, Masons etc.
- Strengthening of important lifeline buildings which need to be functional after a disaster. Upgrade level of safety of hospital, fire service buildings etc.

- Reduce possible damages from secondary effects such as like fire, floods, landslides etc., *e.g.*, identify potential landslide sites and restrict construction in those areas.

Community Based Mitigation

Community preparedness along with public education is vital for mitigating the earthquake impact. Earthquake drills and Public awareness programme.

Community based Earthquake Risk Management Project should be developed and sustainable programmes launched. Retrofitting of schools and important buildings, purchase of emergency response equipment and facilities, establishing proper insurance can be the programmes under Earthquake Risk Management Project. A large number of local masons and engineers will be trained in disaster resistant construction techniques. A large number of masons, engineers and architects can get trained in this process.

TSUNAMI HAZARDS AND DISASTERS

TSUNAMI is a Japanese word meaning "harbour wave". These waves, which often affect distant shores, originate from undersea or coastal seismic activity, landslides and volcanic eruptions. Whatever the cause, sea water is displaced with a violent motion and swells up, ultimately surging over land with great destructive power.

26th December, 2004, A massive earthquake of Magnitude 9.0 hit Indonessia generating Tsunami waves in South-east Asia and Eastern Coast of India. Height of tsunami waves ranged from 3 - 10 m affecting a total coastal length of 2260 km in the States of Andhra Pradesh, Tamil Nadu, Kerala and UTs of Pondicherry Andaman and Nicobar Islands.

Tsunami waves travelled upto a depth of 3 km from the coast killing more than 10,000 people and affected more than lakh of houses leaving behind a huge trail of destruction.

Onset Type and Causes

If the earthquake or under water land movement is near the coast then tsunami may strike suddenly and if the earth movement is far in the sea then it may take few minutes to hours before striking the coast. The onset is extensive and often very destructive. The general causes of Tsunamis are geological movements. It is produced in three major ways. The most common of these is fault movement on the sea floor, accompanied by an earthquake. To say that an earthquake causes a tsunami is not completely correct. Rather, both earthquakes and tsunamis result from fault movements.

Probably the second most common cause of tsunamis is a landslide either occurring underwater or originating above the sea and then plunging into the water. The third major cause of tsunamis is volcanic activity. The flank of a volcano, located near the shore or underwater, may be uplifted or depressed similar to the action of a fault. Or, the volcano may actually explode. In 1883, the violent explosion of the famous volcano, Krakatoa in Indonesia, produced tsunamis measuring 40 meters which crashed upon Java and Sumatra. over 36,000 people lost their lives as a result of tsunami waves from Krakatoa.

Warning

Tsunami is not a single giant wave. It consists of ten or more waves which is termed as a "tsunami wave train".

Since scientists cannot predict when earthquakes will occur, they cannot predict exactly when a tsunami will be generated. Studies of past historical tsunamis indicate where tsunamis are most likely to be generated, their potential heights and flooding limits at specific coastal locations. With use of satellite technology it is possible to provide nearly immediate warnings of potentially tsunamigenic earthquakes. Warning time depends upon the distance of the epicenter from the coast line.

The warning includes predicted times at selected coastal communities where the tsunami cold travel in a few hours. In case of tsunamigenic earthquakes or any other geological activity people near to the coastal areas may get very little time to evacuate on receiving of warning.

Elements at Risk

All structures located within 200 m of the low lying coastal area are most vulnerable to the direct impact of the tsunami waves as well as the impact of debris and boulders brought by it. Settlements in adjacent areas will be vulnerable to floods and scour. Structures constructed of wood, mud, thatch, sheets and structures without proper anchorage to foundations are liable to be damaged by tsunami waves and flooding. Other elements at risk are infrastructure facilities like ports and harbours, telephone and electricity poles, cables. Ships and fishing boats/nets near the coast also add to the destruction caused by tsunami waves.

Typical Effects

Physical Damage. Local tsunami events or those less than 30 minutes from the source cause the majority of damage. The force of can raze everything in its path. It is the flooding effect of a tsunami, however, that most greatly effects human settlements by water damage to homes and businesses, roads, bridges and other infrastructure. Ships, port facilities, boats/ trawlers, fishing nets also get damaged.

Environmental Damage. There is evidence of ever increasing impact upon the environment on account of the effects of tsunamis. The range varies from generation of tonnes of debris on account of structural collapse of weaker buildings, release of toxic chemicals into the environment on account of chemical leak/spillage/process failure/utility breakages/ collateral hazards and negative impact on the already fragile ecosystems.

Casualties and Public Health. Deaths occur principally from drowning as water inundates homes or neighbourhoods. Many people may be washed out to sea or crushed by the giant waves. There may be some injuries from battering by debris and wounds may become contaminated.

Water Supply. Sewage pipes may be damaged causing major sewage disposal problems. Drinking water shortage arises due to breakage of water mains and contamination. Open wells and ground water may become unfit for drinking due to contamination of salt water and debris.

Standing Crops and Food Supplies. Flooding by tsunami causes damage to the standing crops and also to the food supplies in the storage facilities. The land may be rendered infertile due to salt water incursion from the sea.

Specific Preparedness Measures

Hazard Mapping. A hazard map should be prepared with designated areas expected to be damaged by flooding by tsunami waves. Historical data could be of help ion showing areas inundated in the past. Keeping in mind the vulnerable areas, evacuation routes should be constructed and mapped. The plan should be followed by evacuation drill.

Early Warning Systems. A well networked system in place can warn the communities of the coastal areas when the threat is perceived. Tsunami warning should be disseminated to local, state, national as well as the international community so as to be prepared as they are capable of crossing across continents. The information can be broadcasted to the local emergency officers and the general public. On receiving of the warning the action should be to evacuate the place as decided in the evacuation plan. Community Preparedness - communities in the coastal areas are faced by the wrath of cyclones, storm surge and tsunami waves. It is important that the community is better prepared to take suitable actions on receiving of the threat and follow emergency evacuation plans and procedures. a community which choose to ignore warning may get severely effected if they are not prepared to take immediate measures.

Main Mitigation Strategies

Site Planning and Land Management. Within the broader framework of a comprehensive plan, site planning determines the location, configuration and density of development on particular sites and is, therefore, an important tool in reducing tsunami risk. The designation and zoning of tsunami hazard areas for such open-space uses as agriculture, parks and recreation, or natural hazard areas is recommended as the first land use planning strategy. This strategy is designed to keep development at a minimum in hazard areas.

In areas where it is not feasible to restrict land to open-space uses, other land use planning measures can be used. These include strategically controlling the type of development and uses allowed in hazard areas and avoiding high-value and high-occupancy uses to the greatest degree possible.

Site Selection. Avoid building or living in buildings within several hundred feet of the coastline as these areas are more likely to experience damage from tsunamis.

Construct the structure on a higher ground level with respect to mean sea level.

Engineering Structures. As most of the structures along the coast area comprises of fisherman community, which are constructed of light weight materials without any engineering inputs. Therefore, there is an urgent need to educate the community about the good construction practices that they should adopt such as:

Elevate Coastal Homes. Most tsunami waves are less than 3 meters in height. Elevating house will help reduce damage to property from most tsunamis. Structural columns resist the impact while other walls are expendable. It is important to also take note that adequate measures are also brought into the design to cater for earthquake forces. Construction of water breakers to reduce the velocity of waves. Use of water and corrosion resistant materials for construction.

Construction of community halls at higher locations, which can act as shelters at the time of a disaster.

Flood Management. Flooding will result from a tsunami. Tsunami waves will flood the coastal areas. Flood mitigation measures could be incorporated. Building barriers or buffers such as special breakwaters or seawalls can be an effective risk reduction measure against gushing waters in case of Tsunami/Storm surge during cyclones.

Onset Type and Warning

Though they occur gradually, however, sudden failure (sliding) can occur without warning. They may take place in combination with earthquakes, floods and volcanoes. There are no clearly established warnings in place indicating occurrence of landslide and hence, difficult to predict the actual occurrence. Areas of high risk can be determined by use of information on geology, hydrology, vegetation cover, past occurrence and consequences in the region.

Causes of Landslides

Geological Weak Material. Weathered materials, jointed or fissured materials, contrast in permeability and contrast in stiffness (stiff, dense material over plastic materials).

Intense Rainfall. Storms that produce intense rainfall for periods as short as several hours or have a more moderate intensity lasting several days have triggered abundant landslides.

Erosion. Wave erosion of slope toe, glacial erosion of slope toe, sub-terranean erosion (Deposition loading slope or its crest, Vegetation removal.

LANDSLIDE HAZARDS AND DISASTERS

Landslides are slippery masses of rock, earth or debris which move by force of their own weight down mountain slopes or river banks In the picture:

(Top) House wrecked in landslide. Twenty-five residents of a private building in the heart of the Shimla town had a miraculous escape when a major portion of house collapsed following a landslide. The landslide was triggered by haphazard cutting of the hill below it for construction of a hotel.

(Bottom Left). The Varunavat mountain rising on the edge of Uttarkashi town. Huge cracks on its side have set off several landslides. A building in danger of being buried.

(Bottom Right). A building partly buried under rocks and other debris.

Bhachau Landslide. The land slipped during the 26th January 2001 earthquake event in Bhachau. Note people are still camped beneath. Monsoon rains could possibly wash the soil downslope.

Human Excavation of slope and its toe, Loading of slope/toe, draw down in reservoir, mining, deforestation, irrigation, vibration/blast, Water leakage from services.

Earthquake shaking has triggered landslides in many different topographic and geologic settings. Rock falls, soil slides and rockslides from steep slopes involving relatively thin or shallow disaggregated soils or rock, or both have been the most abundant types of landslides triggered by historical earthquakes. Volcanic eruption Deposition of loose volcanic ash on hillsides commonly is followed by accelerated erosion and frequent mud or debris flows triggered by intense rainfall.

Elements at Risk

The most common elements at risk are the settlements built on the steep slopes, built at the toe and those built at the mouth of the streams emerging from the mountain valley. All those buildings constructed without appropriate foundation for a given soil and in sloppy areas are also at risk. Roads, communication line and buried utilities are vulnerable.

Indian Landslides

Landslide constitute a major natural hazard in our country, which accounts for considerable loss of life and damage to communication routes, human settlements, agricultural fields and forest lands. The Indian sub-continent, with diverse physiographic, seismotectonic and climatological conditions is subjected to varying degree of landslide hazards; the Himalayas including Northeastern mountains ranges being the worst affected, followed by a section of Western Ghats and the Vindhyas. Removal of vegetation and toe erosion have also triggered slides Torrential monsoon on the vegetation cover removed slopes was the main causative factors in the Peninsular India namely in Western Ghat and Nilgiris. Human intervention by way of slope modification has added to this effect.

Typical Effects

Physical Damage. Landslides destroy anything that comes in their path. They block or bury roads, lines of communication, settlements, river flow, agricultural land, etc., It also includes loss to agricultural production and land area. In addition physical effects such as flooding may also occur. The Malpa village as on 17 August 1998, a few hours before the rock avalanche wiped out the village around 0300 hours on the 18 August, 1998. The two pictures were taken from the same location upstream of Kali River. They provide a direct comparison of scenarios before and after the event.

Landslide in Kerala

In the Kerala part of the Western Ghats several types of mass movements/landslides have been recorded. The most prevalent, recurring and disastrous type of mass movements noted in Kerala are the "debris flows". The swift and sudden down slope movement of highly water saturated overburden containing a varied assemblage of debris material ranging in size from soil particles to huge boulders destroying and carrying with it every thing that is lying in its path. Note the boulder movement along the path.

Casualties. They cause maximum fatalities depending on the place and time of occurrence. Catastrophic landsides have killed many thousands of persons, such as the debris slide on the slopes of Huascaran in Peru triggered by an earthquake in 1970, which killed over 18,000 people.

Community Based Mitigation

The most damaging landslides are often related to human intervention such as construction of roads, housing and other infrastructure in vulnerable slopes and regions. Other community based activities that can mitigate landslides are education and awareness generation among the communities, establishing community based monitoring, timely warning and evacuation system.

Communities can play a vital role in identifying the areas where there is land instability. Compacting ground locally, slope stabilization (procedures such as terracing and tree planting may reduce damages to some extent) and avoiding construction of houses in hazardous locations are something that the community has to agree and adhere to avoid damage from the possible landslides. This would also reduce the burden of shifting of settlements from hazardous slopes and rebuild in safe site as it is less practical to do in large scale.

Debris Flows or Mudslies

Fast-moving flows of mud and rock, called debris flows or mudslides, are among the most numerous and dangerous types of landslides in the world. They are particularly dangerous to life and property because of their high speeds and the sheer destructive force of their flow.

Hazardous Areas

Debris flows start on steep slopes-slopes steep enough to make walking difficult. Once started, however, debris flows can travel even over gently sloping ground. The most hazardous areas are canyon bottoms, stream channels, areas near the outlets of canyons and slopes excavated for buildings and roads.

(a) Canyon bottoms, stream channels and areas near the outlets of canyons or channels are particularly hazardous. Multiple debris flows that start high in canyons commonly funnel into channels. There, they merge, gain volume and travel long distances from their sources.

(b) Debris flows commonly begin in swales (depressions) on steep slopes, making areas downslope from swales particularly hazardous.

(c) Roadcuts and other altered or excavated areas of slopes are particularly susceptible to debris flows. Debris flows and other landslides onto roadways are common during rainstorms and often occur during milder rainfall conditions than those needed for debris flows on natural slopes.

(d) Areas where surface runoff is channeled, such as along roadways and below culverts, are common sites of debris flows and other landslides.

Onset Type

They strike suddenly although it takes time to build up. They can be tracked on the development but accurate landfall is predictable barely few hours. The onset is extensive and often very destructive.

Warning

Low pressure and the development can be detected hours or days before its damage effects start. Satellite tracking can track the movement since the build up and the likely path is projected. Warning and evacuation is done along the projected path. It is difficult to predict the accuracy. Accurate landfall predictions can give only a few hours' notice to threatened populations. In addition, people generally opt to wait until the very last minute before abandoning their home and possessions. Deaths from drowning in the high tides and sudden flooding and material losses are therefore, often very high.

The India Meteorological Department (IMD) issues warning against severe weather phenomena like tropical cyclones, heavy rains and snow, cold and heat waves, etc., which cause destruction of life and property. Cyclone warning is disseminated by several means such as satellite based disaster warning systems, radio, television, telephone, fax, high priority telegram, public announcements and bulletins in press. Advancement in Information Technology in the form of Internet, Geograhical Information System (GIS), Remote Sensing, Satellite communication, etc., can help a great deal in planning and implementation of hazards reduction schemes.

CYCLONE HAZARDS AND DISASTERS

CYCLONES a violent storm, often of vast extent, characterized by high winds rotating about a calm center of low atmospheric pressure. This center moves onward, often with a velocity of 50 km an hour.

29th October 1999, Supercyclone with winds 260-300 km/hour hit the 140 km coast of Orissa with a storm surge that created the Bay of Bengal water level 9 metres higher than normal. The super storm traveled more than 250 km inland and within a period of 36 hrs ravaged more than 200 lakh hectares of land, devouring trees and vegetation, leaving behind a huge trail of destruction. The violent cyclone was merciless and giant, broke the backbone of Orissa state and killed thousands and devastated millions.

Elements at Risk

All lightweight structures and those built of mud, wood, older buildings with weak walls and structures without proper anchorage to the foundations will be at great risk. Settlements located in low lying coastal areas will be vulnerable to the direst effects of the cyclones such as wind, rain and storm surge. Settlements in adjacent areas will be vulnerable to floods, mudslides or landslides due to heavy rains. Other elements at risk are fences, telephone and electricity poles, cables, light elements of structures - roofs, signboards, hoardings, coconut crowns, fishing boats and large trees.

Typical Effects

First, in a sudden, brief onslaught, high winds cause major damage to infrastructure and housing, in particular fragile constructions. They are generally followed by heavy rains and floods and, in flat coastal areas by storm surge riding on tidal waves and inundating the land over long distances of even upto 15 km inland..

Physical Damage. Structures will be damaged or destroyed by the wind force, flooding and storm surge. Light pitched roofs of most structures especially the ones fitted on to industrial buildings will suffer severe damage.

Casualties and Public Heath. Caused by flooding and flying elements, contamination of water supplies may lead to viral outbreaks, diarrhea and malaria.

Water Supplies. Ground and piped water supply may get contaminated by flood waters

Crops and Food Supplies. High winds and rains will ruin the standing crop and food stock lying in low lying areas. Plantation type crops such as banana and coconut are extremely vulnerable. Salt from the sea water may be deposited on the agricultural land and increase the salinity. The loss of the crop may lead to acute food shortage.

Communication. Severe disruption in the communication links as the wind may bring down the electricity and communication towers, electricity and telephone poles, telephone lines, antennas and satellite disk and broadcasting services. Transport lines (road and rail) may be curtailed. Relief materials may not reach the affected site.

Indian Cyclones

The coastal areas are subjected to severe wind storms and cyclonic storms. A full-grown cyclone is a violent whirl in the atmosphere 150 to 1000 km across, 10 to 15 km high. Gale winds of 150 to 250 kmph or more spiral around the center of very low pressure area. Torrential rains, occasional thunder and lightning flashes - join these under an overcast black canopy. Through these churned chaotic sea and atmosphere, the cyclone moves 300 to 500 km, in a day to hit or skirt along a coast, bringing with it storm surges as high as 3 to 12 metres, as if splashing a part of the sea sometimes up to 30 km inland leaving behind death and destructions. A storm surge is the sudden abnormal rise in the sea level caused by cyclone. The sea water flows across the coast as well as inland and then recedes back to the sea. Great loss of life and property takes place in the process.

A bridge destroyed by the high-velocity winds and floods during the cyclone. A helicopter turned turtle at the Bhubaneshwar airport during the cyclonic storm of 1999.

East Coast. Cyclones affect both the Bay of Bengal and the Arabian Sea. They are rare in Bay of Bengal from January to March. Isolated ones forming in the South Bay of Bengal move west north westwards and hit Tamil Nadu and Sri Lanka coasts. In April and May, these form in the South and adjoining Central Bay and move initially northwest, north and then recurve to the northeast striking the Arakan coasts in April and Andhra Pradesh-Orissa-West Bengal-Bangladesh coasts in May. Most of the monsoon (June - September) storms develop in the central and in the North Bay and move west-north-westwards affecting Andhra Pradesh-Orissa-West Bengal coasts. Post monsoon (October-December) storms form mostly in the south and the central Bay, recurve between 15° and 18° N affecting Tamil Nadu-Andhra Orissa-West Bengal-Bangladesh coasts.

West Coast. Cyclones do not form in Arabian Sea during the months of January, February and March and are rare in April, July, August and September. They generally form in southeast Arabian Sea and adjoining central Arabian Sea in the months of May, October, November and December and in east central Arabian Sea in the month of June. Some of the cyclones that originate in the Bay of Bengal travel across the peninsula, weaken and emerge into Arabian Sea as low pressure areas. These may again intensify into cyclonic storms. Most of the storms in Arabian Sea move in west-north-westerly direction towards Arabian Coast in the month of May and in a northerly direction towards Gujarat Coast in the month of June. In other months, they generally move northwest north and then recurve northeast affecting Gujarat-Maharashtra coasts; a few, however, also move west north westwards towards Arabian coast.

Main Mitigation Strategies

Hazard Mapping. Meteorological records of the wind speed and the directions give the probability of the winds in the region. Cyclones can be predicted several days in advance. The onset is extensive and often very destructive. Past records and paths can give the pattern of occurrence for particular wind speeds. A hazard map will illustrate the areas vulnerable to the cyclone in any given year. It will be useful to estimate the severity of the cyclone and various damage intensities in the region. The map is prepared with data inputs of past climatological records, history of wind speed, frequency of flooding etc.

Land use control designed so that least critical activities are placed in vulnerable areas. Location of settlements in the flood plains is at utmost risk. Siting of key facilities must be marked in the land use. Policies should be in place to regulate land use and enforcement of building codes. Vulnerable areas should be kept for parks, grazing or play grounds. Engineered structures - structures need to be built to withstand wind forces. Good site selection is also important. Majority of the buildings in coastal areas are built with locally available materials and have no engineering inputs. Good construction practice should be adopted such as:

- Cyclonic wind storms inundate the coastal areas. It is advised to construct on stilts or on earth mound.
- Houses can be strengthened to resist wind and flood damage. All elements holding the structures need to be properly anchored to resist the uplift or flying off of the objects. *For example,* avoid large

overhangs of roofs and the projections should be tied down.

- Buildings should be wind and water resistant.
- Buildings storing food supplies must be protected against the winds and water.
- A row of planted trees will act as a shield. It reduces the energy.
- Provide strong halls for community shelter in vulnerable locations.
- Protect river embankments. Communication lines should be installed underground.

Flood Management. Flooding will result from a cyclonic storm. Storm surge will flood the coastal areas. Heavy rains will bring in flash floods. There are possibilities of landslides too. Flood mitigation measures could be incorporated (see section on floods for additional information). Improving vegetation cover - improvement of the vegetation will increase water infiltaration capacity of the soil. The roots of the plants and trees will keep the soil intact and prevent erosion and slow runoff to prevent or lessen flooding. The use of tree planted in rows will act as a windbreak. Coastal shelterbelt plantations can be developed to break severe wind speeds. It minimizes devastating effects. The Orissa calamity has also highlighted the need for urgent measures like shelterbelt plantation along cyclone-prone coastal areas. Species chosen for this purpose should not only be able to withstand the impact of strong cyclonic winds, but also check soil erosion.

Community Based Mitigation

Construction of cyclone resistant houses and strengthening of existing houses can be done through community participation. Local engineers and masons can take part in the construction of the buildings in their area and demonstrate to the people about disaster resistant construction methods. Construction of multipurpose cyclone shelters in the vulnerable locations are desirable. During normal time these buildings can be used as schools or as community centres. In case of cyclones or floods, community can take shelter in these designed buildings. The local communities will be responsible for the maintenance and management of these community shelters.

Protection measures need to be taken for the livestock, the boats, fishing nets, household items and other possessions.

Other activities that can be taken up as part of the community based mitigation are construction of saline embankments for protection against sea water ingress, reforestation, conservation of green belt areas and participating in coastal shelterbelt plantation programme. Community based mitigation activities relating to floods can also be taken up (for more details on community based mitigation on floods, refer the flood section for additional information).

FLOOD HAZARDS AND DISASTERS

Floods is a temporary inundation of large regions as the result of an increase in reservoir, or of rivers flooding their banks because of heavy rains, high winds, cyclones, storm surge along coast, tsunami, melting snow or dam bursts.

Flash floods defined as floods which occurs within six hours of the beginning of heavy rainfall and are usually associated with cloud bursts, storms and cyclones requiring rapid localized warnings and immediate response if damage is to be mitigated. Wireless network and telephone connections are used to monitor flood conditions. In case of flash floods, warnings for timely evacuation may not always be possible.

Elements at Risk

Anything in the flood plains will get inundated. Buildings built of earth, weak foundations and water soluble materials will collapse endangering humans and their property. Basements of buildings are under risk. Utilities such as sewerage, water supply, communication lines and power are put at risk. Food stock in the godowns, agricultural fields, salt pans, livestock, vehicles, machinery and equipments mounted on the ground, fishing boats are also put at risk.

Indian Floods

Floods occur in almost all rivers basins of the country. Heavy rainfall, inadequate capacity of rivers to carry the high flood discharge, inadequate drainage to carry away the rainwater quickly to Streams/Rivers are the main causes of floods. Ice jams or land slides blocking streams; typhoons and cyclones also cause floods. Excessive rainfall combined with inadequate carrying capacity of streams resulting in over spilling of banks is the cause for flooding in majority of cases. Rashtriya Barh Ayog (RBA) constituted by the Government of India in 1976 carried out an extensive analysis to estimate the floodaffected area in the country. RBA in its report (1980) has assessed the area liable to floods as 40 million hectares. It was determined by summing up the maximum area affected by floods in any one year in each state during the period from 1953 to 1978 for which data was analysed by the Ayog. This sum has been corrected for the area that was provided with protection at that time and for the protected area that got affected due to failure of protection works during the period under analysis to arrive at the total area liable to floods in the country as per break-up.

Typical Effects

Physical Damage. Structures damaged or collapsed by washing waters, landslide triggered on account of water getting saturated. Boats and fishing equipments may be lost or damaged in coastal areas.

Casualties and Pubic Health. People and livestock deaths caused by drowning, very few serious injuries. Outbreak of epidemics, diarrhea, viral infections, malaria.

Water Supplies. Contamination of water (wells, ground water, piped water supply). Clean water may be unavailable.

Crops and Food Supplies. Sudden food shortage can be caused due to loss of entire harvest, spoiling of grains when saturated in water alongwith loss of animal fodder. The crop storage facilities and godowns may get submerged resulting in immediate food shortage. Floods may also affect the soil characteristics.

The land may be rendered infertile due to erosion of top layer or may turn saline if sea water floods the area.

Potential for Reducing Hazard

Embankments along the rivers, sea walls along the coasts may keep water away from the flood plains. Water flow can be regularized through construction of the reservoirs, check dams, alternate drainage channels/routes, increasing vegetation cover and by providing storm drains.

Main Mitigation Strategies

Mapping of the flood prone areas is a primary step involved in reducing the risk of the region. Historical records give the indication of the flood inundation areas and the period of occurrence and the extent of the coverage. The basic map is combined with other maps and data to form a complete image of the floodplain. Warning can be issued looking into the earlier marked heights of the water levels in case of potential threat. In the coastal areas the tide levels and the land characteristics will determine the submergence areas.

Flood hazard mapping will give the proper indication of water flow during floods.

Land use control will reduce danger of life and property when waters inundate the floodplains and the coastal areas. The number of casualties is related to the population in the area at risk. It's better to reduce the densities in areas where neighborhoods are to be developed. In areas where people already have built their settlements, measures should be taken to relocate to better sites so as to reduce vulnerability. No major development should be permitted in the areas which are subjected to high flooding. Important facilities should be built in safe areas. In urban areas, water holding areas can be created in ponds, lakes or low-lying areas.

Construction of engineered structures in the flood plains and strengthening of structures to withstand flood forces and seepage. The buildings should be constructed on a elevated area. If necessary build on stilts or platform. Flood Control aims to reduce flood damage. This can be done by Flood Reduction by decreasing the amount of runoff by treatment like reforestation (to increase absorption could be a mitigation strategy in certain areas), protection of vegetation, clearing of debris from streams and other water holding areas, conservation of ponds and lakes etc. Flood Diversion include levees, embankments, dams and channel improvement. Dams can store water and can release water at a manageable rate. But failure of dams in earthquakes and operation of releasing the water can cause floods in the lower areas. Flood Proofing reduces the risk of damage. Measures include use of sand bags to keep flood water away, blocking or sealing of doors and windows of houses etc. Houses may be elevated by building on raised land. Buildings should be constructed away from water bodies.

Flood Management in India, systematic planning for flood management commenced with the Five Year Plans, particularly with the launching of National Programme of Flood Management in 1954. During the last 48 years, different methods of flood protection structural as well as non-structural have been adopted in different states depending upon the nature of the problem and local conditions. Structural measures include storage reservoirs, flood embankments, drainage channels, anti-erosion works, channel improvement works, detention basins etc., and non-structural measures include flood forecasting, flood plain zoning, flood proofing, disaster preparedness etc., The flood management measures undertaken so far have provided reasonable degree of protection to an area of 15.81 million hectares through out the country.

DROUGHT HAZARDS AND DISASTERS

Drought is an insidious natural hazard that results from a departure of precipitation from expected or normal that, when extended over a season or longer period of time, is insufficient to meet the demands of human, plant and animal activities.

Typical Effects

Drought, different from other natural disasters, do not cause any structural damages. The typical effects include loss of crop, dairy, timber (forest fires) and fishery production; increase in energy demand for pumping water; reduced energy production; increased unemployment, loss of biodiversity, reduced water, air and landscape quality; groundwater depletion, food shortage, health reduction and loss of life, increased poverty, reduced quality of life and social unrest leading to migration.

Main Mitigation Strategies

Drought monitoring is continuous observation of rainfall situation, water availability in reservoirs, lakes, rivers and comparing with the existing water needs of various sectors of the society.

Water supply augmentation and conservation through rainwater harvesting in houses and farmers' fields increases the content of water available. Water harvesting by either allowing the runoff water from all the fields to a common point (*e.g.,* Farm ponds) or allowing it to infiltrate into the soil where it has fallen (in situ) (*e.g.,* contour bunds, contour cultivation, raised bed planting etc.) helps increase water availability for sustained agricultural production.

Expansion of irrigation facilities reduces the drought vulnerability. Land use based on its capability helps in optimum use of land and water and can avoid the undue demand created due to their misuse.

Livelihood planning identifies those livelihoods which are least affected by the drought. Some of such livelihoods include increased off-farm employment opportunities, collection of non-timber forest produce from the community forests, raising goats and carpentry etc.

Drought Planning

The basic goal of drought planning is to improve the effectiveness of preparedness and response efforts by enhancing monitoring, mitigation and response measures. Planning would help in effective coordination among state and national agencies in dealing with the drought. Components of drought plan include establishing drought taskforce which is a team of specialists who can advise the Government in taking decision to deal with drought situation, establishing coordination mechanism among various agencies which deal with the droughts, providing crop insurance schemes to the farmers to cope with the drought related crop losses and public awareness generation.

Public Awareness and Education

Educating the masses on various strategies you learned above would help in effective drought mitigation. This includes organizing drought information meetings for the public and media, implementing water conservation awareness programs in the mass media like television, publishing and distributing pamphlets on water conservation techniques and agricultural drought management strategies like crop contingency plans and rainwater harvesting and establishing drought information centers for easy access to the farmers.

Watersheds: For Water Supply Augmentation and Conservation

Watersheds are the geographic areas where the water flows to a common point. To mitigate the drought impact, all kinds of soil and water conservation measures are taken up with the involvement of the local communities. This approach helped these areas to manage efficiently the soil, vegetation, water and other resources.

By conserving scarce water sources and improving the management of soil and vegetation, watersheds have the potential to create conditions conducive to higher agricultural productivity while conserving natural resources. Checkdams (Bhanadaras) These are check dams or diversion weirs built across rivers. A traditional system found in Maharashtra, their presence raises the water level of the rivers so that it begins to flow into channels.

They are also used to impound water and form a large reservoir. Where a bandhara was built across a small stream, the water supply would usually last for a few months after the rains.

What a Mitigation Approach can Do

The people of Ralegan Siddhi in Maharashtra transformed the dire straits to prosperity. Twenty years ago the village showed all traits of abject poverty. It practically had no trees, the topsoil had blown off, there was no agriculture and people were jobless. Anna Hazare, one of the India's most noted social activists, started his movement concentrating on trapping every drop of rain, which is basically a drought mitigation practice. So the villagers built check dams and tanks. To conserve soil they planted trees. The result: from 80 acres of irrigated area two decades ago, Ralegan Siddhi has a massive area of 1300 acres under irrigation. The migration for jobs has stopped and the per capita income has increased ten times from ₹ 225 to 2250 in this span of time. The entire effort was only people's enterprise and involved no funds or support from the Government.

FOREST FIRE HAZARDS AND DISASTERS

Forest Fire/Wild Fire is one of the destructive natural forces known to mankind. While sometimes caused by lightning, nine out of ten wildfires are human-caused. "Wild Fire" is the term applied to any unwanted and unplanned fire burning in forest, shrub or grass.

Wildfire Statistics

In India there are no comprehensive data to indicate the loss to forests in terms of area burned, values and volume and regeneration damaged by fire. The available forest fire statistics are not reliable because they under estimate fire numbers and area burned. The reason behind this is attributed to the fear of accountability. However, Forest Survey of India in a country-wide study in 1995 estimated that about 1.45 million hectares of forest are affected by fire annually. According to an assessment of the Forest Protection Division of the Ministry of Environment and Forests, Government of India, 3.73 million hectares of forests are affected by fires, annually in India.

The Forest Survey of India, data on forest fire attribute around 50% of the forest areas as fire prone. This does not mean that country's 50% area is affected by fires annually. Very heavy, heavy and frequent forest fire damages are noticed only over 0.8%, 0.14% and 5.16% of the forest areas respectively. Thus, only 6.17% of the forests are prone to severe fire damage. In the absolute term, out of the 63 million ha. of forests, an area of around 3.73 million ha can be presumed to be affected by fires annually.

In India there are very few cases of fire due to natural causes. The majority of the forest fires (99 percent) in the country are human caused. It is widely acknowledged that most of these fires are caused by the people deliberately and have a close relationship to their socio-economic conditions. Grazing, shifting cultivation and collection of minor forest products by villagers are major causes of fires in India. Carelessness of the picnickers, travellers and campers are also responsible for forest fires.

Forest Fire Damages in India

Forest fires are a major cause of degradation of India's forests. While statistical data on fire loss are weak, it is estimated that the proportion of forest areas prone to forest fires annually ranges from 33% in some states to over 90% in others. Forest Fires cause wide ranging adverse ecological, economic and social impacts. In a nutshell, fires cause:

- Loss of valuable timber resources and depletion of carbon sinks.
- Degradation of water catchment areas resulting in loss of water.
- Loss of natural regeneration and reduction in forest cover and production.
- Loss of biodiversity and extinction of plants and animals.
- Loss of wildlife habitat and depletion of wild life.
- Loss of carbon sink resource and increase in percentage of CO_2 in the atmosphere.

- Global warming resulting in rising temperature.
- Soil erosion affecting productivity of soils and production.
- Change in micro climate of the area making it unhealthy living conditions.
- Ozone layer depletion.
- Health problems leading to diseases.
- Indirect affect on agricultural production: Loss of livelihood for the tribals as approximately 65 million people are classified as tribals who directly depend upon collection of non-timber forest products from the forest areas for their livelihood.

Various regions of the country have different normal and peak fire seasons, which normally vary from January to June. In the plains of northern and central India, most of the forest fires occur between February and June. In the hills of northern India fire season starts later and most of the fires are reported between April and June. In the southern part of the country, fire season extends from January to May. In the Himalayan region, fires are common in May and June.

Operational Fire Management Systems and Organizations

According to the Constitution of India, the central and state Governments in the country are enabled to legislate on forestry issues. The implementation part of the forest policy/ programmes lies with the state Government. Thus, fire prevention, detection and suppression activities are the responsibility of the State Governments' forestry departments. The policy, planning and financing are the primary responsibility of the Central Government.

The regular staff of the forest departments in the states carries out various activities of forest fire management. During forest fire seasons in some of the divisions, fire watchers are recruited by the State Governments as a special provision. At the central level, the Ministry of Environment and Forests is the ministry responsible for forest conservation and protection. Forest fire management is administered by the "Forest Protection Division" of the Ministry, which is headed by a Deputy Inspector General of Forests. The Ministry is implementing a plan called "Modern Forest Fire Control Methods" in India under which State Governments are provided financial assistance for fire prevention and control. This assistance is being used by the State Governments for procuring hand tools, fire resistant clothes, firefighting tools, radios, fire watch towers, fire finders, creation of fire lines, research, training and publicity on firefighting.

Community Involvement

In India, Joint Forest Management (JFM) Committees have been established at the village level to involve people in forest protection and conservation. At present there are 36,165 JFM committees throughout the country, covering an area of more than 10.24 million hectares. These JFM committees also have been given responsibilities to protect the forests from fires. For this purpose, the Modern Forest Fire Control plan is being revised and JFM is being made an integral component of the forest fire prevention strategy. Use of aircraft and helicopters has not been very cost effective in the fire management program and the Air Operation Wing is being closed down. For emergency purposes, however, a provision for hiring aircraft for transportation of crews and water is being maintained.

The Government of India has issued national forest fire prevention and control guidelines. Salient features of the guidelines include identification of vulnerable areas on maps, creation of a data bank on forest fires, evolving fire dangers, fire forecasting system, provisions for a crisis management group, involvement of JFM committees and efficient enforcement of legal provisions.

Public Policies Concerning Fire

India's National Forest Policy, 1988 presents a visionary strategy for forest conservation and management and emphasizes protection of forests against encroachment, fire and grazing. It states that "The incidence of forest fires in the country is high. Standing trees and fodder are destroyed on a large scale and natural regeneration annihilated by such fires. Special precautions should be taken during the fire season. Improved and modern management practices should be adopted to deal with forest fire". This policy provides a positive step towards protection of forests from fire.

Needs of the Fire Management

The incidence of forest fires in the country is on the increase and more area is burned each year. The major cause of this failure is the piecemeal approach to the problem. Both the national focus and the technical resources required for sustaining a systematic forest fire management programme are lacking in the country. Important forest fire management elements like strategic fire centres, coordination among Ministries, funding, human resource development, fire research, fire detection system by using satellite images, fire management and extension programmes are missing. Taking into consideration the serious nature of the problem, it is necessary to make some major improvements in the forest fire management strategy for the country.

The Ministry of Environment and Forests (MOEF), Government of India, has prepared a National Master Plan for Forest Fire Control. This plan proposes to introduce a well-coordinated and integrated firemanagement programme that includes the following components:

Prevention of human-caused fires through education and environmental modification. It will include silvicultural activities, engineering works, people participation and education and enforcement. It is proposed that more emphasis be given to people participation through Joint Forest Fire Management for fire prevention.

Prompt detection of fires through a well coordinated network of observation points, efficient ground patrolling and communication networks. Remote sensing technology is to be given due importance in fire detection. For successful fire management and administration, a National Fire Danger Rating System (NFDRS) and Fire Forecasting System are to be developed in the country.

- Fast initial attack measures.
- Introducing a forest fuel modification system at strategic points.
- Vigorous follow up action.
- Firefighting resources.

Each of the above components plays an important role in the success of the entire system of fire management. Special emphasis is to be given to research, training and development.

CHEMICAL AND INDUSTRIAL ACCIDENTS

Bhopal Chemical Gas leak Disaster (2-3 December 1984) one of the worst industrial disasters of all time occurred in Bhopal. The tragedy was a technological accident in which 45Tonnes of highly poisonous methyl isocyanate (MIC) gas along with Hydrogen Cyanide and other reaction products leaked out of the pesticide factory of Union Carbide into the night air of Bhopal at around 12.30 a.m. The official death toll reached 3,598 in 1989. Thousands, who survived, however, face a fate worse than death.

In the event of fires, chemical leaks or explosions occurring in industrial facilities, people are exposed to the following dangers:

- The fire spreading in the industry and the residential areas nearby.
- Heat conditions.
- Chemical gas leak (poisonous).
- Combustion of various products and heat waves.
- Low oxygen levels.
- Falling of structural elements and machinery.
- Contamination of the nearby environment (land, water and air).

Onset Type and Warning

Onset in case of industrial disaster can be either rapid (minutes or hours) or sudden (no warning) depending on the nature of occurrence. As there is a series of processes and reactions involved the onset may vary accordingly. Release of chemicals may be because of human error, technological failure or natural activities which include geological activity like earthquakes, natural fires, floods etc. The industrial facility should have monitoring and warning systems for fire and building up of dangerous conditions. Explosion in some of the cases can be anticipated.

Elements at Risk

The industrial set-up and its near environment is under immediate threat. Employees of the work place, residents of nearby settlements, livestock and crops in the nearby vicinity are at risk. The environment which includes land, water and air will get polluted. Hazardous substance released into the air or water can travel long distances and cause contamination of air, water supply and land, making it uninhabitable for humans. Large scale disasters will threaten the ecological system.

Typical Effects

Physical Damage. Damage to structures and infrastructure. In case of explosion, fire, or release of toxins in the air the geographical spread can be high.

Casualties. Many people may be killed, injured and would require immediate treatment. The routes of exposure in chemical accidents are inhalation, eye exposure, skin contact and ingestion. Health effects are described in terms of the system or organ getting affected and may include cancer, heart failure, brain damage, disfunction of immune system, deformation, genetic disorders, congenital (present since birth) disorders etc. Fire can spread to a large area and may cause deaths by burns and asphyxiation.

Environmental. Contamination of air, water, land and standing crops may occur. Particular areas may become uninhabitable due to the damage caused to the environment.

Possible Risk Reduction Measures

Hazard Mapping. Inventories and maps of storage locations of toxins or hazardous substances alongwith the possible characteristics should be displayed and known to all. The community staying in the immediate vicinity should be aware of this hazard and possible effects in case of an accident should be known. The map should also determine the area that may get affected in case an accident occurs. Hazard map should determine possible zone getting affected and safe route for evacuation should be marked.

Land Use Planning. Densely populated residential areas should be separated far away from industrial areas. A buffer zone (green belt) should separate the industrial and the residential zone.

Community Preparedness. The community should be aware of the hazardous installations and know how to combat the situation. The local community has to be informed about the response steps to be taken in case of an accident.

Community members should monitor the pollution levels of the industry and participate in mock drills.

Other Possible Risk Reduction Measures. Maintain the wind flow diagram of the region, improve fire resistance and warning systems, improve fire fighting and pollution dispersion capabilities, develop emergency relief and evacuation planning for employees and nearby settlements, limit storage capacity of the toxic substances, insurance for industries and safety legislation the infectious agent (bacteria, viruses, parasites, or fungi or their products) and the environment that promotes the exposure (refer to the figure below) is upset.

OTHER TYPES OF HAZARDS AND DISASTERS

An Epidemic is defined as the occurrence of an illness or other health-related event that is clearly in excess of unexpected occurrence.

The Surat plague outbreak killed 56 people nationwide. This outbreak served as a chilling reminder of how rapid urbanization and deterioration of the urban environment can bring people into contact with forgotten disease vectors.

Causes

The main cause for an epidemic is the pathogen (virus, bacteria, protozoa or rarely fungi). Reports of outbreaks of communicable diseases are increasing in number and reported in many of the national dailies. This is because of a number of reasons. For instance poor sanitary conditions may contaminate food and water and also suffice the environment for breeding conditions for the vector. Other factors include the seasonal changes that favour the breeding of an insect vector such as mosquito in the rainy season, exposure of non-immune persons say tourists and migrants, poverty, overcrowding etc. Poverty is one of the major factor contributing to the vulnerability. Impact of natural disasters on the environment also leads to outbreak of epidemic. Part of the increase in the number of outbreaks is due to exposure of unreported cases of diseases as a result of better reporting and increased coverage of health services.

Elements at Risk

Population or a particular community is under risk. It can be localized or pandemic (spread across countries).

Typical Effects

Epidemics cause illness and death. There are other secondary effects such as disruption in the society and economic losses. Vulnerability is high among those are poorly nourished, people living in unhygienic sanitary conditions, poor water supply, individuals who do not have an access to the health services or those who have weak immune systems. The outbreak of an epidemic in situations where already a natural calamity has struck will cause life threatening situations.

Potential Risk Reduction Measures

Structuring the health services is important to have clear understanding of roles and responsibilities of the public health system. Organizational preparedness and the coordination mechanism is required right from the State and District to the sub center level which is manned by the Village Health Nurses or the Health Workers.

Contingency Plan for response should be prepared after identifying the epidemics that are likely to occur in the region. Early warning system through a surveillance system is the primary requirement so as to have an effective response and prevent any outbreaks. For this, surveillance need to be carried out at a regular basis through the routine surveillance system by involving the health tier system. Maps of all the health facilities in the region with an inventory of drugs and vaccines, laboratory set ups, list of number of doctors and supporting staff etc., need to be kept ready and updated at regular intervals. Training need to be given to so as to build the capacity at all levels. Training will help to cope better during the emergency response period for epidemics.

Personnel protection through vaccination is an effective mitigation strategy and will protect the persons at risk.

Environment

Shelter, altitude humidity, sanitation food supply, water supply temperature overcrowding essential services

Population

Age genetic susceptibility nutritional status previous exposure immunisation status general physical condition Equilibrium between the Population, Infectious Agent and the Environment Common sources of infection carriers can be tackled by many measures. Strategies included are improving the sanitary conditions, drive to check and fumigate breeding places of any vector (source of infection), improving disposal methods of waste, disinfecting the water source etc.

Heatwave Dangers and Effects

Human Effects. In many parts of the country and the world, every summer thousands of people suffer from heat stress when the bodies absorb more heat than they can dispel. Unless prompt preventive/treatment is received, they suffer the serious or even fatal consequences of heat stroke. Regardless of these statistics, heatwave is probably the most under rated of all natural hazards. The level of discomfort experienced in warm, moist tropical and sub-tropical conditions is determined by a range of climatic variables, principally air temperature, humidity and wind; as well as cultural variables including clothing, occupation and accommodation; and physiological variables such as health, fitness, age and the level of becoming accustomed. The main factor involved in the degree to which we feel uncomfortable in such conditions is not so much because we feel hot, but rather we sense how difficult it has become for us to lose body heat at the rate necessary to keep our inner body temperature close to 37°C.

The body responds to this stress progressively through three stages:

- **Heat Cramps.** Muscular pains and spasms caused by heavy exertion. Although heat cramps are the least severe stage they are an early signal that the body is having trouble with the heat;
- **Heat Exhaustion.** Typically occurs when people exercise heavily or work in a hot, humid place where body fluids are lost through heavy sweating. Blood flow to the skin increases causing a decrease of flow to vital organs. This results in mild shock with the symptoms of cold, clammy and pale skin together with fainting and vomiting. If not treated the victim may suffer heat stroke;
- **Heat Stroke.** Is life threatening the victims temperature control system, which produces sweating to cool the body, stops working. The body temperature may exceed 40.6°C potentially causing brain damage and death if the body is not cooled quickly. (**Source:** American Red Cross Website) Agriculture: animals suffer the same way as humans do, particularly when left without shade and adequate water. During heatwaves, especially in times of drought, livestock losses can be very high.

A Heatwave is a complex phenomenon resulting from a certain combination of temperature, huimidity, air movement and duration. Simply stated, a heatwave is an extended period of very high summer temperatures with the potential to adversely affect communities.

Heatwave claims several lives at different locations across the country. News report as on October 2004 put across fierce heat wave that left at least 622 dead over the past week as unseasonably dry winds push temperatures to sweltering levels in southern India. The deadly conditions, causing temperatures to soar as high as 46 degrees Celsius and above, have affected mainly the most vulnerable populations: the poor, elderly and outdoor workers, such at street vendors and farmers. Nearly 100 others have suffered heat-related deaths in the northern states of Punjab, Haryana and Orissa.

Plants, crops and vegetables are also subject to the effects of the heat. The damage to the standing crops is a common feature during such events.

Infrastructure. It is observed that during heatwaves railway lines can expand to the point where they buckle and cause derailments of trains. Road damage can also occur, where bitumen melting and concrete expanding and cracking occur. This may lead to disruption of traffic.

Forecasting and Warnings

The National Centre for Medium Range Weather Forecasting (NCMRWF) of Department of Science of Technology is the premier institution in India to provide Medium Range Weather Forecasts through deterministic methods and to render Agro Advisory Services (AAS) to the farmers. Advice will be included in the weather forecasts advising of the dangers of heat stress.

Agricultural Meteorology Division, India Meteorological Department (IMD), Pune looks into minimizing the impact of adverse weather on crops and to make use of crop-weather relationships to boost agricultural production. The Agricultural Meteorology Division was established at Pune in 1932 and from its inception the Division supports and participates in multi-disciplinary activities in this field. It is also the centre for research programmes in agricultural meteorology and has field units in various parts of the country. Besides, forecasts and advisories for farmers are issued by IMD's Forecasting Offices located at different State capitals.

Community Awareness

There appears to be a significant lack of community awareness of the risks associated with heat wave, even though several parts of the country experience such events with some regularity. It is a widely overlooked, even unknown, killer. It is ideal to create awareness among the communities and ask them to take suitable pre-cautionary steps during the peak summer months. Media and Community education can be launched prior to the onset of the heatwave conditions.

URBAN STRUCTURE FIRES

Fires are very dangerous. It is an event of something burning and is often destructive taking up toll of life and property. It is observed that more people die in fires than in cyclones, earthquakes, floods and all other natural disasters combined.

The most common human-caused hazard is fire in large occupied buildings and in slums built of combustible materials. Causes can be accidental or deliberate, but unless structures are built to safe fire standards as mentioned in the National Building Code and sound emergency procedures are used, heavy loss of life can result.

There are numerous causes of Fire. It could be:

1. Rubbish and Waste Materials that are left to accumulate can easily contribute to the spread of

fire; they are also a place for malicious fires to be started. Make sure that you remove all waste materials from the workplace on a regular basis and place them in a suitable container located in a safe position outside the building premises. Do not burn rubbish on bonfire, even if it is thought safe to do so. They can easily get out of control and spread fire to nearby buildings or structures.

2. Heating sources are often causes of Fire. Space heaters, electric heaters and fireplaces should be used with caution.
3. Cooking accidents are a major cause of home fires and cause us a lot of concern. Fires can result due to unattended cooking or due to mechanical failure of the stove or any cooking equipment.
4. Electrical wiring can cause a fire if it is not large enough to carry the load being supplied. Overheating of electrical appliances, poor wiring connections, use of unauthorized appliances, multi-point adaptors can result in fires starting.
5. Hazardous Materials such as paints, solvents, adhesive, chemicals or gas cylinders should be kept in separate storage areas and well away from any sources of ignition.
6. Arson and Deliberate Fire Setting is also a cause.
7. Smoking is also a major cause of fire.
8. Combustible Materials such as packing materials, glues, solvents, flammable liquids or gases stored in work place can be extremely dangerous. It is recommended to store materials both in terms of required quantity and in a secure area outside the premises.

Transport Accidents

Many factors govern the safety of passenger in an aircraft. It include technical problems, fire, landing and take off conditions, the environment an airline operates in (mountainous terrain or frequent storms), factors like airport security in cases of hijackings, bombing attempts etc.

The most common types of rail accident are derailment due to lack of maintenance, aging infrastructure, collateral hazards (ground shaking during an earthquake, rock fall on tracks after a landslide etc., causing damage to railway tracks) human error or sabotage. Various type of dangerous cargo are also transported such as fuel oil products, etc.

The main causes are the violation of traffic regulations, speeding, drunk driving and poor maintenance of the vehicle and the roads. All these reasons add to the rising number of accidents and road fatalities.

India has one of the highest accident rates in the world. Every year more than 300.000 accidents are reported. Fatality rate is as high as 60,000. Studies on accidents, the world over, have shown that the human factor is responsible for a majority of accidents.

In India, vehicle users are the causative factor, in 70% of the road accidents. Pedestrians are responsible for 4.1% of the road accidents and poor condition of the roads accounts for about 0.4% of the accidents. It is evident, that nearly 80% of the accidents occur due to bad driving habits and human error.

EFFECTS OF NATURAL HAZARD

While no country in the world is entirely safe, lack of capacity to limit the impact of hazards remains a major burden for developing countries. An estimated 97% of natural disaster related deaths each year occur in developing countries and, although smaller in absolute figures, the percentage of economic loss in relation to the Gross National Product (GNP) in developing countries far exceeds the ones in developed countries.

Natural disasters are a potentially serious shock to an economy. The United Nations estimated the total cost of disasters worldwide during the 1980s at $120 billion (in constant (1990) US dollars). Moreover, there is clear evidence of a rising trend, with total costs increasing from $70 billion in the 1970s and $40 billion in the 1960s.

These figures are typically based on only the direct, visible, financial impacts of a disaster such as damage to homes, hospitals, schools, factories, infrastructure and crops.

The true costs of disasters, taking into account less quantifiable effects such as the loss of personal belongings or jobs, widening trade or Government budget deficits, or the increasing scale and depth of poverty, are even higher.

Vulnerability

Vulnerability to disasters is a function of human action and behaviour. It describes the degree to which a socio-economic system or physical assets are either susceptible or resilient to the impact of natural hazards. It is determined by a combination of several factors, including awareness of hazards, the condition of human settlements and infrastructure, public policy and administration, the wealth of a given society and organized abilities in all fields of disaster and risk management.

Lack of awareness among the public and decision-makers about factors and human activities that contribute to environmental degradation and disaster vulnerability are aggravating these trends.

There is a close correlation between the trends of increased demographic pressure especially in developing countries and particularly in least developed countries, escalated environmental degradation, increased human vulnerability and the intensity of the impact of hazards. *For example,* river and lake floods are aggravated or even caused by deforestation, which causes erosion and clogs rivers, siltation of riverbeds and other factors.

The accelerated and often uncontrolled, growth of cities has contributed to the ecological transformation of their immediate surroundings (pressure on scarce land, deforestation, etc.) In addition, the lack of appropriate drainage systems and/or sealing (use of concrete and asphalt) increase the volume and speed of rainfall runoff thus, making many cities more vulnerable to flash floods. Recent catastrophic earthquakes highlight other key deficiencies and trends in the approach to disaster risk reduction, such as a poor understanding by decision-makers of seismic related risk, as well as the tendency of some builders, to use the cheapest designs and construction materials to increase shortterm economic returns on their investment.

Economic Vulnerability

The degree of severity and nature of impact of a disaster depend on a range of factors. These include the type of hazard, the size of the economy and its economic structure and the sectors affected by the disaster.

Looking at hazard types, we see that droughts do not damage buildings or physical structures but their lengthy duration creates other problems: *For example,* agricultural households may be forced into considerable debt following the loss of crops and livestock. In contrast, sudden-onset disasters such as floods or earthquakes have a direct impact on infrastructure and productive facilities and resources, as well as on social resources and infrastructure, especially housing. The economic costs of disasters can be broken down into three types.

Direct Costs

- Relate to the capital cost of assets (such as buildings, other physical infrastructure, raw materials and the like) destroyed or damaged in a disaster. Crop losses are often included in such calculations.

Indirect Costs

- Refer to the damage to the flow of goods and services. They include, *for example,* lower output from factories that have been destroyed or damaged; loss of sales income due to damaged infrastructure such as roads and ports; and the costs associated with having to purchase more expensive materials or other inputs where normal - cheaper - sources of supply are affected. They also include the costs of medical expenses and lost productivity arising from increased disease, injury and death.

Secondary Effects

- Concern the short and long-term impacts of a disaster on overall economic performance. These may include deterioration in external trade and Government budget balances, the reallocation of planned Government spending and increased indebtedness. Disasters can also affect the pattern of income distribution or the scale and incidence of poverty.

Some sectors of the economy are more vulnerable to hazards than others. Most obviously, the agricultural sector is potentially vulnerable, implying that countries which rely heavily on agriculture may be particularly threatened by hazards.

However, even here, the types of crops cultivated and techniques for growing them play a role in determining the scale of vulnerability. As the Philippines has learnt to its expense, new hybrid varieties of coconut trees, while giving high yields, are much more vulnerable to typhoons than traditional varieties which have longer root systems and so are better able to withstand very strong winds.

Economic Loss as an Indicator of Disaster Impact

Economic losses are often reported with reference to only the direct losses from infrastructure and assets destroyed during large-scale disasters. They seldom take into account the economic implications of reduced levels of production linked to damage in productive assets or infrastructure that in turn access to raw materials, energy labour or markets.

The use of economic loss indicator of disaster impact on development varies for different natural hazards. *For example,* earthquakes often appear to trigger the most expensive disasters, but losses are concentrated. Individual floods may not record large losses, but total human impact may be higher. Asian countries experience the greatest collective economic losses to disaster.

Economic Development Social Development Disaster Limits Developments Destruction of fixed assets. Loss of production capacity, market access or material inputs. Damage to transport, communications or energy infrastructure. Erosion of livelihoods, savings and physical capital.

Development causes disaster risk Unsuitable development practices that create wealth for some at the expense of unsafe working or living conditions for others or degrade the environment. Development paths generating cultural norms that promote social isolation or political exclusion.

Destruction of health or education infrastructure and personnel. Death, disablement or migration of key social actors leading to an erosion of social capital.

Development reduces disaster risk Access to adequate drinking water, food, waste management and a secure dwelling increases people's resiliency. Trade and technology can reduce poverty. Investing Building community cohesion, recognizing excluded individuals or social groups (such as women) and providing opportunities for greater in financial mechanisms and social security can cushion against vulnerability. involvement in decision-making, enhanced educational and health capacity increases resiliency.

Disaster Limits Economic Development

Disasters can wipe out the grains of economic development. Catastrophic disasters result in the destruction of fixed assets and physical capital, interruption of production and trade, diversion and depletion of savings and public and private investment. While absolute level of economic loss are greater in developed countries due to the far higher density and cost of infrastructure and production levels, less developed countries suffer higher levels of relative loss when seen as a proportion of Gross Domestic Product (GDP).

At the local level, disasters can seriously impact household livelihoods and push already vulnerable groups into poverty. The loss of income earners, through death or injury, the interruption of production or access to markets and the destruction of productive assets, such as home-based workshops, are all examples of ways in which disasters affect local and household economies. The capacity of a household or local community to absorb the impact and recover from a major natural hazard will be seriously limited if already weakened overtime by a series of smaller-scale losses.

Disaster Limits Social Development

A population that has weakened and depleted by natural disaster, particularly when it coincides with losses from malnutrition etc., will be less likely to have the organizational capacity to maintain irrigation works, bunds in fields for water harvesting, hillslope terraces, shelter belts. Without these social assets communities become more vulnerable. In addition to the loss of social assets themselves, there are many examples of disaster events destroying the gains of the health, sanitation, drinking water, housing and education sectors that underpin social development. Examples include the Kutch-Bhuj earthquake in 2001, which completely damaged district hospital, 992 primary schools and 18 secondary schools; or the cyclone that hit Orissa, India in 1999, which led to the contamination of drinking water wells and damaged many schools in the direct impact of a single event.

Women suffer additional stresses in disaster situations and also bear a disproportionate burden of the additional domestic and income-generating work necessary for survival following a disaster event. When women are exposed to additional stresses, the level of social development is reduced.

Development Projects

Projects should take into account risk assessment at the appraisal stage. Environmental Impact Reviews should systematically include a section on hazard proneness and consider disaster reduction measures where appropriate, with particular regard to the protection of lifeline infrastructure and critical facilities. In rural programmes and drought prone areas, specific regard should be given to food-security and promotion of agriculture techniques and inter-cropping that reduce hazard-related agriculture losses. Disaster reduction policies and measures need to be implemented, with a two-fold aim: to enable societies to be resilient to natural hazards while ensuring that development efforts do not increase the vulnerability to these hazards.

Disaster risk management falls under global trends of causing policy-makers to rethink the institutional setup of Governments and the roles and responsibilities of different levels of Government in achieving developmental objectives. Actors such as local Governments, municipal authorities and local communities play an increasingly important role in emerging national disaster risk management systems. There is a wide variety of ways in which disaster risk can be reduced as part of development policies. These involve institutional reforms, improved analytical and methodological capabilities, education, awareness, financial planning and political commitment.

This must expand beyond traditional response (Relief and Rehabilitation) to defense against the impact of natural hazards, as an ongoing process that does not focus on singular disaster events. Based on the lessons from the International Decade for Natural Disaster Reduction (IDNDR, 1990-99) four overriding objectives have been formulated in order to effectively reduce the impact of disasters, as the guiding principles for the International Strategy for Disaster Reduction. These overall objectives set the stage for the course of action for Governments, regional bodies and civil society organizations:

Obtaining the commitment from public authorities. This objective needs to be addressed through an increased inter-sectoral co-ordination at all levels, risk management strategies, the allocation of appropriate resources including development of new funding mechanisms. Disaster reduction should be dealt with as a separate policy issue as well as cross cutting in relevant fields of Government (public works, rural development, health, agriculture, food security, environment, etc.) aiming at policy integration among the various sectors.

Increasing public awareness and public participation on how to reduce vulnerability to hazards. This involves programmes related to formal and non-formal education and needs to be addressed through public information, education and multi-disciplinary professional training.

Stimulating inter-disciplinary and inter-sectoral partnerships and the expansion of risk reduction networking amongst Governments at national and local levels, greater involvement of the legislators, private sector, academic institutions, NGOs and Community Based Organizations (CBOs). This calls for strong coordination mechanisms, such as appropriate institutional structures for disaster management, preparedness, emergency response and early warning, as well as the incorporation of disaster reduction concerns in national/state planning processes. Efforts to link natural resource management with disaster reduction should also be encouraged.

Fostering better understanding and knowledge of the causes of disasters through the transfer and exchange of experience and greater access to relevant data and information. The issues to be addressed in this context are the assessment and analysis of socio-economic impacts of disasters, disaster databases, coping strategies of different social groups, early warning processes, as well as the promotion of scientific research, valuing of indigenous knowledge and the development and transfer of knowledge and technologies.

The causes and impacts of natural hazards some times occur in a number of neighbouring States, highlighting the need for a harmonized approach in the management of such a phenomenon. Efficiency can be optimized via exchange of experiences amongst states and constructive dialogue amongst stakeholders via participatory processes. Prioritization of tasks in the various phases of disaster management (prevention, preparedness, response, rehabilitation and recovery) has to be agreed upon to cope with such situations.

❋❋❋

2

Disaster and Risk Management Programme

India is one of the most vulnerable developing countries to suffer very often from various natural disasters, namely drought, flood, cyclone, earthquake, landslide, forest fire, hail storm, locust, volcanic eruption, etc. Which strike causing a devastating impact on human life, economy and environment. Though it is almost impossible to fully recoup the damage caused by the disasters, it is possible to:

(i) Minimize the potential risks by developing early warning strategies.

(ii) Prepare and implement developmental plans to provide resilience to such disasters.

(iii) Mobilize resources including communication and telemedicinal services.

(iv) To help in rehabilitation and post-disaster reconstruction.

Space technology plays a crucial role in efficient mitigation of disasters. While communication satellites help in disaster warning, relief mobilization and tele-medicinal support, earth observation satellites provide required database for pre-disaster preparedness programmes, disaster response, monitoring activities and post-disaster damage assessment and reconstruction and rehabilitation. The article describes the role of space technology in evolving a suitable strategy for disaster preparedness and operational framework for their monitoring, assessment and mitigation, identifies gap areas and recommends appropriate strategies for disaster mitigation *vis-a-vis* likely developments in space and ground segments. Various disasters like earthquake, landslides, volcanic eruptions, fires, flood and cyclones are natural hazards that kill thousands of people and destroy billions of dollars of habitat and property each year.

The rapid growth of the world's population and its increased concentration often in hazardous environment has escalated both the frequency and severity of natural disasters. With the tropical climate and unstable land forms, coupled with deforestation, unplanned growth proliferation non-engineered constructions which make the disaster-prone areas mere vulnerable, tardy communication, poor or no budgetary allocation for disaster prevention, developing countries suffer more or less chronically by natural disasters.

Asia tops the list of casualties due to natural disaster. Among various natural hazards, earthquakes, landslides, floods and cyclones are the major disasters adversely affecting very large areas and population in the Indian sub-continent. These natural disasters are of *(i)* geophysical origin such as earthquakes, volcanic eruptions, land slides and *(ii)* climatic origin such as drought, flood, cyclone, locust, forest fire.

Though it may not be feasible to control nature and to stop the development of natural phenomena but the efforts could be made to avoid disasters and alleviate their effects on human lives, infrastructure and property. Rising frequency, amplitude and number of natural disasters and attendant problem coupled with loss of human lives prompted the General Assembly of the United Nations to proclaim 1990s as the International Decade for Natural Disaster Reduction

(IDNDR) through a resolution 44/236 of December 22, 1989 to focus on all issues related to natural disaster reduction. Nevertheless, by establishing the rich disaster management related traditions and by spreading public awareness the IDNDR provided required stimulus for disaster reduction. It is almost impossible to prevent the occurrence of natural disasters and their damages. However, it is possible to reduce the impact of disasters by adopting suitable disaster mitigation strategies.

The disaster mitigation works mainly address the following:

(i) Minimise the potential risks by developing disaster early warning strategies.

(ii) Prepare and implement developmental plans to provide resilience to such disasters.

(iii) Mobilise resources including communication and tele-medicinal services.

(iv) To help in rehabilitation and post-disaster reduction.

Disaster management on the other hand involves:

(i) Pre-disaster planning, preparedness, monitoring including relief management capability.

(ii) Damage assessment and relief management.

(iii) Prediction and early warning.

Disaster reduction is a systematic work which involves with different regions, different professions and different scientific fields and has become an important measure for human, society and nature sustainable development.

Role of Space Technology

The Earth Observation satellites provide comprehensive, synoptic and multi temporal coverage of large areas in real time and at frequent intervals and 'thus'—have become valuable for continuous monitoring of atmospheric as well as surface parameters related to natural disasters. Geo-stationary satellites provide continuous and synoptic observations over large areas on weather including cyclone-monitoring. Polar orbiting satellites have the advantage of providing much higher resolution imageries, even though at low temporal frequency, which could be used for detailed monitoring, damage assessment and long-term relief management.

The vast capabilities of communication satellites are available for timely dissemination of early warning and real-time co-ordination of relief operations.

The advent of Very Small Aperture Terminals (VSAT) and Ultra Small Aperture Terminals (USAT) and phased-array antennae have enhanced the capability further by offering low cost, viable technological solutions towards management and mitigation of disasters.

Satellite communication capabilities-fixed and mobile are vital for effective communication, especially in data collection, distress alerting, position location and co-ordinating relief operations in the field. In addition, Search and Rescue satellites provide capabilities such as position determination facilities onboard which could be useful in a variety of land, sea and air distress situations.

DROUGHT

Drought is the single most important weather-related natural disaster often aggravated by human action. Drought's beginning is subtle, its progress is insidious and its effects can be devastating. Drought may start any time, last indefinitely and attain many degrees of severity. Since it affects very large areas for months and years it has a serious impact on economy, destruction of ecological resources, food shortages and starvation of millions of people. During 1967-1991, droughts have affected 50 percent of the 2.8 billion people who suffered from all natural disasters and killed 35 percent of the 3.5 million people who lost their lives due to natural disasters. Owing to abnormalities in the monsoon precipitation, in terms of spatial and temporal variation especially on the late on set of monsoon, prolonged break and early withdrawal of monsoon, drought is a frequent phenomenon over many parts of India. In India, thirty three percent of the area receives less than 750 mm rainfall and is chronically drought-prone and thirty five percent of the area with 750-1125 mm rainfall is also subject to drought once in four to five years. Thus, 68 percent of the total sown area covering about 142 million hectares are vulnerable to drought conditions.

Drought Preparedness

Drought mitigation involves three phases, namely, preparedness phase, prevention phase and relief phase. In case of drought preparedness, identification of drought prone areas information on land use and land cover, waste lands, forest cover and soils is a pre-requisite. Space-borne multi spectral measurements hold a great promise in providing such information.

Drought Prediction

Remote sensing data provide major input to all the three types rainfall predictions; namely such as long-term seasonal predictions, medium range predictions and short-term predictions. Global and regional atmospheric, land and ocean parameters (temperature, pressure, wind, snow, El-Nino, etc.) required for long-term prediction, could be generated from observations made by geo-stationary and polar orbiting weather satellites such as INSAT and NOAA.

In the medium range weather prediction, the National Centre Medium Range Weather Forecasting (NCMRWF) uses satellite-based sea surface temperature, normalised difference vegetation index, snow covered area and depth, surface temperature, altitude, roughness, soil moisture at surface level and vertical sounding and radio sonde data on water vapor, pressure and temperature.

Drought Monitoring

Drought monitoring mechanisms exists in most of the countries using ground-based information on drought-related parameters such as rainfall, weather, crops condition and water availability, etc. Conventional methods of drought monitoring in the various States in India suffer from limitations with regard to timeliness, objectivity, reliability and adequacy (Jeyaseelan and Thiruvengadachari, 1986). Further, the assessment is generally, influenced by local compulsions. In order to overcome the above limitations,-sponsored a project titled 'National Agricultural Drought Assessment and Monitoring System (NADAMS)' and sponsored by the Department of Agriculture and Cooperation and Department of Space Department of Space (DOS) was taken up by the National Remote Sensing Agency in collaboration with the India Meteorological Department (IMD), Central Water Commission (CWC) and concerned State Government agencies.

The focus has been on the assessment of agricultural drought conditions in terms of prevalence, relative severity level and persistence through the season. Satellite-derived Vegetation Index (VI) which is sensitive to vegetation stress is being used as a surrogate measure to continuously monitor the drought conditions on a real-time basis. Such an exercise helps the decision makers in initiating strategies for recovery by changing cropping patterns and practices. Initially, NDVI derived from NOAA-AVHRR data was used for drought monitoring biweekly drought bulletins have been issued between 1989 to 1991 and reports on monthly detailed crop and seasonal condition during kharif season (June to October) have been brought out since 1992 at district level.

The project covers eleven agriculturally important and drought-vulnerable States of Andhra Pradesh, Bihar, Gujarat, Haryana, Karnataka, Maharashtra, Madhya Pradesh, Orissa, Rajasthan, Tamil Nadu and Uttar Pradesh.

With the availability of Indian Remote Sensing satellite (IRS) WiFS data with 188m spatial resolution, the methodology is being updated to provide quantitative information on sowings, surface water spread and taluk/mandal/block level crop condition assessment alongwith spatial variation in terms of maps. The IRS WiFS-based detailed monitoring has been opertionalised for Andhra Pradesh State in 1998 and subsequently extended to Orissa and Karnataka.

Drought Relief

The State Governments are primarily responsible for both short-term and long-term relief management. The NADAMS provide detailed assessment of drought conditions for providing short-term relief.

Several chronically drought-affected districts in India experience acute shortage of drinking and irrigation water. To address this issue, a nationwide project titled 'Integrated Mission for Sustainable Development (IMSD)' was taken up in collaboration with other DOS centres and State Remote Sensing Applications Centres. The project essentially aims at generating locale-specific action plan for development of land and water resources on a micro watershed basis in drought-prone areas of the country using IRS data. In the first phase, 175 districts covering 84 million ha has been covered (Rao,1998).

For providing safe drinking water to rural masses, a nationwide project titled "National Drinking Water Technology Mission", was launched by Department of Space (DOS) in collaboration with other State Remote Sensing Applications Centres and Central Ground Water Board and State Ground water Departments. Ground water potential maps showing ground water prospect at 1:250,000 scale have been prepared for entire country. The success rate achieved by drilling wells through the use of remote sensing data has been found to be much better than those achieved by conventional means. Furthermore, as a follow-up large scale (1:50,000) mapping of ground water prospects for Rajasthan, Madhya Pradesh Andhra Pradesh, Karnataka and Kerela under Rajiv Gandhi National Drinking Water Mission is in progress.

CYCLONE

The intense tropical storms are known in different part of the world by different names. In the Pacific ocean, they are called 'typhoons', in the Indian ocean they are called 'cyclones' and over North Atlantic, they are called 'hurricane'. Among various natural calamaties, tropical cyclones are known to claim a higher share of deaths and distruction world over. Records show that about 80 tropical cyclones form over the globe every year.

India has a vast coast line which is frequently affected by tropical cyclones causing heavy loss of human lives and property. Cyclones occurs usually between April and May (called pre-monsoon cyclonic storms) and between October and December (called post-monsoon cyclonic storms). While cyclonic storms can't be prevented, the loss of lives and damage to the properties can be mitigated if prompt action is taken after receiving timely warnings.

Cyclone Warning

Meteorologists have been using satellite images for monitoring storms for about thirty years. One of the most important applications in this endeavour is to determine the strength and intensity of a storm. In the late 1960's, meteorologists began observing tropical cyclones at more frequent intervals. The infrared sensors aboard polar orbiting satellites began providing day-and-night observations while geo-stationary satellite provided the continuous coverage during daytime. There exists a very efficient cyclone warning system in India which is comparable to the best known in the world. The approach essentially involves the pre-diction of the track and intensity of the cyclone using conventional as well as satellite and radar-based techniques (Kellar, 1997).

A network of 10-cyclone detection radar covering entire East and West Coasts is being used for cyclone warning each with a range of 400 km. When cyclone is beyond the range of coastal radar, its intensity and movement is monitored with the help of INSAT and NOAA series of satellites. The INSAT provides every three-hourly cloud pictures over the Indian subcontinent. For precise location, every half-an-hour pictures are used. Warnings are issued by the Area Cyclone Warning Centers (ACWS) located at Calcutta, Madras and Bombay; and Cyclone Warning Centers (CWC) located at Bhubaneswar, Visakhapatnam and Ahmedabad. Around 100 disaster warning systems have been installed in cyclone-prone villages of Andhra Pradesh and Tamil Nadu. It is planned to expand such facility with another 100 DWS in Orissa and West Bengal on the East coast. The DWC disseminates warning of impending event to village administration, District Collector, State Government officials, etc. The most memorable use of DWS system has been during the cyclone that hit the Andhra Pradesh coast on may 9, 1990, in evacuating over 1,70,000 people. The information helped saving thousands of lives and livestock in this area. Additional DWS units are being established to cover the entire coastal areas of the country.

Cyclone Management

The most striking advantage of the earth observation satellite data has been demonstrated during the recent Orissa super-cyclone event. A severe cyclonic storm with a wind speed about 260 kmph hit the Orissa coast at Paradip on 29 October, 1999 causing extensive damage to human life, property, live stock and public utilities. The National Remote Sensing Agency acted promptly and provided spatial extent of inundated areas using pre-cyclone IRS LISS-III data collected on 11th October, 1999 and Radarsat Synthetic Aperture Radar (RSAR) data of 2nd November, 1999 since cloud-free optical sensor data over the cyclone-hit area were not available.

The map showing inundated area as on 2nd November, 1999 was drapped over topographical map and was delivered to the Orissa Government on 3rd November,1999. Information, thus, generated, was effectively used by various departments of Orissa Government involved in relief operations. Subsequently, the recession of inundated areas was also studied using Radarsat and IRS data of 5th, 8th,11th,13th and 14th November, 1999. An estimated 3.75 lakh ha. in Jagatsinghpur, Kendrapara, Bhadrak, Balasore, Jajpur, besides Cuttack, Khurda and Puri districts had been found to be inundated. In addition, the crop damage assessment was also made and maps alongwith block-wise statistics derived using pre-and post-cyclone NDVI image from IRS WiFS data were also provided to Orissa Government.

FLOODS

India is the worst flood-affected country in the world after Bangladesh and accounts for one-fifth of the global death count due to floods. About 40 million hectares or nearly 1/8th of India's geographical area is flood-prone. An estimated 8 million hectares of land are affected annually. The cropped area affected annually ranges from 3.5 million ha during normal floods to 10 million ha during worst flood. Flood control measures consists mainly of construction of new embankments, drainage channels and afforestation to save 546 towns and 4700 villages. Optical and microwave data from IRS, Landsat ERS and Radarsat series of satellites have been used to map and monitor flood events in near real-time and operational mode. Information on inundation and damage due to floods is furnished to concerned departments so as to enable them organising necessary relief measures and to make a reliable assessment of flood damage. Owing to large swath and high repetivity, WiFS data from IRS-1C and-1D hold great promise in floods monitoring.

Based on satellite data acquired during pre-flood, flood and post-flood alongwith ground information, flood damage assessment is being carried out by integrating the topographical, hydrological and flood plain land use/land cover information in a GIS environment. In addition, spaceborne multispectral data have been used for studying the post-flood river configuration and existing flood control structures and identification of bank erosion-prone areas and drainage congestion and identification of flood risk zones.

Flood Disaster Impact Minimization

Flood forecasts are issued currently by Central Water Commission using conventional rainfall runoff models with an accuracy of around 65% to 70% with a warning time of six to twelve hours. The poor performance is attributed to the high spatial variability of rainfall not captured by ground measurements and lack of spatial information on the catchment characteristics of the basin such as current hydrological land use/land cover, spatial variability of soils, etc.

Incorporation of remote sensing inputs such as satellite-derived rainfall estimates, current hydrological land use/ land cover, soil information, etc., in rainfall-runoff model subsequently improves the flood forecast. Improvements in flood forecasting was tested in lower Godavari basin in a pilot study titled "Spatial Flood Warning System". Under this project, a comprehensive database including Digital Elevation Model (DEM) generated using Differential Global Positioning System (DGPS), hydraulic/hydrologic modeling capabilities and a Decision Support System (DSS) for appropriate relief response has been addressed in collaboration with concerned departments of Andhra Pradesh Government. Initial results have been quite encouraging. The deviation in the flood forecast from actual river flood has been within 15%.

EARTHQUAKE

Earthquakes are caused by the abrupt release of strain that has built up in the earth's crust. Most zones of maximum earthquake intensity and frequency occur at the boundaries between the moving plates that form the crust of the earth. Major earthquakes also occur within the interior of crustal plates such as those in China, Russia and the southeast United States. A considerable research has been carried out to predict earthquakes using conventional technologies, but the results to date are inconclusive. Seismic risk analysis based on historic earthquakes and the presence of active faults is an established method for locating and designing dams, power plants and other projects in seismically active areas.

Landsat-TM and SPOT images and Radar interferograms have been used to detect the active faults (Merifield and Lamer 1975; Yeats *et al.*1996; Massonnet *et al.* 1993). Areas rocked by Landers earthquake (South California) of magnitude 7.3 were studied using ERS-1 SAR interferometry which matched extremely well with a model of the earth's motion as well as the local measurements (Masonnet and Advagna 1993). Active faults on the seafloor could also be detected by side-scan sonar system.

The earthquake prediction is still at experimental stage. Successful prediction of minor earthquake have, however, been reported. Among the major earthquakes, Chinese scientists predicted an earthquake 1-2 days ahead in 1975 (Vogel, 1980). Information on earthquake is, generally, obtained from a network of seismographic stations. However, very recently the space geodetic techniques and high resolution aerial and satellite data have been used for earthquake prediction. Space geodetic technique with Global Positioning

System (GPS) provides an accuracy of a centimetre over 1000 km and, thus, helps in measuring the surface deformations and monitoring accelerated crystal deformations prior to earth quakes with required accuracy.

Earthquake risk assessment involves identification of seismic zones through collection of geological/structural, geophysical (primarily seismological) and geomorphologic data and mapping of known seismic phenomena in the region, (mainly epicenters with magnitudes). Such an effort calls for considerable amount of extrapolation and interpolation on the basis of available data. There is also a tendency for earthquake to occur in "gaps" which are in places along an earthquake belt where strong earthquake had not previously been observed.

The knowledge of trends in time or in space helps in defining the source regions of future shocks.. Satellite imagery could be used in delineating geotectonic structures and to clarify seismological conditions in earthquake risk zones. Accurate mapping of geomorphologic features adjoining lineaments reveals active movement or recent tectonic activity along faults.

The relationship between major lineaments and the seismic activity has been observed in Latur area of Maharastra, India. Space techniques have overcome the limitations of ground geodetic surveys/measurements and have become an essential tool to assess the movement/displacements along faults/plate boundaries to even millimetre level accuracy.

Using Very Long Baseline Interferometry (VLBI), it has been possible to record accurately the plate movement of the order of centimetre along baseline of hundreds of kilometre. Similarly, satellite-based Global Positioning System (GPS) has emerged as a powerful geodetic tool for monitoring (geological) changes over time which is the key for understanding the long-term geo-dynamical phenomena.

GPS has been particularly useful in measuring the more complex deformation patterns across plate boundaries where large and regional scale strain builds up. Plate movements, slips along faults etc., have been measured using differential GPS to an accuracy of sub-centimetres.

VOLCANIC ERUPTION

Many times precursors of volcanic eruptions have been observed in various areas of volcanic activity. Ground deformations, changes in the compositions of gases emitting from volcanic vents, changes in the temperatures of fumaroles, hot springs and crater lakes as well as earth tremors are preceding volcanic eruptions. Thermal infrared remote sensing has been applied for volcanic hazard assessment. However, deficiencies of equipment and coverage suggest that thermal infrared has not been adequately evaluated for surveillance of volcanoes. The National Remote Sensing Agency has demonstrated the potential of multi-temporal Landsat-TM thermal band data in the surveillance of active volcanoes over Barren island volcano which erupted during March 1991 to September 1991 (Bhatacharya *et al.* 1992). In the last three decades, aircraft and satellite-based thermal infrared (TIR) data have been used extensively to detect and monitor many of the active volcanoes around the world.

Repetitive coverage, regional scale and low cost of thermal infrared images from satellites make it an alternative tool for monitoring volcanoes. Although the spatial resolution of NOAA environment satellite is too coarse to record details of surface thermal patterns, the plumes of smoke and ash from volcanoes could be detected which is useful in planning the rehabilitation of affected areas. Studies have shown that the upward migration of magma from the earth's crust just before eruption inflates the volcanic cone. Such premonitory signs can easily and quickly be detected with the aid of differential SAR interferometry. Extensive calibrations in a variety of test areas have shown that by using this technique, changes on the earth's surface can be detected to a centimetre accuracy.

LANDSLIDES

Aerial photographs and large-scale satellite images have been used to locate the areas with the incidence of landslide. Higher spatial resolution and stereo imaging capability of IRS-IC and-1D enable further refining the location and monitoring of landslides.

A number of studies have been carried out in India using satellite data and aerial photographs to develop appropriate methodologies for terrain classification and preparation of maps showing landslide hazards in the Garhwal Himalayan region, Nilagiri Hills in South India and in Sikkim forest area.

Such studies have been carried out using mostly aerial photographs because of their high resolution enabling contour mapping with intervals of better than 2 m in height. The availability of 1m resolution data from the future IRS mission may help generating contour maps at 2 m intervals making thereby space remote sensing a highly cost effective tool in landslide zonation.

RISK MANAGEMENT PROGRAMME

Through Participation of Communities and Local Self Governments Summary of the Programme: UNDP has been supporting various initiatives of the central and state Governments to strengthen disaster management capacities for nearly a decade. UNDP proposes to accelerate capacity building in disaster reduction and recovery activities at the national level and in some of the most-vulnerable regions in the country through community-based and gender sensitive approaches with two sub-national Networking Hubs. It is designed to assist the states in the country, which are most prone to natural disasters such as Gujarat, Orissa, Bihar, Tamil Nadu, West Bengal, Maharashtra, Delhi, Uttar Pradesh, Uttaranchal, Assam, Meghalaya and Sikkim. The thematic focus will be on awareness generation and education, training and capacity development for mitigation and better preparedness in-terms of disaster risk management and recovery at community, district and state levels and strengthening of state and district disaster management information centers for accurate and timely dissemination of warning. Specialized support to Ministry of Home Affairs (MHA) would be provided to enable them to set-up the institutional and administrative system for disaster risk management.

The overall goal of the programme is "Sustainable Reduction in Disaster Risk in some of the most hazard-prone districts in the selected States of India".

Eastern and Western India have been suggested as the preferred locations of the two Networking Hubs for disaster risk management as they are strategically located in terms of lessons learnt from the disasters they have experienced in the past. They have all the features of 'disaster-prone' areas given their high degree of vulnerability. These two networking hubs will also facilitate better liasioning with state counterparts and would contribute to UNDP's national efforts in strengthening capacities for disaster risk management. This programme would also dovetail all national programmes supported by UNDP, especially pro-poor initiatives, uncertainty reduction and vulnerability adaptation and assessment under the UN Framework for Convention on Climatic Change.

This programme forms the nucleus of a much larger programme for which resources would be mobilized under a multi-donor framework constituted by Government of India to achieve the overall goal of the programme. Government of

India-UNDP have earlier approved US$ 2 million from CCF-I to initiate the programme in 28 Districts of Orissa, Bihar and Gujarat alongwith national level capacity building support to the Ministry of Home Affairs (MHA).

The Community based approach that was envisaged in the programme has been well-received by communities, Panchayati Raj Institutions (PRIs) and State Governments in the 3 pilot states in Phase I, where successful partnerships have been established with Governments, civil society, as well as private sector. A group of International and National experts evaluated the approach and process under this programme and rated it as an effective and sustainable initiative. The team also noted that the approach and scale make it a pioneering initiative. Following the successful initiation of activities in Phase I, The Government of India has formulated The National Disaster Management Framework and Roadmap for the country with UNDP support, making this programme a platform for future National initiatives in disaster risk management. The Government of India has taken initiative in mobilising resources for this programme from bilateral and other funding partners.

Situation Analysis

Frequent disasters lead to erosion of development gains and restricted options for the disaster victims. Physical safety-especially that of the vulnerable groups-is routinely threatened by hazards. These two major disasters have very clearly illustrated that we need multi-hazard prevention, response and recovery plans for natural hazards so that threat to human life and property is minimized.

Disaster risk management is essentially a development problem and thus, any preparedness and mitigation planning will have to be taken up in tandem with environmental concerns that the country is facing today. The Government of India has set-up a National Committee on Disaster

Management (NCDM) under the Chairmanship of the Prime Minister. The recommendations of this National Committee would form the basis of national disaster risk management programme and strengthening the natural disaster management and response mechanisms. The High Powered Committee [HPC] on Disaster Management was earlier constituted in August 1999. The mandate of the HPC was to prepare Disaster Management Plans at National, State and District level and also suggest strengthening of existing arrangements. The recommendations of the HPC relating to the distribution of relief and human resource development that primarily concerns the States have been communicated to the States for appropriate action.

Disaster Management is deemed to be a 'state subject' and different states have initiated efforts to strengthen their agencies responsible for disaster management. Orissa State Disaster Mitigation Authority (OSDMA) and Gujarat State Disaster Management Authority (GSDMA) were constituted after two major disasters that the respective states experienced. They are autonomous agencies of the respective State Governments and UNDP has been working closely with both these agencies.

UNDP's partnerships with the national and state institutions have been based on the links that natural disasters have with scarcity, inequality and vulnerability. This Programme essentially aims at strengthening community, local self-governments and district administrations' response, preparedness and mitigation measures in some of the most vulnerable districts alongwith states' and national response.

The key element of this programme is establishing linkages between the Government and civil society response plans and capacity building of Government institutions and the local self-governments in disaster mitigation, preparedness and recovery. Panchayati Raj and Urban Planning Institutions at all levels in the selected districts would be directly involved in the planning process to ensure sustainability of these initiatives. A wide representation of women is envisaged in this project during the planning process. Self-help groups of women in the programme areas would be directly involved in the disaster risk management programme. This project will work closely relevant Government departments and institutions at the national and State levels. Learnings from this programme will feed into the national capacity building programmes of the Government of India and the global knowledge base on disaster risk management.

Programme Strategy

UNDP intends to support national and state efforts in disaster management with emphasis on the most multi-hazard prone districts by strengthening the capacities of the communities, local-self governments and districts to deal with future disasters. This programme design is based on UNDP support to the states of Orissa and Gujarat after the two disasters these states experienced. There is a need for capacity building at each level: community and local self-governments in both urban and rural areas, district and state administration and national institutions.

On the basis of the Vulnerability Atlas prepared by Building Materials Promotion and Technology Council (BMPTC), Government of India, UNDP and Ministry of Home Affairs have identified 199 multi-hazard prone districts in the country. UNDP would focus on all multi-hazard prone districts in select States, which are extremely vulnerable to natural hazards such as Gujarat, Orissa, Bihar, Tamil Nadu, West Bengal, Maharashtra, Delhi, Uttar Pradesh, Uttaranchal, Assam, Meghalaya and Sikkim for a comprehensive programme on disaster risk management. In this programme, a multi-pronged strategy would be adopted:

- Support National Government efforts in strengthening its role in community and local self-governments' preparedness and response, including support to National Civil Defense College [NCDC] and National Fire Service College [NFSC].

- Support to Ministry of Home Affairs for ensuring administrative, institutional, financial and legal mechanisms for disaster risk management.
- Comprehensive disaster risk management programme in the selected 125 most vulnerable districts falling in Gujarat, Orissa, Bihar, Tamil Nadu, West Bengal, Maharashtra, Delhi, Uttar Pradesh, Uttaranchal, Assam, Meghalaya and Sikkim in two phases.

These states are exposed to various natural disasters and strengthening disaster prevention, response and recovery in all multi-hazard prone districts would minimize disaster risk. The programme components would include the following:

- Development of disaster risk management and response plans at Village/Ward, Gram Panchayat, Block/Urban Local Body levels.
- Development of state and district disaster management plans.
- Capacity building of Disaster Management Teams at all levels. Special training for women in first aid, shelter management, water and sanitation, rescue and evacuation, etc.
- Constitutions of Disaster Management Teams and Committees at all levels with adequate representation of women in all committees and team. (Village/Ward, Gram Panchayat, Block/Urban local body, District and State.)
- Capacity building in cyclone and earthquake resistant features for houses in disaster-prone districts,

training in retrofitting and construction of technology demonstration units.

- Integration of disaster management plans with development plans of local self-governments.

The Super Cyclone (1999) and the floods of 2001 in Orissa have many lessons to offer in design of effective disaster management systems for cyclones and floods. Similarly, Gujarat has many best practices to offer in earthquake response and recovery. UNDP has been working very closely with the key stakeholders in these two states. UNDP would support Governments, civil society organizations and institutions in the programme states, in replicating and enhancing the successful initiatives in community based disaster reduction and recovery in Orissa and Gujarat in the 125 most hazard-prone districts. Disaster Risk Management can be addressed in three ways: Structural measures, non-structural measures and establishing failsafe communication networks.

Structural measures would reduce the impact of disasters and non-structural measures would enhance the management skills and improve capacities of the community, local self-governments, urban bodies and the State authorities to prepare, prevent and respond effectively to disasters. Non-structural measures are of utmost importance and include vulnerability mapping, risk assessment analysis, hazard zoning, inventory of resources to meet the emergency, etc.

The project envisages the following:

(a) Appropriate specialized support to Ministry of Home Affairs (MHA) for setting-up the system and framework for disaster risk management.

(b) Support to include disaster management in school curriculum and schedule to drills in disaster prevention and response for schools.

(c) Development of national/state database on vulnerability, disaster risk management and sustainable recovery.

(d) Awareness campaigns on disaster mitigation and preparedness for each programme state.

(e) Strengthening National and State Governments through support for hardware and software for disaster risk management and capacity building of institutions.

(f) Promoting partnerships with academic institutions and private sector in development of disaster risk management plans.

(g) Capacity building activities for all stakeholders including civil society organizations in the rescue, relief and restoration in disaster situations and the use of equipment involved.

(h) Development of training manuals in Disaster Management for District, Block, Gram Panchayat, Villages/Wards for each State in vernacular languages.

(i) Strengthening disaster management information centers in programme states and districts for accurate dissemination of early warning and flow of information for preparedness and quick recovery operations.

(j) Dissemination of cost effective alternate technologies for hazard resistant housing-including retrofitting/ roof top rainwater harvesting features as long-term mitigation measures.

(k) District multi-hazard preparedness and mitigation plans intergrating Block/ULB, Gram Panchayat,

Village/Ward plans which would involve vulnerability mapping, risk assessment and analysis, hazard zoning, resource inventory, response structure, etc

Resource Mobilization Strategy

This programme would be initiated with US$ 2 million from CCF-I and US $ 5 million from CCF-II and would form the nucleus of a much larger Government of India initiative for disaster risk reduction and sustainable recovery. MHA aims to address the disaster risk management needs of the most multi-hazard prone districts in 12 states of India through this programme. The resources required for the programme would be US$ 27 million approximately, over a period of six years. Multi-donor meetings would be held by Ministry of Home Affairs with UNDP support to mobilize funds for this programme.

GOALS AND OBJECTIVES

Goal. Sustainable Reduction in Disaster Risk in some of the most hazard prone Districts in selected States of India

Indicators. The indicators of achievement of this goal would be:

(a) Risk reduction factored in rapid disaster recovery.

(b) Disaster mitigated and development gains protected.

(c) Disaster risk considerations mainstreamed into development.

(d) Gender equity in disaster preparedness.

PSO-I

National capacity building to institutionalize the system for natural disaster risk management in Ministry of Home Affairs.

PSO-II

Environment building, education, awareness programmes and strengthening capacities at all levels in natural disaster risk management and sustainable recovery. [Development of manuals and training modules, information, education and communication materials and their dissemination, awareness campaign strategy and implementation for disaster reduction and recovery.]

PSO-III

Multi-hazard preparedness, response and mitigation plans for disaster risk management at state, district, block, village and ward level in 125 most multi-hazard prone districts of 12 selected states.

PSO-IV

Networking knowledge on effective approaches, methods and tools for disaster risk management, developing and promoting policy frameworks at State and National levels. The activities envisaged are as follows:

Activities under PSO-I

- Capacity building of functionaries at National level to sustain the programme.
- Supporting the Ministry of Home Affairs for establishment of institutional, administrative, financial and legal systems for disaster risk management, with built-in mechanisms to ensure adequate representation of women at community level.
- Support for outlining the development of policy initiatives for disaster risk management in the country, building on the work of High Powered Committee report and with a conscious effort to

mainstream gender (by giving special thought to the needs of women and disabled persons in policy, in preparedness, mitigation as well as response) and decentralization (by ensuring PRIs' ownership in disaster management activities and plans at community level) at all levels of disaster management.

- Exposure visits to understand the best practices in the area of disaster risk management and sustainable recovery.

Activities under PSO-II

- Consultations with National and State Governments, NGOs, training institutions, private sector etc., at state, district and sub-district levels for area specific disaster reduction and recovery strategies.
- Finalization of districts for the programme in the selected States.
- Formulation of state specific awareness campaigns and strategies for implementation for disaster risk management in the selected districts.
- Sensitization of all stakeholders, including women representatives and PRIs on the need for disaster risk management and mitigation.
- Awareness generation programmes at all levels including all villages/wards in selected districts through workshops/seminars/training, posters/ leaflets, wall painting and observation of disaster risk management day/week.
- Development of school primers on disaster management, training of teachers in curricula, preparedness and response activities, mock drills in schools, etc.

- Development of manuals for design and construction of hazard-resistant houses in the selected districts.
- Development of manuals for District, Block, Gram Panchayat, Community and Ward level for preparing disaster risk management and response plans.
- Development of user-friendly manuals for retrofitting, roof top rainwater harvesting features, etc.
- Manuals for training and orientation of Disaster Management Teams [DMT] at all levels in dissemination of accurate warning, search and rescue operations, first aid, water and sanitation, shelter management, counselling and damage assessment for early response and recovery, proper utilization and better co-ordination of relief materials during crisis time.
- Training of all stakeholders on the process of development of village/ward based disaster risk management and response plans.

Activities under PSO-III

- Identification and establishment of working networks of nodal agencies and partners at different levels for implementation of the programme. Formations of committees to look at gender mainstreaming.
- Formation of State, District, Block, Gram Panchayat, Village/Ward Disaster Management Committees [DMC], which would include all concerned Government Departments/functionaries, Senior Citizens, National Cadet Corps (NCC), National Social Service (NSS), Nehru Yuva Kendra Sangathan (NYKS), Zilla Sainik Board, elected members (PRIs), NGOs, Community Based Organizations (CBOs) and

other civil society response groups. Each DMC would have equal representation of women and at community level, would include school teachers, disabled persons, village volunteers and members of isolated hamlets.

- Development of disaster management plans at district, block, municipality, gram panchayat, village/ ward levels. Women and disabled persons, socially marginalised sections, etc., would be an integral part of the plan preparation activity.
- Vulnerability mapping and risk assessment in all the multi-hazard prone districts with special emphasis on vulnerability and risk of women, disabled persons and children, to help in formulating gender equitable and sustainable community plans for disaster preparedness.
- Development of disaster response structure from village/ward to district level.
- Disaster Response Mock drills at all levels-National, State, Districts, Block, Gram Panchayat and village/ ward levels.
- Identification aprons and emergency response kits for DMT members.
- Formation and training of Disaster Management Teams [DMT] at all levels. Each DMT would ensure adequate representation of women. Members of DMTs at all levels would be sensitised to response and recovery needs of special groups.
- Training of masons and engineers to upgrade their skills in the construction of cost effective disaster resistant houses and in retrofitting features. Women construction workers would be encouraged to train

as masons and training sessions would ensure women's participation

- Enable citizen's access to disaster risk management and development related information at District Disaster Management Information Centers.
- Model technology demonstration units showing retrofitting initiatives and rooftop rainwater harvesting features as mitigation measures in the selected districts. Participation of women would be encouraged.

Activities under PSO-IV

- National database on disaster risk management and disaster response plans.
- Capability assessment and national training plan for natural disaster risk management
- Development of Risk and Vulnerability Reduction Indices and annual reports.
- Research and documentation on disaster risk management indices for each State.
- Documentation and sharing of best practices in India in disaster risk management for wider circulation as part of training curriculum.
- Development of GIS based disaster vulnerability database for States and its use to generate risk and vulnerability reports, to be used as policy instruments to direct national and state policy on disaster risk management.
- Development and use of a web-site linking DRM Programme implementation partners (National and State Governments, UNDP, etc.,) to share activities, approaches, methods to mainstream disaster

management, gender, decentralization etc., and exchange best practices and lessons learnt between States.

- Consultations and studies in disaster risk management and global climatic change linkages.

MANAGEMENT ARRANGEMENTS

Execution Arrangements

Ministry of Home Affairs, Government of India would execute this programme under National Execution [NEX] guidelines.

The programme involves partnerships at different levels and with different stakeholders. It aims to reach most multi-hazard prone states and districts and thus, it has a multi-state focus. The programme seeks to establish close partnership with communities and civil society organizations. Programme demands greater flexibility, creativity and innovative approaches for natural disaster risk management. In view of the complexities involved in the implementation.

Institutional Arrangements

1. Co-ordination at the National Level. The Ministry of Home Affairs, Government of India will be the nodal agency at central level for smooth execution of the programme supported out of Country Cooperation Framework resources. There would be a Programme Management Board (PMB) headed by the Secretary, MHA to provide overall guidance to the programme. Programme Steering Committee (PSC) headed by the Joint Secretary [DM] in MHA would be constituted, which will meet in every quarter to review the progress of the programme.

2. Monitoring at the State Level. In each state, a State Steering Committee (SSC) headed by Chief Secretary will review the programme at periodic intervals. The committee may consist of executing agencies, implementing agency and UNDP. A joint UNDP-Government of India assessment would be carried out to examine the effectiveness of the programme at the end of each programme year.

3. The financial arrangement and audit would as per the guidelines of Department of Economic Affairs, UNDP guidelines and procedures established for Country Office Support agreements.

The UNDP Country Office, Delhi would liaise with Central Government for smooth implementation of the programme and provide effective backstopping to the state offices for planning, implementation, resource mobilization and financial management.

Implementation Arrangements

The programme would be implemented by UNDP in partnership with the state nodal institutions and NGOs in Programme states and districts. The national nodal agency, Ministry of Home Affairs would be provided support to develop national disaster risk management framework, strengthen the institutional, administrative, techno-legal and legal systems for disaster risk management. Nodal agencies in each of the twelve states would be provided the support of one trained State Project Officer specialist on Community Based Disaster Risk Management for development of disaster risk management plans. For smooth execution and to ensure sustainability, State nodal agencies will take support of the existing training institutions/resource units in the state for up gradation of the disaster risk management plan and the training capabilities of the different stakeholders.

In addition to this an Engineer specialist on disaster resistant/cost effective technology [National UN Volunteer] would be provided to each programme district to strengthen the technology transfer in housing sector training of masons and engineers for hazard-resistant housing programme, model retrofitting initiates and rooftop rainwater harvesting features. Appropriate programme management system would be put in place for effective implementation of the programme. The entire programme would be overseen and managed by a senior professional of proven project management capabilities. The state offices would also facilitate in undertaking research activities and providing support to each programme state with training manual, guideline and development of database with other UNDP supported programmes such as strengthening of regional resource centers for Panchayati Raj Institutions, support to ATIs under administrative reforms programme, programmes in the energy and environment sector and all community-based pro-poor initiatives etc.

Village/ward based multi-hazard preparedness and response plans would be prepared by the local institutions and linkages with the existing developmental programme would be established to address the causes of vulnerabilities. Local-self governments at all levels would be directly involved in these exercises for sustainability of the programme in long term. Disaster Management Specialists and experienced project management professionals, who have expertise in disaster risk management at the community levels in post-disaster situations, would work with state and district governments, civil society partners and communities.

Implementation Process

The disaster management plan would start from the village/ward level and would be consolidated through similar planning at the Panchayat, Block, District and Urban Local Bodies levels in the selected districts. A cadre of village volunteers would be created to carry out the village based natural disaster risk management programmes in the select programme districts. These Village Volunteers will be drawn from the community with the help of civil society organizations such as NCC, NSS,

NYKS, Scouts and Guides and Civil Defence etc. The plans would focus on the disaster risk prevention and early recovery through community-based preparedness and response plans, skill development for construction of hazard-resistant housing and enhanced access to information as per the need of the community. Twenty Eight districts will be covered under the massive village based disaster preparedness programme including development of village contingency plan, Gram Panchayat, Block and district disaster management plans and formation of Disaster Management Committees and DMTs in the year of 2002-2004 and remaining districts will be covered by the end of 2007 in phases. Under Phase-I, three states namely Orissa, Gujarat and Bihar will be covered all vulnerable villages in the selected 28 districts for development of contingency plans.

Phase I. The programme will strengthen the disaster risk reduction initiatives of the Ministry of Home Affairs [Government of India], the states of Orissa, Gujarat and Bihar and 28 districts from these three states in first two years under CCF-I. Environment building and initiation of the natural disaster risk management programme will be also part of the programme and initiated in all levels simultaneously in these three states alongwith national and state consultation for strategy development for sustainable recovery and massive awareness campaign, transformation of technology, database etc. Some of the activities will be taken up in the third year of the programme implementation depending on the availability of resources.

Phase II. Remaining 97 most vulnerable districts in nine states of India would be covered in Phase II depending on the availability of resources under CCF II and resources mobilized from donors for disaster risk management programme. The State offices would provide required specialized programme implementation support to strengthen the state nodal agencies and civil society partners in the Programme states for implementation of this programme. National Institute of Industrial Security, Hyderabad (CISF)/State Administrative Training Institutes would be entrusted to train the State Government functionaries, Civil Society response groups and state taskforce on disaster management. Research centers and academic institutions in different states would be engaged to carry out studies of existing system for disaster response and recovery in the state alongwith traditional coping mechanism in the communities for development of appropriate strategies and would be followed by field-testing.

The State Nodal Authorities, Panchayati Raj Departments/ Urban Bodies and national organizations such as NYKS and NSS would play major role in the implementation of the programme.

The following activities will carried on in partnership with state nodal agencies and civil society response groups.

Awareness Campaign Strategy

An effective disaster risk management campaign strategy will be developed in consultation with all stakeholders of the selected states for public education to take preventive measures in the wake of natural hazards to minimize the loss. The state nodal agency with the help of civil society response groups would take up a massive awareness campaign through out the selected districts for preparedness through rallies, mass meeting, different competitions like essay, debate, drawing etc., among school students, posters, leaflets Similarly wall paintings will be done in each village explaining Dos and Don'ts of various disasters, showing the safe shelters and safe routes for evacuation etc.

Manuals and Guidelines

Based on the experiences of Orissa and Gujarat disaster preparedness programmes, the state nodal agencies and research units will develop training manuals for Village, Gram

Panchayat, Block, District and State disaster management team, manuals for development of contingency plans for different hazards and Standard Operating Procedures (SOPs) for all levels. The manuals would be printed in vernacular languages after field-testing. Training will be provided to the stakeholders to use the manuals and widely circulated for replication of the programme. In all manuals special column shall be there for coping mechanism of women in disaster situations.

Formation of Disaster Management Team

Disaster Management Teams (DMT) would be formed at different levels to carry out the activities during emergency for sustainable recovery from disaster such as State, District, Municipality, Block, Gram Panchayat, Community and Ward. DMT at village/ward level would comprise of a group of 10-12 people in task-based groups such as Early Warning (EW), Search and Rescue Operation (SRO), First Aid and Water and Sanitation (FAWA), Shelter Management (SM), Trauma Counseling (TC) and Damage Assessment (DA) groups. Similarly, DMT at Gram Panchayat, Municipal and Block level may be formed with the involvement of people' representatives, members from local administrative system like local police, Medical Officer, Junior Engineer from Rural Water Supply and Sanitation, Veterinary Assistance Surgeon/ Inspectors, Revenue Inspector, Block Development Officers (BDO) etc. BDO would be the convener of the team at the Block level.

In addition, there will be an Advisory Committee at each levels to facilitate the preparedness programme and develop the natural disaster risk management and emergency response plans and providing timely support to the DMTs.

Training/Capacity Building

State nodal agency and UNDP will organize the Training of Trainers (ToT) at state, district and block levels to enhance the capacity of disaster management committees and prepare a core team to trainers and training. Training would be a continuous process on disaster risk management programme. The trained cadre will facilitate the process of contingency plan development at different levels.

Selected village volunteers will be provided with three modular training programmes to develop the village contingency plans. One or two volunteers will be selected by the PRIs/CBOs/NGOs from their own locality, based on their past experiences on relief and rehabilitation activities for facilitating the process at village and GP levels. More emphasis will be given to women volunteers in development of village disaster management activities.

Specialized training will be organized at different levels for the disaster management team members for enhancement of skills to effectively carry out their responsibilities such as warning dissemination, search and rescue operation, shelter management, fist aid, trauma counseling and damage assessment etc. The DMT members will be provided a specific type of apron or jacket for easy identification after the training. Adequate training will be provided to the women DMTs to carry out activities during emergency situation. Exposure visit of the Government Officials, PRIs and DMTs will be arranged to the best practice areas in sustainable recovery and preparedness on disaster risk management for capacity building.

Regular studies, research and workshops will be conducted at state and national levels on the vulnerability analysis, existing coping mechanism, revision and modification of the existing administrative, legal, techno-legal and institutional systems, as per the suitability of different localities and need of the areas. Training manuals, standard operating procedures and documentation of the best practices are important components of disaster preparedness programmes and will be developed for different levels for easy adoption, replication and sharing.

Emergency Rescue Kits

Support will be provided to the district administration for having an emergency kit with some essential equipments like a boat, portable power generator set, early warning equipments, tents, power saw etc., to meet the emergency need at the time of natural disasters like cyclones or flood or earthquakes. Each selected district will be provided the equipment kit as per their need. Equipments will procure in consultation with state and district administration and the maintenance will be the responsibility of the district administration.

Demonstration Unit

Construction of demonstration unit on disaster resistant and cost effective technology in housing sector would be done through trained masons and engineers for wider dissemination and adoption of the technology in selected districts, which enable the communities to adopt disaster-resistant and cost-effective technologies. Training and skill up-gradation of engineers and masons in construction of multi-hazard resistant houses would lead to safer habitat for the community. Model retrofitting and roof top rainwater harvesting initiatives in some multi-hazard prone programme districts will facilitate in dissemination of structural mitigation measures.

Resource Inventory Data Base

Support will be provided to each state to have a web enabled resource inventory for mobilization of resources and volunteers for emergency. IT facilitators will support the state government for development of a resource database, which will updated regularly by the nodal agency to know the status of the resource availability. Similarly, each state will have a list of volunteers with specific skill set-those who can be utilized by the state nodal agencies during emergencies.

District Disaster Management Information Centers

Necessary support will be provided in terms of equipments like advance communication equipments such as computer with internet facilities, HAM equipments, FAX etc to the district control room and state control room and training to the functionaries to handle the equipments during emergency. Thus, there will be well-equipped control room at state and district levels to disseminate accurate warning for advance action. These control rooms will also provide platform for the co-ordination during and post emergencies.

Vulnerability and Risk Indexing and Report

Benchmarking of vulnerability and risk would be attempted through national level research on the subject. Vulnerability and Risk Index would evolve through a consultative process. A national database would also be developed for assessment of preparedness and Risk Vulnerability Reports.

Sustainability

Village disaster preparedness and response plans will be approved by the Palli Sabha/Village meeting/assembly to make it a public document. It will establish linkages with the existing development programmes to reduce the vulnerability of the areas. Similarly, the Gram Panchayat disaster management plans will be the compilation of all village plans, which will be approved by the Gram Sabha and Panchayat will endeavor to support mitigation plans under the annual development plans. The Gram Panchayat mitigation plan will be reflected in the Panchayat Samiti plan and Panchayat Samiti plan in the Zillah Parishad plan. This will be an ongoing process at all levels and district mitigation plan would be a sub-set of district annual development plan. Disaster preparedness and mitigation planning will be an integral part of all developmental planning process.

Specifically, the following will be the measurable indicators of success of the programme:

- Preparedness, response and mitigation planning becomes an integral part of Annual Development Planning process at all levels.
- Well equipped and functional state and district disaster management information system [Clear line of command for warning dissemination at different levels].
- Disaster Management Committees and Disaster Management Teams conduct regular mock drills to enhance preparedness.
- Specific modification in building codes and techno-legal systems for risk reduction.
- Manuals and guidelines will be available for all operations for pre-during and post-emergencies.
- Adequate human resource capacity for training and capacity building in disaster preparedness and response functions.
- Trained masons available at village level on alternate and cost effective technology for building a safer habitat.

Exit Strategy

The exit strategy would be based on strengthening local capacities for development and upgradation of disaster preparedness and response plans alongwith regular mock drills. With trained human resource made available in the state and district and the entire planning process linked to development plans, UNDP programme implementation support could be withdrawn gradually from all programme districts.

UNDP implementation strategy is based on partnerships with local institutions and empowering District Disaster Management Committees and Disaster Management Teams at all levels. Mainstreaming risk management and vulnerability reduction activities in the development plans and enhancing capacities of Government functionaries would ensure that the achievements of the programme are sustained, even after the programme duration.

Transparency and Accountability

UNDP will ensure quarterly reporting to the nodal agency in order to maintain better co-ordination and accountability. There will be review committees at state as well as national level to review the implementation of the programme. Progress report alongwith financial report will be shared with all for better understanding and transparency. Utilization of resources under the programme would be based on decisions of the Programme Steering Committee.

✸✸✸

3

Earthquakes and Seismology Designs

Earthquakes are defined as, 'Ground shaking and radiated seismic energy caused mostly by sudden slip on a fault, volcanic or any sudden stress change in the earth'.

Important Definitions

Some of the important definitions involved in the understanding of seismology are given below:

1. Magnitude. It is the quantity to measure the size of an earthquake in terms of its energy and is independent of the place of observation.

2. Richter Scale. Magnitude is measured on the basis of ground motion recorded by an instrument and applying standard correction for the epicentral distance from recording station. It is linearly related to the logarithm of amount of energy released by an earthquake and expressed in Richter Scale.

3. Intensity. It is the rating of the effects of an earthquake at a particular place based on the observations of the affected areas, using a descriptive scale like Modified Mercalli Scale. Epicenter: It is the point on the (free) surface of the earth vertically above the place of origin (hypocenter) of an earthquake. This point is expressed by its geographical latitude and longitude.

4. Hypocenter or Focus. It is the point within the earth from where seismic waves originate. Focal depth is the vertical distance between the hypocenter and epicenter.

Earthquake Occurrence in the World

All places on the earth are not equally seismic. Earthquakes are generally found to occur along specific regions called 'Seismic Belts'. There are three main belts around the globe along which majority of earthquakes have occurred. They are:

1. Circum Pacific Belt or Ring of Fire;
2. Alpide Belt and
3. North and South in the Middle of the Atlantic Ocean.

Earthquake Occurrence in India

In India, the main seismic zone runs along Himalayan mountain range, northeast India Andaman-Nicobar islands and Rann of Kutch region.

Plate Tectonics

The theory of plate tectonics was originally proposed in 1912 by a German scientist, A. Wegner. Plate Tectonics is the theory supported by a wide range of evidence that considers the earth's crust and upper mantle to be composed of several large, thin, relatively rigid plates that move relative to one another. It is based on some theoretical assumptions that explain the forces, which cause accumulation of stresses inside the earth. These assumptions are as given below:

- Shortening of Earth's crust due to cooling and contraction.
- Disturbance of mass distribution on the Earth's surface as a result of erosion of high lands and deposition of sediment in the sea.

- Drifting of continents and mountain building process.
- Generation of heat by radioactive material inside the Earth's crust.

The edges of the oceanic and/or continental plate boundaries mark the regions of destructive earthquake activity and volcanic activity.

About 80% of the seismic energy is released by earthquakes occurring along the plate boundaries. These earthquakes are called as inter-plate earthquake, directly associated with forces related to the interaction of the plates.

Sporadically, earthquakes also occur at rather large distances from the respective plate margins, these so called intra-plate earthquake, show a diffuse geographical distribution.

Earthquakes are usually caused when the underground rocks suddenly break along a plane of weakness, called fault.

FAULTS

A fault is nothing but a crack or weak zone inside the Earth. When two blocks of rock or two plates rub against each other along a fault, they don't just slide smoothly they stick a little. As the tectonic forces continue to prevail, the plate margins exhibit deformation as seen in terms of bending, compression, tension and friction. The rocks eventually break giving rise to an earthquake, because of building of stresses beyond the limiting elastic strength of the rock.

The building up of stresses and subsequent release of the strain energy in the form of earthquake is a continuous process, which keeps on repeating in geological time scale.

Types of Faults

Different types of faults are:

- Dip Slip Faults.
- Normal.
- Reverse.
- Strike Slip Faults.
- Right Lateral.
- Left Lateral.

Earthquake Hazard Maps

Under the initiative of the Ministry of Urban Development, a Vulnerability Atlas of India was prepared in which the earthquake, cyclone and flood hazard maps for every state and Union Territory of India have been prepared to a scale of 1:2.5 million.

Seismology

The term 'Seismology' (Science of Earthquakes) is derived from Greek word Seismo, which means earthquake and logos which means science; hence, the Seismology is Science of Earthquakes.

Seismology can be defined in two ways:

1. The science of earthquakes and the physics of the earth's interior.
2. The science of elastic wave (seismic waves) *i.e.,*
   (a) Their origin (earthquakes, explosions etc.).
   (b) Their propagation through the earth's interior.
   (c) Their recording, including the interpretation of records.

The elastic waves, emanating from an earthquake permit the most reliable studies and conclusions about the internal constitutions of the earth using the records of the seismograph stations around the world. Source parameters of earthquake help us to evaluate the tectonic force.

In addition there is applied seismology, where we can also distinguish between several branches, such as seismic prospecting, *i.e.,* the search by seismic method for economically significant occurrences of salt, oil, mineral ores. Furthermore, depth to bedrock measurements for construction purposes, etc. The problem of distinguishing between earthquakes and explosions can be considered as another branch of seismology.

In brief, seismology deals with the following:

- The practical problem of understanding, reacting and living with earthquakes.
- The use of earthquakes and other natural excitations of the earth to understand the nature of the terrestrial forces involved and the structure of earth.
- The technology of seismic prospecting.

Causes of Earthquakes

An earth shaking may occur due to various reasons: tectonic plate movements, volcanic activity, impact of meteorites, collapse of caves, rock-burst in mines, land slides/rock-falling, nuclear explosion etc.

An earthquake is a phenomenon related to strong vibrations occurring on the ground due to sudden release of energy.

Classification of Earthquakes

Most earthquakes originate within the crust. At depth beneath the Moho, the number falls abruptly and dies down to zero at a depth of about 700 km.

Classification based on Focal Depth

1. Shallow-focus. Shallow-focus earthquakes, which constitute about 80% of total activity, have their foci at a depth between 0 to 70 km and occur at oceanic ridges, collision and subduction zones and transform faults

2. Intermediate-focus. Intermediate-focus earthquakes (focal depth between 71 and 300 km) and

3. Deep-focus. Deep-focus earthquakes (focal depth greater than 300 km) occur at subduction zones

Classification Based on Magnitude

Classification Magnitude (on Richter Scale)

Micro earthquake less than 3.0

Slight 3.1-4.9

Moderate 5.0-6.9

Great 7.0-8.0

Very Great Greater than 8.0

Classification Based on Epicentral Distance

Classification Range

Local shock < 4.0

Near shock 4.0 to 10.0

Distant shock 10.0 to 20.0

Teleseismic shock > 20.0

Earthquake Size

There are two methods of describing how large an earthquake is, as given below:

1. The Intensity of an Earthquake. It is a subjective parameter that is based on an assessment of visible effects. It is therefore depends on factors other than the actual size of the earthquake.

2. The Magnitude of an Earthquake. It is determined instrumentally and is more objective measure of its size.

Intensity. Intensity is the rating of the effects of an earthquake at a particular place based on the observations of the affected areas, using a descriptive scale. Large earthquakes produce alterations to the Earth's natural surface features or severe damage to the man-made structures such as buildings, bridges and dams. Even small earthquakes can result in disproportionate damage to the edifices when inferior construction methods or materials have been utilized. The intensity of earthquake at a particular place is classified on the basis of the local character of the visible effect it produces. Various types of scales have been developed for the classification of intensity, one originally proposed in its original, known as Modified Mercalli (MM) scale is in common use. In map intensity is represented by lines representing equal intensities called as isoseismals.

Magnitude. The strength of an earthquake or strain energy released by it is usually measured by a parameter called 'magnitude' determined from the amplitudes and periods of seismic waves of different types. A magnitude is a logarithmic measure of size of an earthquake or explosion base on instrument measurement. Depending upon the level of magnitudes, epicentral distance and the characteristics of seismographs, there are mainly four magnitude scales in use. They are:

- Local (Richter) magnitude (M_L).
- Body Wave magnitude (m_b).
- Surface Wave magnitude (M_S).
- Moment Magnitude (M_W).

Seismic Waves

We know that, sudden release of energy causes an earthquake. Part of energy released during an earthquake, at its origin, fractures the rock in that region. The rest travels away from the focus in all directions in the form of elastic waves. These are called seismic waves. The velocity of propagation of these waves depends upon the density and the elastic properties of the medium through which they travel. Different types of seismic waves are described below:

Body Waves

Those waves that travel through rocks are called body waves. Body waves are of two kinds, longitudinal and transverse.

Longitudinal Waves. These are sometimes referred to as P waves, or primary waves or push waves. As the wave advances each particle in the solid medium is displaced in the direction of motion of these waves, as in the case of sound waves. Transverse waves: These are also known as S waves or secondary waves. These are like ripples observed in a pond. The particle motion within the transmitting medium is at right angles to the direction of wave propagation. *For example,* the ripples one observes when a stone is thrown in a pond. If a cork is placed in water it moves up and down while the wave travels at right angles to the cork movement. So in any medium the longitudinal wave travels faster than the transverse wave and hence, at any point of observation one first observes longitudinal waves. And as liquids do not have any rigidity, the transverse waves cannot travel through them.

Surface Waves

Those waves that travel on the surface of the earth or elastic boundaries are called surface waves. They travel only at the surface or at the boundary of two different media and not into earth's interior.

Energy Release

The energy released at the time of earthquake is not same for all earthquakes. Some earthquakes are so small that they can be detected only with the help of very sensitive instruments. However, the energy released at the time of a large earthquake is indeed enormous.

To measure the size of an earthquake, seismologists use the Richter magnitude scale. It is a measure of the total energy released during an earthquake and is determined by the maximum amplitude of recorded seismic waves, instrumentally recorded, plus an empirical actor that takes into account the weakening of seismic waves as they spread away from the focus. This logarithmic scale is expressed in Arabic numerals. If the magnitude is increased by a factor of one, the energy released is increased by a factor of 30. There is no longer limit to the magnitude but the upper limit seems to be about 8.9, as earthquakes with magnitude greater than this have not yet been recorded.

SEISMOLOGICAL INSTRUMENTS

Many instruments have been designed to measure ground shaking in detail. Some of them which are used in seismology are given below:

Seismograph

Elastic waves transmitted from a single earthquake can be recorded all over the world using earthquake recording instruments called seismographs.

The prototype of the modern seismograph was built in Japan about 100 years ago. Basically, the seismograph has a mass which is loosely coupled to the earth through a spring. The inertia of the mass keeps it fixed in position as the earth moves.

Modern seismographs are quite complex in the construction and can record very feeble ground motions which have traveled long distances. They can magnify the ground motion upto million times before recording it. A study of seismograms, that is, the records produced by seismographs, can yield information not only about the time and place of occurrence of an earthquake, but also about the rocks through which earthquake energy travels.

Accelerograph

Rate of change of velocity with time is known as acceleration and a strong motion earthquake instrument recording accelerations is called as accelerograph. The record from an accelerograph showing acceleration as a function of time is accelerograms.

Seismoscope

The first earthquake recorder described in any detail was an artistic device invented by the Chinese scholar Chang heng about 132 A.D. Balls were held in dragons' mouths connected by linkages to a vertival pendulum. Shaking released the balls. The instrument was seismoscope, because unlike a seismograph, it could not give the complete time history of the earthquake shaking but simply the direction of the principal impulse due to earthquake.

EARTHQUAKE DESIGN PRINCIPLES

Seismic design principles are derived and updated as the knowledge and understanding of building behaviour under shaking is incremental. A study of structural performance of buildings during the past earthquakes indicates that commonly employed constructions are not earthquake resistant and therefore require improvement in design and construction techniques.

Earthquake resistant design is possible by:

(i) Proper planning.

(ii) Design.

(iii) Construction details to make them collapse proof and withstand damage within acceptable limit. Elastic design is not justified because of prohibitive cost.

Objectives of Earthquake Resistant Design

Objectives of earthquake resistant design are discussed below:

1. The IS 1893 (Part 1): 2002 says that the Design Basis Earthquake (DBE) can be reasonably expected to occur at least once in the design life of the structure. And buildings are expected to withstand DBE without major damages. Maximum Considered Earthquake (MCE) is the most severe earthquake effects considered by this Code to happen to any building and no collapse should happen to it due to MCE.

2. Under minor but frequent shaking (serviceable earthquake, up to intensity VI) :

- The main members of the building that carry vertical and horizontal forces should not be damaged.
- However, building parts that do not carry load may sustain repairable damage.
- In case of buildings of post-earthquake importance even non-structural elements should not undergo any displacement or distortion, otherwise loss of critical function would be incurred.

3. Under moderate but occasional shaking (design earthquake, from intensity VII to VIII):

- The main members may sustain repairable damage.
- The other non-load bearing parts of the building may be damaged such that they may even have to be replaced after the earthquake.

- In case of buildings of post-earthquake importance, non-structural elements should undergo only predicted damage or distortion, otherwise loss of critical function would be coupled with unlimited closure period thus, resulting in higher economic loss.

4. Under strong but rare shaking (maximum limit earthquake, from intensity IX to XII)

- The main members may sustain severe and even irreparable damage.
- But the building should not collapse.
- And people can be safely evacuated.

Implication of objectives of earthquake resistant design is that the maximum expected earthquake load is much larger than Design Earthquake Load.

BASIC TERMINOLOGY

Strength

Ground vibration is random in magnitude and direction and has two horizontal components and one vertical component. Vertical vibration initiates vertical inertia force in the structure, which gets added or subtracted to gravity force. In general, factor of safety adopted for gravity load design is high enough to take care of additive vertical component for a safe structure. Horizontal vibration components introduce horizontal inertia force.

To transfer this load to ground safely, a complete load transfer path is required. The elements in that load path should have adequate strength to combat duly generated stress. Strength is a material property; so selection of material inherently governs the stress limit the element can be subjected to.

Stiffness

Deflection under loading is a measure to understand stiffness of any element. This is a property of an element, its material, cross section, unsupported length or height; Stiffness prevents the structure or its parts from moving out of alignment more than permissible limit. This is also referred as horizontal drift or storey-to-storey drift. In a structural system, relative stiffness or rigidity amongst different elements are of serious concern in seismic analysis; though it is not of same concern in case of gravity load. Conventional assumption is that if a structure is subjected to certain force/s and it is a combination of two or more elements, then load sharing would occur in proportion to their relative stiffness.

Low lateral stiffness leads to large deformation and more damage in inelastic response, significant P-? effect, damage to non-structural elements due to large deformation etc.

Period

One important thing to remember is that, the overall stiffness of a building is measured by its period. Flexible, tall buildings have extended time period.

As per IS 1893 (Part I)—2002, the approximate natural period of vibration (Ta), in seconds, of a moment-resisting frame building without brick infill panels may be estimated by the empirical expression:

$T_a = 0.075\ h_{0.75}$ for RC frame building

$= 0.085\ h_{0.75}$ for steel frame building,

Where, h= Height of building, in m.

(This excludes the basement stories, where basement walls are connected with the ground floor deck or fitted between the building columns. But, it includes the basement stories, when they are not so connected.)

The approximate natural period of vibration (T_a), in seconds, of all buildings, including momentresisting frame building with brick infill panels may be estimated by the empirical expression:

$$T_a = 0.09/\sqrt{d}$$

where,

h = Height of building, in m. (as discussed above).

d = Base dimension of the building at the plinth level, in m, along the considered direction of the lateral force.

Centre of Mass

IS 1893 (Part 1) : 2002 defines Centre of Mass as the Point through which the resultant of the masses of a system acts. This point corresponds to the Centre of gravity of masses of system.

Centre of Rigidity or Stiffness

Centre of rigidity is the geometric centre of the relative rigidities of all elements bracing the structure in both directions. It is also referred as the shear centre or centre of rotation, meaning that during a seismic event the structure would rotate about its centre of rigidity. IS 1893 (Part!): 2002 defines centre of rigidity or stiffness as the point through which the resultant of the restoring forces of a system acts.

Torsion

Centre of gravity or mass of any structure pass through a point where it would be balanced against any rotation. Any load, when uniformly distributed, then the point would coincide with geometric centre of the structure. If this centre of mass coincides with centre of rigidity, then there would be no rotation effect. The earthquake force assumed to act at the centre of mass of the structure and the resistance of the building would pass through the centre of rigidity. Asymmetry as far as mass and rigidity/stiffness distribution is concerned, would experience a rotational problem. This is referred as Torsion. And as a result twisting would occur to it, which is undesirable. Not only in plan form, asymmetry has to be checked in 3 dimensional configuration of a structure to arrest the rotation phenomenon.

Design Eccentricity

The offset between the centre of mass of any structure and the centre of rigidity/stiffness of the safe is referred as eccentricity. IS 1893(Part1): 2002 refers Design Eccentricity (edi) as the value of eccentricity to be used at floor in the torsion calculations for design.

Damping

Damping is an inherent quality of structure and it controls or dampens response of a building during earthquake shaking. This can be visualized by comparing it with a swinging door without and with damper. In the first case it would continue to swing unless the door is being stopped forcefully. This is an example of undamped or under-damped situation (gradually swinging becomes lesser and then stopped). In case of door with damper, the door would be stopped slowly without going for to and movement. It can be said that critical damping has been introduced in the system. Critical damping is defined as the smallest value of damping at which the element or the structure experience no cyclic motion and gradually return to neutral position.

Ductility

A structure or its components whose deformation vanishes rapidly with the disappearance of the loads is said to behave elastically. All structural systems are elastic and that too in a linear fashion to a certain extent. Elements presenting permanent deformations after the disappearance of the loads are said to behave plastically. Although large permanent deformations are to be avoided, it must not be thought that plastic behaviour above the elastic range makes an element or a structure unsuitable for structural purposes; in fact the opposite is true. Above the yield point (where the structure starts behaving in a clearly plastic fashion) deformations increase more rapidly than the loads and eventually keep increasing even if the loads are not increased. This flow or yield is thus, the clearest sign and a healthy warning, that failure is imminent. And this quality if a structural material or a system exhibits it is referred as ductility.

Ductility is one of the strongest tools to design earthquake resistant structure. It offers the element to deform a large extent absorbing energy and thus, can resist earthquake force better deferring collapse mechanism.

Deformation may be measured in terms of deflection, rotation or curvature.

Increasing redundancy in the structure would result in improved ductility. Designers can predetermine for some elements to undergo large inelastic actions. At different level ductility would mean different displacement ratio:

- Section ductility (moment vs. bending or buckling curvature).
- Member ductility (transverse force vs. displacement/rotation).
- Storey ductility (storey shear vs. storey drift) and overall structural ductility (*Base shear vs. roof displacement*).

Response Spectrum

The Response spectra is a plot of maximum response versus T (for fixed ?) for a given ground motion. This is response in terms of force, displacement, acceleration, shear force etc. Design spectrum smoothens out the crest and trough in response spectra. This is specified concurrently with damping to be used, natural period calculation, permissible stress/strain, load factors etc.

Ductility Based Design

Earthquake resistant design philosophy strongly supports that, member elements as well as the entire structure should be strong enough to carry the gravity load safely. But to resist lateral load, structures would rely on ductility, as it provides similar scope for energy absorption, yet at the same time it would fail after sending sufficient warning through deformation. No sudden collapse would occur to the structure. Reliance on ductility in comparison to strength of the structure builds basis of ductility-based design. As ductility has been relied on, ductility reduction factor and over strength factor would influence the design force through introduction of Response reduction factor, R.

The Capacity Design Concept

For Earthquake Resistant Design maximum elastic seismic forces is calculated first (*e.g.*, with help of response spectra method) and then reduce to account for ductility and over-strength. Structure should have adequate strength and good ductility. In capacity design method planning for failure sequence is very important. The hierarchy of failure of elements in a structure is decided on basis of consequence of their failure. Local impact of failure would support the candidature of slab to be failed first. Beam would come next as it would influence two adjacent bays in that story. Then expected sequence would be Column, Foundation and lastly soil. Another assumption has to be made on type of damage. Preferable damage pattern is gradual and ductile one over sudden and brittle one; *e.g.*, beam should fail in flexure yielding rather than local buckling. That emphasize ductile elements should yield prior to failure of brittle elements. Ductility of the structure shows the ductility of its weakest element. So, strong column with weaker beam would be an appropriate strategy for ductility based capacity design.

In a Capacity Design method, followings are the steps:

- Assess required strength of structure from seismic code.
- Apply suitable safety factors on this load and material properties and design and detail out ductile elements.
- Identify a desirable collapse mechanism.
- Assess upper-bound strength (upper bound loads on the structure corresponding to yielding of ductile elements) of the ductile element.
- Design brittle elements corresponding to upper-bound load calculated above; and thus, ensure that brittle elements are elastic when the ductile elements yield.

To improve performance of the structure under earthquake load:

- Increase redundancy is helpful to make the pre-determined elements to undergo large inelastic actions.
- Prevent premature local or member buckling of design elements.
- Ensure that pre-determined locations of inelastic actions can sustain expected large plastic rotations through providing good moment connections.

Human settlements in highly seismic regions of the world by observations in past earthquakes developed an adequate understanding of seismic behaviour of buildings and evolved sound seismic design principles. All the earthquake resistant constructions have to be based on these principles to minimize the damage to buildings during earthquakes.

Various crucial aspects for seismic design principles like strength, stiffness, period, center of mass, center of rigidity or stiffness, torsion, design eccentricity, damping, ductility and response spectrum are discussed in the chapter. It is seen that earthquake resistant philosophy strongly supports that entire structure should be strong enough to carry the gravity load safely and at the same time ductility of the structure is important to take the lateral loads. Ductility of a structure shows the ductility of its weakest elements. Hence, understanding ductility based capacity design concept is important for earthquake resistant design.

✸✸✸

4

Disaster Preparedness and Management

A quantitative risk assessment undertaken in 2003 by the World Bank confirms that natural disasters can have a significant consequence for the economic performance of Central Asian countries. More than 90% of the loss potential is from earthquakes, floods and landslides. A quarter of the total expected loss is caused by events that are predicted to occur on average once every 20 years.

Another 38% originate from events that have a return period of 20-25 years. Catastrophic events with an annual probability of occurrence of 0.5% (events expected to occur once in every 200 years) would have a major impact on already vulnerable economies. Expected economic losses from such events exceed 20% of GDP in Armenia, Azerbaijan and Tajikistan; 10% of GDP in the Kyrgyz Republic; and 5% of GDP in Kazakhstan.

National Preparedness

The Central Asian countries have ministries for emergency situations, which deal with policy aspects, provide training, manage state disaster reserve resources and provide co-ordination among different levels of government in developing and implementing emergency plans. The People's

Republic of China (PRC) has, since January 2005, a State Disaster Reduction Commission.

- **Legal Framework.** Each country has each own decrees, acts and laws that serve as legal basis for disaster management.
- **Hazard/Risk Mapping.** Most countries have risk maps. Those in the Central Asian countries were prepared during the Soviet era, but their scale is not suitable for risk management activities. Most of these maps are outdated.
- **Disaster Preparedness Plans.** Countries in the region have made different levels of progress in developing disaster preparedness plans. The PRC has a capacity-building program and is making safe storage sites for waste products from metal processing.
- **Structural Measures.** In the Central Asian countries, many protective structures remain from the Soviet era-such as dams, dikes for flood protection and sediment control devices. These structures lack maintenance, which not only decreases their protective value but also can amplify a disaster when they collapse.
- **Community Involvement.** General awareness for natural disasters, preparedness and mitigation is very low. In the PRC, a community-based disaster reduction outreach campaign has been launched.

Regional and International Co-operation

The emergency policies of the five Central Asian countries currently include a regional mechanism through the relevant ministries. In 1993, an Interstate Council for Emergency Situations Regarding Natural and Man-made Disasters was established to co-ordinate disaster management policies.

Central Asian countries also co-operate with each other through a number of regional and bilateral agreements, including

- 1996 agreement between Kazakhstan, Kyrgyz Republic and Uzbekistan on joint collaboration for the rehabilitation of tailing sites that have a transboundary impact.
- 1998 agreement between Kazakhstan, Kyrgyz Republic, Tajikistan and Uzbekistan on the joint use of transboundary rivers, water bodies and hydraulic infrastructure.
- 1999 joint program of action to rehabilitate tailing sites in the countries of the Central Asian Economic Community.

Most Central Asian countries participated in the Sub-regional Initiative for Disaster Risk Management organized by the United Nations Development Programme (UNDP) in 2003 in Iran, to consider DRM initiatives in Central Asia and neighbouring countries, including two related subsequent meetings. The PRC is a signing party to the Shanghai Co-operation Organization Agreement on Intergovernmental Mutual Assistance for Disaster Relief and sponsored the Asian Conference on Disaster Reduction, the first ministerial meeting of its kind in Asia.

Central Asian countries are parties to many international declarations and summit agreements that stipulate increased preparedness for natural disasters on a national and regional bases. *For eaxmple,* all Central Asian countries, except Turkmenistan, sent a delegation to the World Conference on Disaster Reduction held in January 2005 in Kobe, Japan and became parties to the Hyogo Framework for Action 2005-2015 (HFA) to pursue "substantial reduction" of disaster losses during that period and which calls for increased international and regional co-operation.

Two good examples of regional co-operative arrangements are the Asian Disaster Preparedness Center (ADPC), a nonprofit organization based in Bangkok, set-up in part by ADB in 1986; and the International Strategy for Disaster Reduction (ISDR). ADPC's main role is to enhance the national and regional disaster management capacities. It undertakes this through a variety of modes, including training programs, promoting and supporting the mainstreaming of DRM in development processes, identifying national and regional DRM issues and assisting development of strategic solutions. The ISDR is the successor to the United Nations's international Decade of Natural Disaster Reduction 1990-1999. The decade was dedicated to promoting solutions to reducing risk from natural hazards. ISDR was created to move this momentum forward by fostering greater awareness, public commitment, knowledge and partnerships to implement risk reduction measures of all kinds, at all levels, in all countries.

On the donor side, many agencies give assistance for preventive as well as humanitarian emergency actions. The Swiss Agency for Development and Co-operation has a regional proactive strategy in operation, while the European has a general humanitarian plan of action. Other agencies are providing country-specific assistance.

ADB has also been active in providing disaster assistance. For ADB, responding to disaster impacts in unprepared Developing Member Countries (DMCs) means diverting badly needed development funds to replace social and economic infrastructure that has been lost or dislocated. Carefully prepared country strategies and plans can be destroyed literally overnight, resulting in a huge loss in effort and time. In 2004, ADB adopted a proactive Disaster and Emergency Assistance Policy (DEAP), which aims to integrate DRM into the development process of DMCs, build DMC disaster and hazard risk management capacity and take disaster risk into account in preparing ADB country strategies and plans and projects. A key element of DEAP is institutionalizing DRM by identifying risks during ADB's country programming schedules and building risk reduction strategies into the project plan. Regarding postimpact recovery, the policy emphasizes *(i)* rehabilitating critical physical and social infrastructure; *(ii)* revitalizing basic services; and *(iii)* jump-starting economic productivity, all in a DRM framework. The principles underpinning DEAP and the action plans stemming from it are similar to the HFA to which ADB, like most nations in this region, is a signatory. ADB is, therefore, assisting DMCs meet their HFA goals.

In spite of these efforts, disaster preparedness remains inadequate in much of the region. At the national level, there are needs to update (and in some cases, initiate) disaster legislation, enhance (and in some cases, establish) the national focal agency and strengthen interinstitutional and inter-governmental (national-regional-local) co-ordination. In addition, there are needs to improve risk mapping, preparedness planning, improve protective infrastructure and increase awareness and preparedness in communities. The need for capacity building underlies effective future actions in these areas.

EFFECTIVE DISASTER MANAGEMENT

An analysis of what transforms a natural event into a human and economic disaster reveals that the fundamental problems of development in Central Asia are the very same problems that contribute to the region's vulnerability to the catastrophic effects of natural hazards.

The principal causes of vulnerability in Central Asia include:

(i) The persistence of widespread urban and rural poverty.

(ii) Inefficient public policies.

(*iii*) Degradation of the region's environment from mismanagement of natural resources.

(*iv*) Lagging and misguided investments in infrastructure.

Development and disaster-related policies have largely focused on emergency response, leaving a serious under-investment in natural hazard prevention and mitigation. It follows that the most effective way to reduce losses from natural disasters is to integrate disaster risk into overall economic and development processes, *i.e.,* mainstreaming DRM.

To mainstream DRM at the national level, the following points comprise a useful general course of action:

(*i*) The first overarching issue is to improve governance for DRM. Most countries in this region still deal with disaster risk through response-focused civil defense type structures. Risk considerations have to be factored in into all aspects and levels of government and society.

(*ii*) Post-disaster recovery, if not undertaken correctly, too often rebuilds risk and creates the conditions for further and worse disasters in the future. The post-disaster period is, therefore, a unique opportunity to factor risk considerations into development.

(*iii*) Disaster risk analysis should be undertaken for all new developments. This not only means ensuring that new development is located and built in such a way as to be more secure but also ensure that new development does not generate new risk.

(*iv*) Treating hazards as dynamic is important: Hazard characteristics change and with it so do the risks. *For eaxmple,* climate change is already altering the frequency, severity and intensity of hydrometeorological hazards.

To give an example of the benefits of mainstreaming a DRM approach, the World Bank recently estimated that, on average, countries can save $7 in disaster recovery costs for every $1 spent on risk reduction measures.

Infrastructure Investment

Infrastructure is a key issue because infrastructure is basic not only for economic growth but also to bring the benefits of a higher economic performance to people living in rural and isolated areas as well as to enable them participate in mainstream economic activities. Moreover, damage to infrastructure can slow down response and recovery operations. Nevertheless, critical infrastructure the systems, facilities and networks that support health, safety and well-being of citizens (*e.g.*, utilities, transport and health services)- is destroyed or incapacitated during disasters. Infrastructure damage is estimated to make up two thirds of all flood losses. About 70% of all damage from the December 2004 tsunami disaster was to infrastructure.

Clearly, critical infrastructure needs to be protected from potential natural disasters. At the national level, mainstreaming DRM implies careful land-use planning of such critical facilities as power plants and major roads with consideration to possible occurrence of natural disasters that would help minimize damage.

Future Regional Co-operation

Since many disasters transcend national borders, mitigation would clearly benefit from regional co-operation by sharing resources, experience and expertise. However, the effectiveness of the existing national and regional mechanisms for natural disaster preparedness in Central Asia is limited due to inadequate funding and capacity, while international development partners, though quick to provide assistance in the event of disaster, have paid little attention to supporting prevention and disaster preparedness.

Similar to the Asia and Pacific region as a whole, disaster management in Central Asia has been badly neglected. ADB estimates that 1% (about $40 billion) of the entire Asia and the Pacific region's gross national income of $4 trillion is needed to put the needed disaster management infrastructure in place.

While developing and mainstreaming national DRM systems are essential, regional initiatives are important. In a region subject to sudden-onset disasters that have wide geographical coverage (earthquakes are the classic example) and where much of the region's transport and communications infrastructure crosses several borders, the need for regional-level services is obvious. Conversely, failure to implement DRM in any one country can affect such infrastructure and, thus, the region as a whole.

Regional co-operation for DRM, including infrastructure development, is essential not only to cope with the impacts of disasters but also to help ensure that the region sustains economic growth. Regional co-operation in DRM in the 21st century is expected to respond to development needs in a more flexible manner than the past. Future regional co-operation is expected to focus on emerging natural hazards of increasing intensity or to be incorporated into the DRM process of regional and national development programs.

From an international development partner perspective, enhanced regional co-operation in DRM offers attractive opportunities to provide resources. Some partners (including ADB) have separate funds for regional versus individual country allocation. Thus, assistance in regional co-operation serves to enhance, not detract from, country assistance. International partners can assist countries in the region to meet their domestic needs and international obligations (*e.g.*, HFA) through technical assistance and loan support for regional co-operation in such areas as the following:

(i) Building Capacity Training and Public Support for Disaster Management and Mitigation. To be successful, regional co-operation needs to build on a strong national institutional base.

(ii) Assistance in Development of National Disaster Management Plans. Harmonization of such plans across the region would greatly enhance mutual understanding and sharing of resources during emergencies. This must be supported by enabling disaster management legislation.

(iii) Development of National Disaster Information Systems. Monitoring and reporting on all data related to disasters is essential, not only of occurrences but also types of hazards, potential risks and available resources and institutions.

(iv) Integration of Disaster Risk Reduction into National Development Processes. As noted, only by such integration can disaster risk management considerations influence decisions of the planning bodies and be supported by adequate investment and expertise in a sustainable manner.

(v) Improving Legislative and Institutional Arrangements and Enhancing Political Will. A co-operative approach to disaster management and mitigation among countries of the region would result in harmonized legislation, enabling cross-border or region-wide actions to proceed rapidly in the event of disaster.

(vi) Scientific and Technical Inputs for Disaster Management (including early warning). There is

great scope not only for new research in disaster management in the region, but also for collation, interpretation, adaptation and application of existing knowledge. Clearly, this would be most effective at the regional level and through regional institutions.

Establishment of a task force to develop a regional strategy and determine priorities from among the many DRM needs would be a most useful first step. A partnership of national stakeholders and international development partners would provide a firm basis for future assistance. In this way, bilateral donors, international agencies and multilateral development banks would be able to co-ordinate and complement each other's activities toward the goal of optimizing DRM in the region.

Asian Development Bank Assistance in Disaster Mitigation and Recovery

The Asian Development Bank (ADB) adopted a policy on disaster rehabilitation assistance in 1987 for small Developing Member Countries (DMCs) and broadened and extended this to all DMCs in 1989. The rationale for assistance was to provide timely interventions that would enable an affected DMC maintain its development momentum. The policy was reviewed in 2002. Analyses showed that three main factors are crucial for project effectiveness:

- Good project design.
- Effective operation and maintenance of mitigation structures.
- Strong institutional development to support structural and preventive measures, *e.g.*, increased disaster awareness, community preparedness, early warning systems, effective land-use planning and sound and enforceable building codes.

Such measures should be part of the core design of natural disaster mitigation projects and should be integrated into country strategies and programs.

A new policy the Disaster and Emergency Assistance Policy was adopted in 2004, which takes a more proactive stance as described in the text. ADB assistance for emergency rehabilitation and disaster mitigation, including conflict and epidemic situations as well as natural disasters, totaled some $3.9 billion during 1987-2005.

APPROACHES FOR REGIONAL CO-OPERATION IN DISASTER PREPAREDNESS AND MANAGEMENT

Initiatives Fostering Regional Co-operation

- Periodic information dissemination in the region, whereby a regional information documentation and dissemination center would disseminate information to improve information exchange.
- Ministerial meetings on disaster management, which would involve organizing a high-level Central Asian Ministerial Meeting on Disaster Management to secure political support for disaster management.
- Multistakeholder conferences, which would be large meetings at the Central Asian level with cross-sectoral participation from government, United Nations agencies, non-government organizations, scientific and technical organizations, donors and regional institutions.
- Preparation of Central Asian and national disaster management reports.
- Vulnerability Atlas for Central Asia, which would map hazards, vulnerabilities and risks in countries of the region, similar to the vulnerability atlas of

India and the hazard atlas of the People's Republic of China.

- Scientific and technical co-operation in disaster management, which would bring existing information on scientific and technical issues into the public domain through dialogue with those national and regional institutions that have hazard, risk and disaster management information.

Capacity Building of National Systems

To be successful, regional co-operation needs to build on a strong national institutional base. Disaster management training and capacity building may be needed to strengthen

(i) National disaster management agencies/committees, which should be established and/or strengthened in every country by developing human resources and enacting necessary enabling national disaster management legislation.

(ii) National disaster management information systems to routinely monitor and report on all data related to hazards and vulnerabilities, resources and organizations.

(iii) Public awareness and media campaigns, which are needed to create a greater constituency for disaster preparedness and mitigation.

(iv) Development of disaster management plans, which are the cornerstone of a national disaster management system and must be backed up by national legislation and prepared at different levels: national, state and district levels.

❋❋❋

5

Disaster Management and Global Development

Five Year Plan documents have, historically, not included consideration of issues relating to the management and mitigation of natural disasters. The traditional perception has been limited to the idea of "calamity relief", which is seen essentially as a non-plan item of expenditure. However, the impact of major disasters cannot be mitigated by the provision of immediate relief alone, which is the primary focus of calamity relief efforts. Disasters can have devastating effects on the economy; they cause huge human and economic losses and can significantly set back development efforts of a region or a State. Two recent disasters, the Orissa Cyclone and the Gujarat Earthquake, are cases in point. With the kind of economic losses and developmental setbacks that the country has been suffering year after year, the development process needs to be sensitive towards disaster prevention and mitigation aspects. There is thus, need to look at disasters from a development perspective as well.

Further, although disaster management is not generally associated with plan financing, there are in fact a number of plan schemes in operation, such as for drought proofing, afforestation, drinking water, etc., which deal with the prevention and mitigation of the impact of natural disasters. External assistance for post-disaster reconstruction and streamlining of management structures also is a part of the Plan. A specific, centrally sponsored scheme on disaster management also exists. The Plan thus, already has a defined role in dealing with the subject.

Recently, expert bodies have dwelt on the role of the Planning Commission and the use of plan funds in the context of disaster management. Suggestions have been made in this regard by the Eleventh Finance Commission and also the High Powered Committee on Disaster Management. An approach on planning for safe development needs to be set out in the light of these suggestions.

The Global Context

There has been an increase in the number of natural disasters over the past years and with it, increasing losses on account of urbanisation and population growth, as a result of which the impact of natural disasters is now felt to a larger extent. According to the United Nations, in 2001 alone, natural disasters of medium to high range caused at least 25,000 deaths around the world, more than double the previous year and economic losses of around US $ 36 billion.

These figures would be much higher, if the consequences of the many smaller and unrecorded disasters that cause significant losses at the local community level were to be taken into account. Devastations in the aftermath of powerful earthquakes that struck Gujarat, El Salvador and Peru; floods that ravaged many countries in Africa, Asia and elsewhere; droughts that plagued Central Asia including Afghanistan, Africa and Central America; the cyclone in Madagascar and Orissa; and floods in Bolivia are global events in recent memory.

Natural disasters are not bound by political boundaries and have no social or economic considerations. They are borderless as they affect both developing and developed countries. They are also merciless and as such the vulnerable tend to suffer more at the impact of natural disasters. *For example,* the developing countries are much more seriously affected in terms of the loss of lives, hardship borne by population and the percentage of their GNP lost. Since 1991, two-third of the victims of natural disasters were from developing countries, while just 2 percent were from highly developed nations. Those living in developing countries and especially those with limited resources tend to be more adversely affected.

As a number of the most vulnerable regions are in India, natural disaster management has emerged as a high priority for the country. Going beyond the historical focus on relief and rehabilitation after the event, we now have to look ahead and plan for disaster preparedness and mitigation, in order that the periodic shocks to our development efforts are minimized.

THE INDIAN EXPERIENCE

Regional Vulnerabilities

Physical vulnerability relates to the physical location of people, their proximity to the hazard zone and standards of safety maintained to counter the effects. For instance, some people are vulnerable to flood only because they live in a flood prone area. Physical vulnerability also relates to the technical capacity of buildings and structures to resist the forces acting upon them during a hazard event.

The extent to which a population is affected by a calamity does not purely lie in the physical components of vulnerability, but is contéxtual also to the prevailing social and economic conditions and it's consequential effect on human activities within a given society. Research in areas affected by earthquakes indicates that single parent families, women, handicapped people, children and the aged are particularly vulnerable social groups. The geophysical setting with unplanned and inadequate developmental activity is a cause for increased losses during disasters. In the case of India, the contribution of overpopulation to high population density, which in turn results in escalating losses, deserves to be noted. This factor sometimes tends to be as important as physical vulnerability attributed to geography and infrastructure alone.

The continent of Asia is particularly vulnerable to disaster strikes. Between the years 1991 to 2000 Asia has accounted for 83 percent of the population affected by disasters globally. While the number of people affected in the rest of the world were 1,11,159, in Asia the number was 5,54,439.Within Asia, 24 percent of deaths due to disasters occur in India, on account of its size, population and vulnerability. Floods and high winds account for 60 percent of all disasters in India. While substantial progress has been made in other sectors of human development, there is need to do more towards mitigating the effect of disasters.

Many parts of the Indian sub-continent are susceptible to different types of disasters owing to the unique topographic and climatic characteristics. About 54 percent of the sub-continent's landmass is vulnerable to earthquakes while about 4 crore hectares is vulnerable to periodic floods. The decade 1990-2000, has been one of very high disaster losses within the country, losses in the Orissa Cyclone in 1999 and later, the Gujarat Earthquake in 2001 alone amount to several thousand crore of Rupees, while the total expenditure on relief and reconstruction in Gujarat alone has been to the tune of ₹ 11,500 crore.

Similarly, the country has suffered four major earthquakes in the span of last fifty years alongwith a series of moderate intensity earthquakes that have occurred at regular intervals. Since 1988, six earthquakes have struck different parts of the country. These caused considerable human and property losses.

Disasters lead to enormous economic losses that are both immediate as well as long-term in nature and demand additional revenues. Also, as an immediate fallout, disasters reduce revenues from the affected region due to lower levels of economic activity leading to loss of direct and indirect taxes. In addition, unplanned budgetary allocation to disaster recovery can hamper development interventions and lead to unmet developmental targets.

Disasters may also reduce availability of new investment, further constricting the growth of the region. Besides, additional pressures may be imposed on finances of the Government through investments in relief and rehabilitation work.

In the recent earthquake in Gujarat, more than 14,000 lives were lost, ten lakh houses were damaged and the asset loss has been indicated to be worth 15,000 crore.

Institutional Arrangements

The country with its federal system of Government has specific roles for the Central and State Governments. However, the subject of disaster management does not specifically find

The country has an integrated administrative machinery for management of disasters at the National, State, District and Sub-District levels. The basic responsibility of undertaking rescue, relief and rehabilitation measures in the event of natural disasters, as at present, is that of the State Governments concerned. The Central Government supplements the efforts of the States by providing financial and logistic support.

Central Level

The dimensions of response at the level of the Central Government are determined in accordance with the existing policy of financing relief expenditure and keeping in view the factors like:

- The gravity of a natural disaster,
- The scale of the relief operation necessary.
- The requirements of Central assistance for augmenting financial resources and logistic support at the disposal of the State Government.

The Contingency Action Plan (CAP) identifies initiatives required to be taken by various Central Ministries and Public Departments in the wake of natural calamities. It sets down the procedures and determines the focal points in the administrative machinery to facilitate launching of relief and rescue operations without delay. The Ministry of Home Affairs is the nodal Ministry for co-ordination of relief and response and overall natural disaster management and the Department of Agriculture and Co-operation is the nodal Ministry for drought management.

The following decision-making and standing bodies are responsible for disaster management at the Central level:

- Union Cabinet, headed by the Prime Minister.
- Empowered Group of Ministers, headed by the Deputy Prime Minister.
- National Crisis Management Committee (NCMC), under the chairmanship of the Cabinet Secretary.
- Technical Organizations, such as the Indian Meteorological Department (cyclone/earthquake), Central Water Commission (floods), Building and Material Promotion Council (construction laws), Bureau of Indian Standards (norms), Defence Research and Development Organization (nuclear/biological), Directorate General Civil Defence provide specific technical support to co-ordination of disaster response and management functions.

- Crisis Management Group (CMG), under the chairmanship of the Central Relief Commissioner comprising senior officers from the various Ministries and other concerned Departments which reviews contingency plans, measures required for dealing with a natural disaster and co-ordinates the activities of the Central Ministries and the State Governments in relation to disaster preparedness response and relief.
- The setting-up of a National Disaster Management Authority (NDMA) is being contemplated by the Ministry of Home Affairs as the proposed apex structure within the Government for the purpose. Amongst other major organizational initiatives, it is proposed to:
    - — Establish a specialised and earmarked response team for dealing with nuclear/biological/chemical disasters.
    - — Establish search and rescue teams in each State.
    - — Strengthen communication systems in the North Eastern Region.

State Government

The responsibility to cope with natural disasters is essentially that of the State Government. The role of the Central Government is supportive in terms of supplementation of physical and financial resources. The Chief Secretary of the State heads a state level committee which is in overall charge of the relief operations in the State and the Relief Commissioners who are in charge of the relief and rehabilitation measures in the wake of natural disasters in their States function under the overall direction and control of the state level committee. In many states, Secretary, Department of Revenue, is also in-charge of relief.

District and Local Level

The district administration is the focal point for implementation of all Governmental plans and activities. The actual day-to-day function of administering relief is the responsibility of the Collector/District Magistrate/Deputy Commissioner who exercises co-ordinating and supervising powers over all departments at the district level. Though it may not be a common phenomenon, there exists by and large in districts also a district level relief committee consisting of officials and non-officials.

The 73rd and 74th Constitutional Amendments recognise Panchayati Raj Institutions as 'Institutions of self- Government'. The amendment has also laid down necessary guidelines for the structure of their composition, powers, functions, devolution of finances, regular holding of elections and reservation of seats for weaker sections including women. These local bodies can be effective instruments in tackling disasters through early warning system, relief distribution, providing shelter to the victims, medical assistance etc. Other than the national, state, district and local levels, there are various institutional stakeholders who are involved in disaster management at various levels in the country.

Armed Forces

The Indian Armed Forces are supposed to be called upon to intervene and take on specific tasks only when the situation is beyond the capability of civil administration. In practice, the Armed Forces are the core of the Government's response capacity and tend to be the first responders of the Government of India in a major disaster. Due to their ability to organize action in adverse ground and the resources and capabilities at their disposal, the Armed Forces have historically played a major role in emergency support functions such as communications, search and rescue operations, health and medical facilities, transportation, power, food and civil supplies, public works and engineering, especially in the immediate aftermath of disaster.

External Linkages

The Government of India is a member of various international organizations in the field of disaster response and relief. While, as a policy, no requests for assistance or appeals are made to the international community in the event of a disaster, assistance offered suo moto is accepted. Linkages exist with the following organizations:

(a) UN Office for Co-ordination of Humanitarian Affairs (UN OCHA), which has been made responsible by UN General Assembly mandate for all international disaster response.

(b) United Nations Development Programme (UNDP), responsible for mitigation and prevention aspects of disaster management.

(c) UN Disaster Assessment and Co-ordination (UNDAC) System.

Streamlining Institutional Arrangements for Disaster Response

Institutional arrangements for disaster response are the heart of disaster management systems. There is no dearth of personnel, both civilian and military, experienced in handling situations arising out of natural disasters. However, there certainly is a pressing need for improvement and strengthening of existing institutional arrangements and systems in this regard to make the initial response to a disaster more effective and professional. Most of the resources and expertise needed already exist with the Government. What needs to be streamlined is how they should be integrated, trained and deployed. Some of the areas where improvement is urgently needed are:

(*a*) Integrated planning for disasters, including the integration of relevant Armed Forces formations into disaster management planning at all levels from District to State and Central Government.

(*b*) Establishment of a national stand by, quick reaction team composed of experienced professionals, both military and civilian, drawn from Central and State Government staff to respond immediately by flying in a matter of hours an experienced response team to the locations when a disaster strikes. This team can be organized and run professionally on the same lines as the United Nations Disaster Assessment and Co-ordination (UNDAC) teams.

(*c*) Setting-up of a modern, permanent national command centre or operations room, with redundant communications and data links to all State capitals. The national command centre or operations room needs to be manned on a 24-hour basis by professionals to cater for instant integrated response. There needs to be a properly equipped operations room at the State level as well.

(d) Creation of urban search and rescue capacity at all levels, by establishing a fully equipped Search and Rescue unit, as part of the fire service in all State capitals, with trained staff and modern equipment such as thermal imagers, acoustic detection devices etc. This is of immediate relevance since a major weakness exposed in the Gujarat earthquake was a lack of specialised urban search and rescue capability in India.

(*e*) Media policy geared to handling the growing phenomenon of real time television reporting, which generates enormous political pressures on a Government to respond rapidly and efficiently.

(*f*) Standard procedures for dealing with domestic humanitarian and relief assistance from non-government sources. Procedures and systems need to be set out to avoid confusion and ensure best utilisation of the assistance being offered, just as in the case of systems for international assistance.

(*g*) Closer interface with and better understanding of the international system for disaster response and putting in place, systems for dealing with international assistance once it comes in *e.g.*, customs, immigration, foreign policy implications etc. A greater appreciation is needed of the speed and automation of modern international response to a natural disaster.

(*h*) Modern unified legislation for disaster management. In view of the current division of responsibilities between the State and Central Government into state, central and concurrent lists, there is a need to create a body of legislation dealing with response to natural disasters and other emergencies, clearly delineating responsibilities and powers of each entity and specifying what powers or actions would need to be triggered on declaration of a disaster by the Government of India or a State Government. This legislation should also incorporate the current legislation dealing with chemical emergencies that has been created by the Ministry of Environment so that all emergencies are dealt with under one law.

FINANCIAL ARRANGEMENTS

Financing of Relief Expenditures

The policy arrangements for meeting relief expenditure related to natural disasters are, by and large, based on the recommendations of successive finance commissions. The two main windows presently open for meeting such expenditures are the Calamity Relief Fund (CRF) and National Calamity Contingency Fund (NCCF). The Calamity Relief Fund is used for meeting the expenditure for providing immediate relief to the victims of cyclone, drought, earthquake, fire, flood and hailstorm.

Expenditure on restoration of damaged capital works should ordinarily be met from the normal budgetary heads, except when it is to be incurred as part of providing immediate relief, such as restoration of drinking water sources or provision of shelters etc., or restoration of communication links for facilitating relief operations. The amount of annual contribution to the CRF of each State for each of the financial years 2000-01 to 2004-05 is as indicated by the Finance Commission. Of the total contribution indicated, the Government of India contributes 75 percent of the total yearly allocation in the form of a non-plan grant and the balance amount is contributed by the State Government concerned. A total of ₹ 11,007.59 crore was provided for the Calamity Relief Fund from 2000-05.

Pursuant to the recommendations of the Eleventh Finance Commission, apart from the CRF, a National Calamity Contingency Fund (NCCF) Scheme came into force with effect from the financial year 2000-01 and would be operative till the end of the financial year 2004-05. NCCF is intended to cover natural calamities like cyclone, drought, earthquake, fire, flood and hailstorm, which are considered to be of severe nature requiring expenditure by the State Government in excess of the balances available in its own Calamity Relief Fund. The assistance from NCCF is available only for immediate relief and rehabilitation. Any reconstruction of assets or restoration of damaged capital should be financed through re-allocation of Plan funds. There is need for defining the arrangements in this regard. The initial corpus of the National Fund is ₹ 500 crore, provided by the Government of India. This fund is required to be recouped by levy of special surcharge for a limited period on central taxes. An amount of about ₹ 2,300 crore has already been released to States from NCCF. A list of items and norms of expenditure for assistance chargeable to CRF/NCCF in the wake of natural calamities is prescribed in detail from time to time.

Financing of Disaster Management Through Five Year Plans

Although not specifically addressed in Five Year Plan documents in the past, the Government of India has a long history of using funds from the Plan for mitigating natural disasters. Funds are provided under Plan schemes *i.e.*, various schemes of Government of India, such as for drinking water, employment generation, inputs for agriculture and flood control measures etc. There are also facilities for rescheduling short-term loans taken for agriculture purposes upon certification by the District/State administration. Central Government's assets/infrastructure are to be repaired/rectified by the respective Ministry/Department of Government of India. Besides this, at the occurrence of a calamity of great magnitude, funds flow from donors, both local and international, for relief and rehabilitation and in few cases for long-term preparedness/preventive measures. Funds for the latter purposes are also available from multilateral funding agencies such as the World Bank. These form part of the State Plan.

There are also a number of important ongoing schemes that specifically help reduce disaster vulnerability. Some of these are: Integrated Wasteland Development Programme (IWDP), Drought Prone Area Programme (DPAP), Desert Development Programme (DDP), Flood Control Programmes, National Afforestation and Ecodevelopment Programme (NA&ED), Accelerated Rural Water Supply Programme (ARWSP), Crop Insurance, Sampurn Grameen Rozgar Yojana (SGRY), Food for Work etc.

Planning for Safe National Development

Development programmes that go into promoting development at the local level have been left to the general exercise of planning. Measures need also to be taken to integrate disaster mitigation efforts at the local level with the general exercise of planning and a more supportive environment created for initiatives towards managing of disasters at all levels: National, state, district and local. The future blue-print for disaster management in India rests on the premise that in today's society while hazards, both natural or otherwise, are inevitable, the disasters that follow need not be so and the society can be prepared to cope with them effectively whenever they occur. The need of the hour is to chalk out a multi-pronged strategy for total risk management, comprising prevention, preparedness, response and recovery on the one hand and initiate development efforts aimed towards risk reduction and mitigation, on the other.

Disaster Prevention and Preparedness

Disaster prevention is intrinsically linked to preventive planning. Some of the important steps in this regard are:

(a) Introduction of a comprehensive process of vulnerability analysis and objective risk assessment.

(b) **Creating state-of-the-art infrastructure:** The entire disaster mitigation game plan must necessarily be anchored to frontline research and development in a holistic mode. State-of-the art technologies available worldwide need to be made available in India for upgradation of the disaster management system; at the same time, dedicated research activities should be encouraged, in all frontier areas related to disasters like biological, space applications, information technology, nuclear radiation etc., for a continuous flow of high quality basic information for sound disaster management planning,

(*c*) **Building a robust and sound information database:** A comprehensive database of the land use, demography, infrastructure developed at the national, state and local levels alongwith current information on climate, weather and man-made structures is crucial in planning, warning and assessment of disasters. In addition, resource inventories of Governmental and non-governmental systems including personnel and equipment help in efficient mobilisation and optimisation of response measures.

(*d*) Establishing Linkages between all knowledge- based institutions: A National Disaster Knowledge Network, tuned to the felt needs of a multitude of users like disaster managers, decision-makers, community etc., must be developed as the network of networks to cover natural, manmade and biological disasters in all their varied dimensions,

Capacity Building, Training and Education

Personnel involved in the exercise have to draw upon knowledge of best practices and resources available to them. Information and training on ways to better respond to and mitigate disasters to the responders go a long way in building the capacity and resilience of the country to reduce and prevent disasters. Training is an integral part of capacity building as trained personnel respond much better to different disasters and appreciate the need for preventive measures. The directions in this regard are:

(*a*) The multi-sectoral and multi-hazard prevention based approach to disaster management requires specific professional inputs. Professional training in disaster management should be built into the existing pedagogic research and education. Specialised courses for disaster management may be developed by universities and professional teaching institutions and disaster management should be treated as a distinct academic and professional discipline, something that the American education system has done successfully.

(*b*) The focus towards preventive disaster management and development of a national ethos of prevention calls for an awareness generation at all levels. An appropriate component of disaster awareness at the school level will help increase awareness among children and, in many cases, parents and other family members through these children. Curriculum development with a focus towards dissemination of disaster related information on a sustained basis, covering junior, middle and high schools may be worked out by the different school boards in the country.

(*c*) Training facilities for Government personnel involved in disaster management are conducted at the national level by the National Centre for Disaster Management (NCDM) at the Indian Institute of Public Administration, in New Delhi which functions as the nodal institution in the country for training, research and documentation of disasters.

(*d*) Capacity building should not be limited to professionals and personnel involved in disaster management but should also focus on building the knowledge, attitude and skills of a community to cope with the effects of disasters. Identification and training of volunteers from the community towards first response measures as well as mitigation measures is an urgent imperative. A programme of periodic drills should be introduced in vulnerable areas to enable prompt and appropriate community response in the event of a disaster, which can help save valuable lives.

Capacity building for effective disaster management therefore needs to be grounded and linked to the community and local level responders on the one hand and also to the institutional mechanism of the State and the Nation on the other.

Community Level Initiatives

The goal of any disaster management initiative is to build a disaster resistant/resilient community equipped with safer living and sustainable livelihoods to serve its own development purposes. The community is also the first responder in any disaster situation, thereby emphasising the need for community level initiatives in managing disasters. To encourage such initiatives, the following are required:

(a) Creating awareness through disaster education and training and information dissemination are necessary steps for empowering the community to cope with disasters.

(b) Community based approach followed by most NGOs and Community Based Organizations (CBOs) should be incorporated in the disaster management system as an effective vehicle of community participation.

(c) Within a vulnerable community, there exist groups that are more vulnerable like women and children, aged and infirm and physically challenged people who need special care and attention especially during disaster situations. Efforts are required for identifying such vulnerable groups and providing special assistance in terms of evacuation, relief, aid and medical attention to them in disaster situations.

Management of disasters should therefore be an interface between a community effort to mitigate and prevent disasters as also an effort from the Government machinery to buttress and support popular initiatives.

Strengthening of Plan Activities

Given the pervasive nature of disasters and the widespread havoc caused by some of them, planned expenditure on disaster mitigation and prevention measures in addition to the CRF is required. The Central Sector Scheme of Natural Disaster Management Programmes has been implemented since 1993-94 by the Department of Agriculture and Co-operation with the objective to focus on disaster preparedness with emphasis on mitigation and preparedness measures for enhanced capability to reduce the adverse impact of disasters.

The major activities undertaken within this scheme include the setting-up of the National Centre for Disaster Management (NCDM) at the Indian Institute of Public Administration, creation of 24 disaster management faculties in 23 states, research and consultancy services, documentation of major disaster events and forging regional co-operation. The Eighth Plan allocation of ₹ 6.30 crore for this scheme was increased to ₹ 16.32 crore in the Ninth Plan. Within this scheme, NCDM has conducted over 50 training programmes, training more than 1000 people, while 24 disaster management centres with dedicated faculty have been established in the states. Over 4000 people have been trained at the State level. In addition, some important publications and audio-visual training modules have been prepared and documentation of disaster events has been done.

Though limited in scope and outlays, the Scheme has made an impact on the training and research activities in the country. Creation of faculties in disaster management in all 28 states is proposed to be taken up in the Tenth Plan in addition to community mobilisation, human resource development, establishment of Control Rooms and forging international co-operation in disaster management. There is also an urgent need for strengthening the disaster management pedagogy by creating disaster management faculties in universities, rural development institutes and other organizations of premier research.

Sustainability is the key word in the development process. Development activities that do not consider the disaster loss perspective fail to be sustainable. The compounded costs of disasters relating to loss of life, loss of assets, economic activities and cost of reconstruction of not only assets but of lives can scarcely be borne by any community or nation. Therefore, all development schemes in vulnerable areas should include a disaster mitigation analysis, whereby the feasibility of a project is assessed with respect to vulnerability of the area and the mitigation measures required for sustainability. Environmental protection, afforestation programmes, pollution control, construction of earthquake resistant structures etc., should therefore have high priority within the plans.

The aim of a mitigation strategy is to reduce losses in the event of a future occurrence of a hazard. Structural mitigation may comprise construction of individual disaster resistant structures like retrofitted or earthquake-resistant buildings or creation of structures whose function is primarily disaster protection like flood control structures, dykes, levees, infiltration dams etc.

Mitigation measures on individual structures can be achieved by design standards, building codes and performance specifications. Building codes, critical front-line defence for achieving stronger engineered structures, need to be drawn up in accordance with the vulnerability of the area and implemented through appropriate techno-legal measures.

Mitigation measures need to be considered in land use and site planning activities. Constructions in hazardous areas like flood plains or steep soft slopes are more vulnerable to disasters. Necessary mitigation measures need to be built into the design and costing of development projects.

Insurance is a potentially important mitigation measure in disaster-prone areas as it brings quality in the infrastructure and consciousness and a culture of safety by its insistence on following building codes, norms, guidelines, quality materials in construction etc. Disaster insurance mostly works under the premise of 'higher the risk higher the premium, lesser the risk lesser the premium', thus, creating awareness towards vulnerable areas and motivating people to settle in relatively safer areas.

The Path Ahead

For addressing natural calamities such as floods and drought, there already exist a number of plan schemes under which a lot is being done and can be done. State Governments need to make full use of the existing plan schemes and give priority to implementation of such schemes that will help in overcoming the conditions created by the calamity. In some cases this implies possible diversion of the funds from other schemes to those schemes the implementation of which will help meeting the situation. There may also be need in a crisis situation for certain re-appropriations/reallocations among the different departments.

The Planning Commission will aim at responding quickly to the needs of the Central Ministries/Departments/States in matters relating to the Plan for meeting situations arising out of natural disasters, by enabling adjustment of schemes to meet the requirements as far as possible. A mechanism will be evolved to take expeditious decisions on proposals which involve transfer of funds from one scheme to another, or any other change which involves departure from the existing schemes/pattern of assistance, new schemes and relaxation in procedures, etc., in the case of natural disasters.

As the first responder in any disaster situation, however, each State needs to build a team, skilled personnel, make provision for specialised equipments, efficient communication network and relevant, intelligent and easily accessible database. There is also a need to consider creation of a plan scheme in each state basically to meet the minimum requirements for strengthening communications and emergency control rooms, thereby improving co-ordination and response to disasters. No new institutional structures need be created in such a scheme.

In particular, with regard to major disasters, it is also necessary for disaster mitigation components to be built into all development projects. In order to save larger outlays on reconstruction and rehabilitation subsequently, a mechanism would need to be worked out for allowing components that specifically help projects coming up in highly disaster prone areas withstand the impact of natural disasters as part of approved project cost for projects financed under the Plan. The message for the Tenth Plan is that in order to move towards safer national development, development projects should be sensitive towards disaster mitigation. With the kind of economic losses and developmental setbacks that the country has been suffering year after year, it makes good economic sense to spend a little extra today in a planned way on steps and components that can help in prevention and mitigation of disasters, than be forced to spend many multiples more later on restoration and rehabilitation. The design of development projects and the process of development should take the aspect of disaster reduction and mitigation within its ambit; otherwise, the development ceases to be sustainable and eventually causes more hardship and loss to the nation.

Guidelines to State Governments

1. The State Department of Relief and Rehabilitation may be converted into Department of Disaster Management with the responsibility of looking at the whole cycle of disaster management- prevention, mitigation, preparedness, response, relief and

rehabilitation. Steps for prevention/mitigation will need to be taken across a number of Departments. The Department of Disaster Management will co-ordinate the steps taken by the different Department of the Government in these spheres.

2. It has been decided that fire services may be trained and equipped to function as all hazard response units as in other countries. This will necessitate some additional equipment and training to the fire units for carrying our search and rescue in all types of disasters. The Government of India will be initiating a separate project for this.

3. It has been noticed that while the local administration has the requisite skills and capabilities for carrying out search and rescue in recurrent types of disaster like flood, there is lack of capability for specialised search and rescue. Each State may consider setting-up specialised search and rescue teams. The teams would need to be composite with one coy of the State Armed Police trained and equipped to carry out specialised search and rescue; one mobile engineering unit with necessary equipment and one medical assistance team. These teams may be constituted and trained together so as to function as a unit under the overall charge of a designated officer. Guidance/advise required with reference to training and equipment will be provided by the Disaster Management Division of the Ministry of Home Affairs, Government of India.

4. The Ministry of Home Affairs had advised the State Governments that composite control rooms may be set-up at the State level and at the district levels under the District Magistrates for co-ordinating law and order as well as disaster management and that

allocations under the Modernisation of Police Forces Schemes may be used for the this purpose. Steps may be taken to put such control room in place quickly with standby communication systems.

5. Disaster mitigation concerns/aspects may be made an essential term of reference for every plan project/ development scheme in the areas vulnerable to disasters. In other words, every plan project will need to state as to how is addresses mitigation concerns. Plans/projects specifically addressing mitigation/prevention may be given a priority.

6. Funds available under the ongoing schemes may be used for mitigation/preparedness. *For example,,* funds under the rural development scheme can be used for construction of cycle shelters in areas prone to cyclones. Similarly, sites and designs of primary school buildings in flood prone areas may be so selected so that they can serve as shelters in times of floods. The design requirements for primary school building and hospitals and other important public buildings in seismic zones V and IV would need to be in accordance with BIS norms for construction in these zones.

7. State in seismic zones V and IV may ensure that the BIS building codes for these zones have been adopted and are rigorously enforced by the municipal bodies. All construction in the Government sector in these areas must conform to the BIS code.

8. Every hazard prone district may draw up specific hazard related plans. These plans may be reviewed/ updated in the months of April and May each year.

9. Every district located in area prone to hazard will need to maintain an on line inventory of resources

available in the Government, public and private sector. This will enable easy and quick mobilization of resources in case of need. A State-wide on line resources inventory would enable the mobilization of resources from neighbouring districts in cases of need.

10. The initial training curriculum of the field staff—VLWs, Karamcharis, Patwaris, Talhatis, Block Agriculture Officers, Block Animal Husbandry Officers other Block Supervisors, State Civil Service Officers, Constables, Sub-inspectors, Dy S.Ps etc., in the States vulnerable to hazards may include capsules on basic dos and don'ts in case of disasters; disaster mitigation and response, search and rescues techniques etc. In-service training may be organized for staff already in service.

11. AICTE have been advised to include engineering aspects of disaster mitigation in the engineering courses at the undergraduate level. State Governments may take similar action with reference to engineering colleges under their universities.

12. CBSE have been advised to include basic disaster related material in text books for classes 8th, 9th and 10th—the basic dos and don'ts/precaution to be taken etc. State Government may advise their Secondary Boards of Education to include similar in their textbooks.

13. Special efforts may be put in for education and awareness. This should include awareness of basic design requirements for constructing private housing in seismic zones IV and V as well as in the belt vulnerable to cyclones.

***

6

Social Responsibility and Disaster Management

India has been traditionally vulnerable to natural disasters on account of its unique geo-climatic conditions. In view of India's high vulnerability profile, the recurrent phenomena of a range of geophysical as well as hydro-meteorological hazards impact millions across the country leaving behind a trail of heavy loss of lives, property and livelihoods. In many areas of the country, disaster losses tend to outweigh the development gains.

The economic and social costs on account of losses caused by natural disasters continue to mount year after year as disasters occur with unfailing regularity encompassing every segment of national life including the industrial and corporate sector. Traditionally, India had been 'reactive' in its approach towards disasters - with precious resources being spent on relief, rehabilitation and reconstruction efforts. Today, after considerable and meticulous planning and a concerted effort, a paradigm shift in the approach of the Government departments and agencies as well as of other stakeholders including the community, the corporate sector and others has been brought about for building holistic capabilities for disaster management.

The focus has shifted to a balanced approach including pre-disaster aspects such as disaster prevention, mitigation and preparedness since it is felt that appropriate mitigation measures can substantially, if not wholly, reduce the heavy toll of lives and property, the dissipation of developmental, industrial and infrastructural gains and the hard-earned socio-economic infrastructure.

For long, the corporate sector had been viewed as a separate entity perennially ranged at the other end of the spectrum *vis-a-vis* the society. Over the past few decades, this perception has undergone a complete metamorphosis and the existence of corporate sector is today intimately intertwined with the safety and well-being of the society. Rather the community today is the very raison d'etre of its being. It is the crux lending credence and substance to the world view of the corporates. The corporate sector and the society are being seen as complementary to each other—heavily dependent upon each other for mutual existence and prosperity. The high vulnerability profile of India also enhances the susceptibility of the corporate sector to multiple disasters and impacts it similarly. The rising ferocity and magnitude of natural disasters and the expanding human and economic infrastructure over the last few decades has led to a greater exposure of the same to hazards of nature. The only way of safeguarding the precious physical infrastructure is to integrate disaster prevention, mitigation and preparedness measures into them.

The involvement and association of the corporate sector with national risk reduction and risk management initiatives and with dissemination of appropriate and practical structural and non-structural disaster prevention and mitigation measures necessary for their safe and disaster-free functioning has been accorded priority as part of a strategy to systematically mainstream holistic disaster management into the functioning of the corporate sector.

The ever-expanding extent, sweep and scale of natural disasters has made it imperative for the corporate sector to initiate and integrate disaster risk prevention and mitigation measures in all facets of their functioning and operations with the objective of safeguarding the painstakingly built industrial assets from the impact of natural disasters. During the last decade, the frequency and fury of disaster occurrences in different parts of the country has imposed a colossal economic cost in terms of financial losses, disruption in industrial activities, retardation of expansion and growth plans and dissipation of investment and precious resources on rebuilding the same assets and infrastructure to make the operations sustainable.

Today, the corporate sector has become an inalienable part of our socio-economic and national life and a vibrant industry is not only better placed to make itself sustainable but can also act as a composite foil to the Governmental efforts at holistic disaster management. Recognizing the importance of integrating the corporate sector and their nodal organizations in disaster prevention, mitigation and preparedness agenda, the National Disaster Management Framework drawn up by the Ministry of Home Affairs, Government of India envisages "involvement of corporate sector in awareness generation and disaster preparedness and mitigation planning" through sensitization, training and co-opting of the corporate sector and their nodal bodies in planning process and response mechanisms. Similarly, the GoI-UNDP Disaster Risk Management Programme also entails promotion of partnerships with the private sector in awareness generation and sensitization leading to development of disaster risk management plans. The recent major disasters have clearly indicated the need for interweaving of disaster risk reduction and management concerns in order to minimize the losses both human and economic.

ROLE OF CORPORATE SECTOR

In keeping with the paradigm shift in its approach to disaster management brought about by the Government of India and the recurring phenomenon of natural disasters impacting all sectors of socio-economic life, including the corporate sector and inflicting heavy economic losses, focused attention has been given to risk mitigation endeavors to systematically reduce the vulnerabilities. The new approach stems from the premise that development in any sector, more so in the corporate world, cannot be sustainable and viable unless risk reduction and mitigation measures are built into the development processes and that investments in mitigation are much more cost-effective than expenditure on relief, rehabilitation and reconstruction.

Recognizing the gargantuan proportions of the challenge posed by recurring incidence of natural catastrophes, association and involvement of corporate sector and their representative nodal organizations for initiating disaster risk management measures has been considered as integral to success of disaster management initiatives.

The corporates in every country have always played a major role in post-disaster relief, rehabilitation and reconstruction efforts in the affected regions. In India, the contribution of the corporate sector has been notable especially in the aftermath of the devastating super-cyclone in Orissa in 1999 and the Bhuj earthquake (Gujarat) in 2001. The industrial and corporate organizations like the Confederation of Indian Industry (CII), the Federation of Indian Chambers of Commerce and Industry (FICCI), the PHD Chambers of Commerce and Industry and other industry and area-specific manufacturers and traders associations have been in the forefront of providing much-needed succor to the affected populace for ameliorating their sufferings. The Confederation of Indian Industry (CII), with a direct membership base of nearly five thousand industrial and corporate houses and an indirect associate membership of around fifty thousand companies from 283 national and regional sectoral associations, was the first industry organization to constitute a Disaster

Management Committee in May 2001 as part of its corporate set-up to advise and assist its member industries in initiating disaster risk reduction steps to insulate industrial establishments, infrastructure and processes from the vagaries and damaging potential of natural and man-made (industrial/technological) disasters.

Earthquake - adopting villages and contributing to the reconstruction of social and community assets. Apart form addressing natural disasters, CII has established an Environment Management Division (EMD) involved in research and propagation of environmentally sound industrial systems and processes. It has been deeply involved in advising and developing systems and methodologies for safer and disaster-free handling of chemicals and other hazardous substances in production processes and procedures.

The EMD has also been assisting the industries in development and implementation of on-site and off-site disaster management plans for ushering into an environment friendly industrial scenario, especially in the light of experience of the Bhopal Gas Tragedy. In addition, many area-specific industrial and commercial associations have also been contributing towards the well-being of the community around them by adopting socio-economic practices aimed at improving the living conditions and generally benefiting the people at large. *For example,* the Ankleshwar Environment Preservation Society in Ankleshwar, Gujarat alongwith Ankleshwar Industrial Association has set-up joint effluent treatment plants for medium and small-scale industries in the industrial belt with predominantly chemical industries and has also taken up disposal and treatment of solid and hazardous waste generated by industries and the cities with their own expertise and finance. Industries at Ankleshwar have shown that through a proactive and collaborative approach, environmental problems can be addressed in a constructive manner.

The corporate sector possesses huge resources - human, material, technical and financial and has significant presence in every region in the country. It also works and interacts with the community very closely and has an important stake in the well-being and prosperity of the community as its own progress and viability is largely dependent upon a resilient and safe community. The accountability of the corporate sector in terms of its Corporate Social Responsibility (CSR) has also increased as the value and reputation of a company is being increasingly adjudged by its social behaviour and by its contribution to the economic well-being and development of the communities in which it operates.

However, in keeping with the change in focus to the pre-disaster aspects of prevention, mitigation and preparedness to mount an allround assault on vulnerabilities and building of capacities at all levels, a lot of emphasis has been laid on integrating the disaster risk reduction and risk management aspects into the functioning and processes of industries. With a view to achieve this objective, active collaboration with representative industrial organizations like the CII, FICCI etc., is being forged for assessing and meeting the needs of corporates to have their assets and infrastructure analyzed from the point of view of retrofitting of existing structures and ensuring safety of upcoming industrial assets and establishments against the vagaries of nature.

The strategic framework envisages involvement of corporate bodies in entire gamut of issues connected with integrating disaster management concerns in the developmental efforts of the private sector - with a specific emphasis on pre-disaster aspects. Moreover, the corporate sector organizations have linkages with other similar organizations in different countries and regularly exchange and supplement each others' information and resources in times of need. It is, therefore, imperative for the success of initiatives in the area of disaster risk management that corporate sector organizations and their networks are associated with different facets of disaster management.

CORPORATE SOCIAL RESPONSIBILITY AND DISASTER MANAGEMENT

Corporate Social Responsibility (CSR) permeates every aspect of the functioning of corporate sector. The corporates always look for ways and means to enhance the brand value of their company and their products. It is in this context that corporate social responsibility makes good business sense. It is a business strategy that works. Now-a-days, the value and reputation of a company are increasingly being seen as its most valuable assets for retaining the loyalty and trust of the public to ensure a bright and sustainable future.

The business corporations, because of their high visibility, are being adjudged not merely on the basis of their bottom lines but also on their social behaviour. By integrating CSR into its business strategy as a core value, the corporates not only make a significant contribution to a better society but are also recognized for doing so. This has obvious benefits for the company. In fact, enormous rewards are there both for the business/industrial community as well as the society. The companies are motivated to achieve profitability, sustainable growth and human progress by placing corporate social responsibility in the mainstream of their business practice.

As part of their corporate social responsibility, the companies are encouraged to conduct business responsibly by contributing to the economic health and development of communities in which they operate; create healthy and safe working conditions to attract and retain a quality workforce; manage risk more efficiently and minimize the negative impact of its activities on the environment and its resources; be accountable to all stakeholders through dialogue and transparency regarding economic, social and environmental impacts of business activities; operate a good governance structure and uphold the highest standards and ethics while conducting business. The corporate sector is an integral part of the society.

It can play a leading role in supporting and building the knowledge, capacity and skills of the community in comprehensive risk-based disaster management activities ranging from prevention, mitigation and preparedness to response and recovery. It can offer human and financial resources and can also be a precious source of technical know-how, as *for example,* in the case of identification and research on technological solutions to prepare for and respond to natural disasters.

In addition, the recovery of the community cannot be complete if the business community itself is seriously affected as disasters can have serious negative fall-out on the corporate sector. For them to acquire capacity in disaster risk management would also entail protection of their employees and dependents. Corporate sectors' co-operation in reducing people's vulnerabilities to natural disasters would also help it in protecting its market catchment areas. In the aftermath of a catastrophe, the resources of the community are more likely to be utilized in protecting and rebuilding livelihoods rather in acquiring goods and services offered by the corporate sector.

Thus, their involvement in minimizing the impact of a natural event or in facilitating speedy and sustainable recovery should be viewed as a form of investment in protecting and securing its own "sources of livelihood".

INDIA INC.' RESPONSE—CONTRIBUTION TO TSUNAMI DISASTER RELIEF AND REHABILITATION ENDEAVOR

The President of the Confederation of Indian Industry (CII) has invoked the corporate sectors' social responsibility and appealed for liberal contributions and support to the relief and rehabilitation efforts in the aftermath of the Tsunami tragedy. The gargantuan scale of death and devastation in its wake across countries has been unprecedented. The CII has set-up "Tsunami Relief Fund" and has activated helpline offices in Delhi, Chennai and Hyderabad. It has also set-up an Outreach Inc. office in Virginia, USA to mobilize resources.

The Confederation is in touch with the Central and State (Provincial) Governments and is collecting feedback on the extent of damage and the immediate requirements of the affected people. Considering the tsunamic proportions of the tragedy and an acute shortage of drinking water especially in the island areas as well as in Tamil Nadu, CII has operationalized four easyto use water treatment plants, courtesy a member industry of the CII, in the Andaman and Nicobar Islands to provide clean drinking water to the affected people. Light trucks, generators, pumps and other industrial equipment has also been sent. CII has also deputed volunteers to manage distribution of relief materials through its warehouses.

ECONOMIC IMPACT ON CORPORATE SECTOR

At the global level, nearly 700 major catastrophes take place every year affecting billions in different countries. The disasters periodically visit the same geographical regions and set the development clock back by decades. It is similar to taking two steps forward and one step backwards. In some countries, this equation even gets reversed. The repeated occurrence of natural catastrophes undermines the economic viability of the communities as well as the corporate sector—further impoverishing the impoverished and sapping the very soul.

It is estimated that 28 developing countries, including India, suffered direct losses of over 1billion USD each during the past twenty years. In respect of some countries, it amounts to an erosion of over 1% of their annual GDP. In India, the natural disasters eroded 2% of the GDP during 1996-2001 and consumed 12% of the Government revenue during the same period. On an average, the disasters have been affecting nearly six million people annually in India and over six percent of the population is directly hit. In addition, the natural disasters pose a major threat to economic development in India as disaster-loss figures are rapidly increasing. *For example,* during 1965-1980, the losses were to the tune of 2.9 billion USD while during 1981- 1995, the same increased to 13.4 billion USD. However, this was overtopped in six years during 1996-2001 with loss figures touching 13.8 billion USD. The table below shows the catastrophe losses in India during the period in million USDs.

The compounded losses suffered by the industries including direct, indirect and secondary losses are colossal and virtually incalculable.

At the global level too, the basic disaster frequency and the losses imposed by them are steadily mounting as evidenced by the table below:

> A study reveals that forty three (43%) percent of the industries experiencing a disaster never re-open and twenty nine (29%) percent close for good within two years even if they mobilize resources to restart operations.

The increasing incidence, frequency and severity of natural catastrophes has resulted in steadily mounting monetary losses, as per the table given below:

> Amounting to Rupees 100 crore and Gujarat State Fertilizer Corporation's output was disrupted to the tune of 2,000 tonnes per day. The wind lifted the heavy cranes and machinery and twisted the transmission towers.

THE ORISSA SUPER-CYCLONE, 1999

The Orissa Super-Cyclone in 1999 inflicted a cumulative loss of nearly 1,000 crores on the industrial sector. The major industries like the Paradeep Port, Oswal Fertilizers and CESCO suffered heavy losses. A large number of industrial units remained inundated for days together.

During 1990s, there were three times more incidents of natural disasters and eight times increase in disaster costs as compared to the 1960s.

The three major natural disasters in recent years to have caused massive losses to the industries and the corporates have been the Gujarat Cyclone of 1998, the Orissa Super-Cyclone of 1999 and the Bhuj Earthquake of 2001.

The Gujarat Cyclone, 1998

The Gujarat Cyclone of 1998 with two landfalls and a wind velocity between 170-200 kmph, ripped through the industrial heart of Gujarat and inflicted an economic loss of nearly ₹ 2,500 crores. The Kandla Port, gateway to the granaries of north India and the industrial belt of west and north India and neighbouring facilities suffered extensive damage and a loss of nearly 600 crores. The corporate sector including Reliance Industries' Jamnagar oil refinery suffered losses.

The Bhuj Earthquake (Gujarat), 2001

However, it was during Bhuj Earthquake, 2001 that the need for a comprehensive strategy and planning targeted at safeguarding the industrial and lifeline infrastructure was underscored. The earthquake caused nearly ten thousand industrial units to go out of production as it struck the industrial heartland of the State. The total economic loss was assessed at over Rupees five thousand crores. The entire spectrum of industries including the lifeline structures like bridges, roads, power, rail network telecommunication, air control towers and aerodromes suffered damages and hampered restoration and rehabilitation activities.

The performance of lifeline and industrial structures left much to be desired and underlined the need to integrate risk reduction and mitigation measures while planning and settingup industrial units.

It is estimated that nearly ten thousand industrial units went out of production at the hands of the earthquake and an overwhelming majority of the remaining ones operated at only fifty percept of their output capacity. The economic loss on account of disruption of industrial and commercial activity for over a month is pegged at more than rupees two thousand crores.

Industrial and Chemical Disasters

In addition to the onslaught of natural disasters casting a long shadow over the viability of the economic sector, susceptibility to industrial and chemical hazards also poses a major threat to the healthy and safe functioning of corporate sector. The industries employ many production processes involving a wide range of chemicals and hazardous raw materials, intermediates, waste and final products.

These disasters, though normally caused by irresponsible handling of hazardous substances or due to their improper and unauthorized use or due to inadequate attention to maintenance of manufacturing processes, have the potential to substantially undermine the very functioning of industries in the region in the aftermath of any untoward incident since such incidents have widespread ramifications and long-term impact on the society and environment.

Between 1970 and 1990, about 180 severe industrial accidents occurred worldwide, leading to the release of various chemical compounds into the environment and killed nearly eight thousand people, injured more than twenty thousand and led to hundreds of evacuations involving thousands of people. The scenario becomes scary and horrendous if one takes into account the generational and genetic impact on the community for years to come.

The Bhopal Gas Tragedy of 1984, involving a sudden release of about 30 tonnes of methyl isocynate (MIC) at the Union Carbide plant due to poor safety management practices, poor early warning systems and lack of community preparedness led to death of nearly three thousand people, caused severe health and respiratory problems and birth of deformed and still-born children.

It is estimated that the incident caused damages varying between USD 30 million to as high as USD 3 billion. The deleterious effects of the tragedy can still be felt even after twenty years.

It is the world's worst industrial and chemical disaster. Toxic gas leakage from the poorly maintained and understaffed plant has rendered over one hundred twenty thousand people chronically ill. The safety systems designed to prevent such a disaster at the plant had been shut down to save money. The survivors, denied adequate compensation, suffer from debilitating illnesses and the heavily polluted site of the plant has not been cleaned up and poisonous chemicals continue to seep into the ground water further compounding the misery of the residents.

The Bhopal Gas Tragedy has highlighted the responsibilities of units handling hazardous substances including development of on-site and off-site emergency plans, notifying the authorities and the community around about the processes and materials used, their storage, handling and transportation and the possible hazards emanating there from and the requisite precautionary measures.

However, even after the worst chemical tragedy, forty two major industrial disasters have taken place since then taking a toll of over two hundred fifty persons in India and exposure to hazardous materials and wastes to explosives in metal scrap continues unabated. In spite of numerous environmental and regulatory laws, the chemical and hazardous industries continue to generate and discharge tonnes of potentially dangerous wastes every day, posing a grave danger to people's health, lives and environment.

In spite of stupendous human and economic cost of natural phenomena in myriad forms resulting in breakdown of support infrastructure and services compounding loss and trauma of the affected, the factors aggravating these continue to multiply introducing newer hazards and accentuating the vulnerabilities of human and industrial infrastructure.

The situation is leading to an enhanced expenditure on emergency response and relief and diversion of developmental resources as reinvestment in restoration of socio-economic infrastructure. It has impeded and retarded industrial growth leading to a fall in industrial production and revenues generated there from. The corporate sector as well as the community has to depend increasingly upon external borrowings to meet its immediate needs and to make the industrial units operational.

The natural as well as man-made disasters cast a tremendous social, human and developmental cost with a major impact on the overall human development indices and industrial growth, stability and prosperity in the affected regions. It is only through adoption and integration of comprehensive disaster risk reduction and mitigation measures that the long shadow of the deleterious impact of natural and industrial/ chemical catastrophes can be contained.

***

7

Earthquake Resistance Buildings

Earthquake motion is chaotic, at times violent and it involves translation and rotation of the ground in all directions, simultaneously. This pattern of ground motion is neither unique nor uniform. It varies from one earthquake to another. Its magnitude and intensity depends on the varying soil properties starting from the focus of the earthquake, which invariably is deep inside the earth, to the epicenter, which is on the crust and then to the point where a building is located. It also depends on the properties of soil on which the building is constructed.

To the complexity of the ground motion is added the complexity of the response of the structure. This response depends on its shape, form, structural system of the superstructure, type of foundation, type of finishes, details of finishes, cladding materials, construction materials and, finally, the quality of construction. Added to this, is the problem of limitations on accurately modeling a structure mathematically to predict its response to such chaotic ground motions in elastic as well as in inelastic range.

Even though the knowledge to predict response in elastic range of a structure has advanced considerably, but that to predict its response in inelastic range is still meager. However, in case of a very severe earthquake, a structure would definitely move into the inelastic range because a number of elements and joints will yield. It is, therefore, very important to provide sufficient strength in members and joints so that even after yielding they do not completely fail and the structure does not collapse.

Earthquake Codes

Scientists have been able to identify the range of earthquakes of different magnitudes and different intensities, which could be, expected in different parts of the country and also to some extent the probable frequency of occurrence of the highest range of earthquake in a specific region. This knowledge forms the basis of earthquake codes, which divide the country in different zones where earthquakes of a specific magnitude and a specific intensity could be expected.

The Codes also give guidelines for design of buildings with different materials, of different shapes and forms and with different structural systems. Considering the unpredictable nature of earthquake, in its occurrence, its magnitude, its intensity and its duration, the Codes are very guarded in undertaking complete responsibility of the safety of a structure, even if it is designed following all its provisions rigorously. This is a stand taken by the codes all over the world, not only just in India. The philosophy of design adopted by all these codes is, that if a building is designed properly and constructed properly on the basis of the code, it should not suffer any damage under a mild earthquake, should suffer damage of only non-structural elements and finishes etc., which can easily be repaired under an earthquake of medium to high intensity and should suffer damage of structural elements, without collapse, under very severe earthquake.

None of the codes states that if a building is designed following provisions of the code and built properly, nothing will happen to it under any earthquake that can possibly occur in that region. Because those who frame these codes realize that if they had to make this statement, the cost of the buildings would be prohibitive. The buildings would have to be designed for earthquakes of very high intensity and magnitude, the probability of occurrence of which may be only once in fifty years, or once in hundred years.

It is interesting to trace the history of the process of making these earthquake codes. Early codes were based directly on the practical lessons learned from earthquakes, relating primarily to types of construction. In some cases they placed limitations on the height of buildings.

This process started in Italy way back in 1783 when a severe earthquake in "Calabrian" prompted the engineers to think of Earthquake (EQ) resistant buildings. On the basis of observations, the engineers stipulated that:

- All buildings which had failed and survived be built with timber frame, in-filled with stone embedded in mortar.
- The maximum height of buildings be two storeys.

However, these stipulations were not rigorously followed as the years, decades and a century went by, during which period there was extensive seismic activity in the region but of small to medium intensity and magnitude. Later in 1908 a severe earthquake occurred in "Messina-Reggio", during which 160,000 persons lost their lives in a relatively small area. Most of the collapsed buildings were in masonry and had not followed the stipulations framed in 1784.

A fter this earthquake, a commission of nine practicing engineers and five distinguished university professors were assigned the task of identifying methods to design buildings which were cheap, could be built easily an could also resist earthquakes. The commission gave two proposals:

1. Isolate the building from the ground and place it on a compacted layer of sand or on spherical rollers.
2. Construct the building with timber frame and in-built rubble masonry but design it to withstand horizontal force equal to 1/12 of its dead weight. This force was later changed to a horizontal design load of 1/12 of the weight above for the ground floor and 1/8 of the weight above for 2nd and 3rd floor.

Proposal (2) was generally adopted. These were intuitive recommendations based on observations and these concepts of designing a building to withstand a stipulated horizontal force or isolating it from the ground are still valid.

Japan also has a long history of earthquakes, which had intuitively led them to construct very light buildings in timber. Some of the wooden pagodas constructed before 15th century are amongst the tallest wooden structures in the world and have withstood many earthquake without any reported damage. Here, again, a commission was set-up which observed that buildings built in wood and steel had fared much better than those in concrete.

It is interesting to note that three buildings designed by one Dr. Tachu Naito, Professor of Architecture at Waseda University in Tokyo, withstood the 1923 earthquake remarkably well. These three buildings were the Japan industrial Bank, 100ft high in steel frame, Jitsugyo Building in reinforced concrete frame and the Kalenki Theatre in a combination of concrete and steel. All these buildings had been designed to withstand a lateral force equal to 1/15 of their dead weight. By 1880 a Seismological Programme had been set-up and some empirical criteria for design of earthquake had been developed.

In 1923 a very severe earthquake took as many as 1,40,000 lives in Japan. By then, a number of building in steel and reinforced concrete had also been built, most of which withstood the earthquake fairly well. On account of success of these buildings to resist earthquake forces, Dr. Naito was considered an authority on the subject. He had laid down four very simple principles to be followed for earthquake resistant buildings:

1. A building should be as rigid as possible with rigid joints and generous bracings or shear walls. This will ensure short building period and prevent resonance with ground motion.

2. Use a closed plan layout, rather than an open U, L, T or H shapes.

3. Rigid walls or bracings should be placed symmetrically in plan.

4. Lateral force allocation to different frames of a building is done based on their rigidities.

The famous Imperial Hotel designed by Frank Lloyd Wright survived this 1923 earthquake in Japan without too much damage. It was a fairly rigid two storied building supported on short 8' long piles at 2' × 2' grid. In the USA, a very severe earthquake occurred in 1906 in San Francisco. But it did not result in seting-up any commission to make recommendations. Instead, the regular building code made a provision to design all buildings for a horizontal load of 30 pounds per square foot to cater for wind and earthquake forces.

It was only at 1925 "Santa-Barbara" earthquake that work to frame a seismic design code was undertaken which resulted in a "Uniform Building Code" published in 1927. The provisions in this code were, however, casual, to cater for a specified horizontal force and were not mandatory. A subsequent "Long-Beach" earthquake in 1933, made the authorities serious.

1933—Important buildings like schools, hospitals, places of assembly for 10% (Dead + some Live load) all other buildings 2% to 5% (Dead + some Live load)

1943—Horizontal load each floor = C × dead load above C = 0.6/(N + 4.5), N = No. of stories above. Thus, for a one storey building (N = 0) C = 0.133 and a 13 storeys building (N = 12) C = 0.0364

1947—Horizontal load varies form 3.7 to 8% of design vertical load depending on number of storeys and soil conditions

1948—Base shear V=CW

W = dead load + 0.25 live load

C = 0.015/T

T = fundamental period = 0.05H

H = height in ft.

D = plan dimension in the direction of earthquake in ft.

1956—V same as above, but

C = 0.02/T

A number of subsequent revisions took place. The latest uniform building code is of 1997 edition. The name of this code has been changed to "International Building Code of USA" in 2000, the latest edition of which is of 2003.

The first Indian code for design of EQ resistant buildings was framed in 1962, which was subsequently revised in 1966, 1970, 1975, 1984 and finally in 2002. With every revision, revisions were modified on the basis of the latest available knowledge. However, with every such revision provisions of the code became more stringent.

Originally, the country had been divided in 7 zones. Starting with EQ of very mild intensity in Zone-0, the intensity kept on increasing in Zones-I, II, III, IV and V with the heaviest in Zone-VI.

Subsequently in 1984 these seven zones were reduced to five. Zone-0 was merged into Zone-I and Zone-VI in Zone-V. Recently in 2002 the zones have further been reduced to four. Zone-I has been merged into Zone-II. The latest seismic zoning map of India showing four different zones (zones II, III, IV and V). The magnitude of seismic force experienced by a building varies with its configuration, construction materials, height and number of floors, structural system and type of foundation and soil characteristics.

It is directly related to the intensity of earthquake. Actual forces that a structure is subjected to during an earthquake may be far greater than those specified in this Code. However, ductility, arising from inelastic material behaviour and detailing and over strength arising from the additional reserve strength in a structure, over and above the design strength, are relied upon to withstand these additional forces.

The strength requirement of a building to withstand earthquake-generated forces can be assessed based on a "Static Approach" or a "Dynamic Approach".

In the static approach, it is assumed that earthquake vibrations subject a building to horizontal forces along its height. The magnitude and distribution of such horizontal forces is related to the construction materials, height and number of floors, foundation system, soil characteristics and the Earthquake zone in which the building is located. The total design lateral load is termed as the design seismic base shear.

In the Dynamic Approach, vibration analysis of the building is carried out to establish the base shear and its distribution over the height of the building. The Code specifies that all buildings can be designed with the static approach, except for buildings higher than 40 m in Zones IV and V and higher than 90 m in Zones II and III which need to be designed with the dynamic approach. But if a building is irregular it has to be designed according to dynamic approach, if it is higher than 12 m in Zones-IV and V and higher than 40 m in zones II and III.

The Code has very stringent provisions to cater for torsion effects of earthquake forces. It also has equally stringent provisions to analyze and design irregular buildings.

Uniform Philosophy of Design

The philosophy of design against earthquake forces in all the codes is more or less the same which has been given earlier and which states that, the buildings designed according to codes should be able to resist minor earthquakes undamaged, resist moderate earthquakes without significant damage and resist severe earthquakes without collapse.

The codes do not guarantee that a structure would never be subjected to higher forces than stipulated in any earthquake. All the Codes have similar equations to compute the base shear and its distribution over the height of a building. This distribution is either triangular or parabolic, with the highest value at the top and least at the bottom. Some of the codes also specify a small component of the base shear to act as a point load at the top.

Provisions for variation of base shear related to importance of the building, structural system, structural material, soil properties etc., are also similar. Considering regions of different intensity of earthquake and buildings of different height, different flexibility and on different soil conditions, the base shear could vary from 2% to 14% of the total gravity and part live load of a building. This range is also more or less similar.

It is interesting to compare this range with that specified intuitively by Italian and Japanese engineers long ago, which varied from 7% to 12%. All Codes have fairly stringent provisions for analyzing and designing irregular buildings. All Codes ascribe to the concept of inelastic response of the Structure and Ductility.

Choice of Strucutral Materials

The preferred materials for medium to high-rise buildings in earthquake regions are concrete and steel. With the help of both these materials the desired level of flexibility or rigidity can be provided. Both these materials if detailed properly retain their integrity even after a large number of stress reversals and have high level of ductility.

A precast system or a combination of prestressed and precast system is not considered very suitable but cannot be ruled out. In Russia it has been used quite successfully in regions of high seismic activity. The joints need special consideration and very careful detailing so as to be ductile and not lose integrity under cycles of reversal of stresses.

For low-rise buildings masonry or a combination of masonry with concrete frames is most popular.

CHOICE OF STRUCUTRAL SYSTEMS

Guide Lines for Planning Earthquake Resistant Buildings

As we have seen in chapter 5 that poor form cannot be ordered to behave satisfactorily in an earthquake. Therefore in order to predict response of a form to earthquake, it should be sound and symmetrical and honor the following design principles.

(*a*) Be simple.

(*b*) Be symmetrical.

(*c*) Not be too elongated in plan or too slender in elevation.

(*d*) Have continuous and uniform distribution of strength.

(*e*) Have horizontal members which form hinges before the vertical members.

(*f*) Have its stiffness related to sub soil properties.

Horizontal and Vertical Members

One of the essential design principles of earthquake engineering is that horizontal members should fail before vertical members. This increases the capacity of a building to keep absorbing earthquake motions even after hinges are formed in the beams, but not in the columns. Collapse would occur only after hinges are formed in the Columns.

Uniform and Continuous Distribution of Strength

The behaviour of a structure is far closer to its analysis and it has far greater chances of withstanding earthquake-induced forces properly without much damage if it follows the following design principles:

(*a*) The load bearing members are uniformly distributed in plan.

(*b*) All columns and walls are continuous and without offsets from roof to foundation.

(*c*) All beams are free of offsets.

(*d*) Columns and beams are co-axial.

(*e*) A principal member should not change section suddenly.

(*f*) Columns and beams are of nearly the same width.

(*g*) The structure is continuous and monolithic with rigid joints

The more these principles are followed, the less would be the cost of the structure, the detailing would be easier to plan and construct and its behaviour under an earthquake would be much better.

IS 1893 : 2002 CRITERIA FOR EARTHQUAKE RESISTANT DESIGN

Inelastic Seismic Response of Structures and Ductility

Under sustained loading a member suffers elastic deformations, which keep on increasing linearly with the load, upto the yield stress of the material. After this is a stage called "Plastic Stage" in which the member keeps deforming without any additional load, which is followed by a "Strain hardening" stage in which the member capacity slightly increases and finally the "strain softening" stage in which the member collapses.

Load Combinations

In the limit state design of reinforced concrete structures, following load combinations shall be accounted for

1. 1.5 (DL + IL)
2. 1.2 (DL + IL ± EL)
3. 1.5 (DL ± EL)
4. 0.9 DL ± 1.5EL

When the lateral load resisting elements are oriented along orthogonal horizontal direction, the structure shall be designed for the effects due to full design earthquake load in one horizontal direction at time. When the lateral load resisting elements are not oriented along the orthogonal horizontal directions, the structures shall be designed for the effects due to full design earthquake load in one horizontal direction plus 30% of the design earthquake load in the other direction. For instance, the building should be designed for (±ELx ± 0.3ELy) as well as (± 0.3ELx ± Ely), where x and y are two orthogonal horizontal directions.

Distribution of Shear in Multi-Storied Building

Vertical distributions of Base shear to different floor levels of a multistoried building have been referred in IS 1893 (Part I): 2002. The design Base Shear (V_b) computed in 7.6.4 shall be distributed along the height of the building as per the following expression:

where, Q_i = Design lateral force at floor, i.

W_i = Seismic weight of the building.

h_i = Height of floor I measured from base.

n = number of storeys in the building is the number of levels at which masses are located.

Estimation of Base Shear

The total design lateral force or design seismic base shear (V_b) along any principal direction shall be determined by the following expression:

$$V_b = A_h W$$

where, A_h = Design horizontal acceleration spectrum value Ta in the considered direction of vibration

W = Seismic weight of the building

Estimation of Earthquake Loading

For the purpose of determining seismic forces, the country is classified into four seismic zones.

The buildings shall be designed for lateral force as calculated below:

$$V_B = AhW$$

where, V_B = Base shear

W = Seismic weight = Dead load + part of super/imposed load.

This design base shear is distributed along the height of the building as given below:

Q_i = Design lateral force at floor i.

W_i = Seismic weight of floor i.

h_i = height of floor I.

n = number of stories.

The total shear in any horizontal plane shall be distributed to the various vertical element of lateral force resisting system (shear walls, bracing).

TYPES OF CONSTRUCTION

Framed Construction

This type of construction is suitable for multistoried and industrial buildings. Vertical Load Carrying Frame Construction consists of frames with flexible (hinged) joints and bracing members. Such buildings shall be adequately strengthened against lateral forces by shear walls and/or other bracing systems in plan, elevation and sections such that EQ forces shall be resisted by them in any direction.

Moment Resistant Frames With Shear Walls

The frames may be of reinforced concrete or steel with semi-rigid or rigid joints. The walls are rigid capable of acting as shear walls and may be of reinforced concrete or of brickwork reinforced or unreinforced bounded by framing members through shear connectors. The shear walls should extend from the foundation either to the top of the building or to a lesser height as required from design consideration. In design, the interaction between frame and the shear walls should be considered properly to satisfy compatibility and equilibrium conditions.

Box Type Construction

This type of construction consists of prefabricated or in-situ masonry, concrete or reinforced concrete wall along both the axes of the building. The walls support vertical loads and also act as shear walls for horizontal loads acting in any direction.

All traditional masonry construction falls under this category. In prefabricated construction attention shall be paid to the connections between wall panels so that transfer of shear between them is ensured.

CATEGORIES OF BUILDINGS

For the purpose of specifying the earthquake resisting features in masonry, the buildings have been categorized in five categories A to E based on the value of Ah

$$A_h = ao\ I\ b$$

where, A_h = Design seismic coefficient for the building

a_o = Basic seismic coefficient for the seismic zone in which the building is located.

I = Importance factor applicable to the building

b = Soil foundation factor

DUCTILE DETAILING OF RC STRUCTURES

Ductility

The main structural elements and their connection shall be designed to have a ductile failure. This will enable the structure to absorb energy during earthquakes to avoid sudden collapse of the structure. Providing reinforcing steel in masonry at critical sections, as provided in this standard will not only increase strength and stability but also ductility.

IS 13920 suggests ductile detailing of reinforced concrete structures subjected to seismic forces.

Flexure Members

Standards provided by IS Codes for design of flexure members are:

- The member should preferably have a width-to-depth ratio of more than 0.3.
- The width of member should not be less than 200 mm.
- The depth of member should preferably be not more than ¼ of the clear span.

Longitudinal Reinforcement

- At least two bars throughout the member length at top and bottom.
- Positive steel at a joint face must be at least equal to 1/2 the negative steel at that face.
- Steel provided at each of the top and bottom face of the member at any section along its length should be at least equal to 1/4 of the maximum negative moment steel provided at the face of either joint.

The longitudinal bars should be spliced, only if hoops are provided over the entire splice length, at spacing not exceeding 150 mm.

The lap length should not be less than the bar development length in tension. Lap splices should not be provided:

- Within a joint.
- Within a distance of 2d from joint face.
- Within a quarter length of the member where flexural yielding may generally occur under the effect of earthquake forces.

Web Reinforcement

The spacing of hoops over a length of 2d at either end of a beam should not exceed

- d/4
- 8 times the dia of the smallest longitudinal bar.

However, it need not be less than 100 mm. The first hoop should be at a distance not exceeding 50 mm from the joint face. Vertical hoops at the same spacing as above should also be provided over a length equal to 2d on either side of a section where flexural yielding may occur under the effect of earthquake forces. Elsewhere, the beam should have vertical hoops at a spacing not exceeding d/2.

Transverse Reinforcement

The parallel legs of rectangular hoop shall be spaced not more than 300 mm center to center. If the length of any side of the hoop exceeds 300 mm, a crosstie shall be provided.

Alternatively, a pair of overlapping hoops may be provided within the column. The hooks shall engage peripheral longitudinal bars.

Special Confining Reinforcement

Special confining reinforcement shall be provided over a Length 'lo' from each joint face, towards mid span and on either side of any section, where flexural yielding may occur under the effect of earthquake forces. The length 'lo' shall not be less than:

- Larger lateral dimension of the member at the section where yielding occurs.
- 1/6 of clear span of the member.
- 450 mm.

When the calculated point of contra-flexure, under the effect of gravity and earthquake loads, is not within the middle half of the member clear height, special confining reinforcement shall be provided over the full height of the column.

Also, special confining reinforcement shall be provided over the full height of a column, which has significant variation in stiffness along its height. This may result in variation in stiffness.

❋❋❋

8

Disaster Prevention and Management

Natural hazards cause a high number of lives to be lost, but relatively small property losses, in the least developed and developing countries. In the relatively developed countries, on the other hand, where disaster prevention and mitigation measures are adequately established, the loss of lives is relatively small but the damage to property can be high. Losses may of course vary considerably within a given country. China's structure of land use dictates the disaster composition of the country. In terms of the geographical extent of vulnerability, the bulk of farmland and pastures are the main areas threatened by natural hazards. In the event of a disaster, therefore, peasants and herdsmen are affected the most and in case of a destructive disaster, thousands upon thousands of households may be adversely affected. However, in terms of total losses, those resulting from disasters in urban areas will usually be much heavier.

The effect of natural hazards on the loss of human lives is directly related to the poverty levels in a given country. National and regional efforts for natural disaster reduction should therefore be closely linked with poverty alleviation and economic and social development activities.

Another factor that exacerbates the effects of natural hazards is the environmental degradation taking place in many countries of the region. The damage caused by natural hazards is higher in countries where environmental degradation is rampant. Deforestation, erosion, overgrazing, overcultivation and incorrect agricultural practices and the degradation of natural buffers amplify the effects of natural hazards. Table shows the relative intensity of hazards faced by some countries in Asia and the Pacific.

All in all, therefore, the potential for the occurrence of devastating natural disasters is much greater in the countries of Asia and requires particular attention if the severe toll of these events on life and property is to be significantly reduced. It is the purpose of this report to examine the extent of these disasters in further detail, to report upon the progress that has been made during the Decade to cope with the problems they bring and to suggest improved ways and means of doing so.

STEPS FOR FUTURE DISASTERS

Risk Management

The countries of the ESCAP region are exposed to a high proportion of water-related disasters, brought about by cyclones, storm surges, floods, landslides and droughts. The effectiveness of disaster reduction measures will be dependent upon a quantification of the nature and occurrence of these hazards. A description and analysis of natural hazards and the consequent risks associated with them are an essential step in assessing the strategies required to mitigate their effects. This process is usually termed "risk management".

In essence, disaster risk management involves an analysis of the exposure to risk of the disaster prone community, *i.e.*, a disaster risk analysis followed by the identification and implementation of appropriate measures in order to manage existing, future and residual disaster risks and to reduce their effects to acceptable levels. The modern risk management approach involves recognition of:

(i) The need to investigate the entire range of the particular disaster up to the maximum probable event.

(ii) The importance of public consultation to encourage ownership of the resulting mitigation plan.

(iii) The risk relating to developments in the disaster prone area.

(iv) The need to implement a comprehensive public education and awareness programme.

All the elements that contribute risk to the situation must be carefully identified and the order of their importance established. The elements can also evaluated with respect to their potential to cause damage to the existing development. Once the major hazards are identified, the risk analyses will aim to determine their magnitude and frequency.

This general risk management process can be applied to all types of risk and to the organizations exposed to these risks. The detailed process consists of the following steps:

(i) Identify the stakeholders exposed to or affecting the risk of the disaster.

(ii) Estimate the disaster risk, *i.e.,* the likelihood and consequences of the disaster.

(iii) Identify public and private property, social systems and environmental elements at risk.

(iv) Assess the acceptability of the disaster risk.

(v) Monitor and review disaster risks and the effectiveness of risk treatment.

(vi) Define disaster risk treatment strategies.

(vii) Communication between the community and risk management agencies.

Hazard and Vulnerability

Disaster risk management involves the assessment of hazard and vulnerability.

Hazard assessment is concerned with defining the properties of the hazard and its direct effect. The first step in hazard assessment is data collection and recording. Tropical cyclones pose three threats, namely, wind, flood and storm surge. The intensity of a tropical cyclone is measured by its wind characteristics which are described by velocity and direction. Evaluation of the hazard associated with cyclones therefore involves the measurement of wind direction, velocity and frequency at a number of meteorological stations.

The assessment of the flood hazard involves the identification of:

(a) Flood behaviour.

(b) Topography.

(c) Population at risk.

When combined, these elements define the nature and extent of the flood hazard at a particular locality. Generally, this information is presented in map form showing the areas which are likely to be inundated to a given depth with a specified frequency.

For hazard evaluation of storm surge, it is necessary to determine the frequency of intense winds, the topography of the continental shelf and adjacent coastline and the normal tidal behaviour.

In evaluating the relationship of hazards to the elements at risk, it is important that the analysis is applied to the entire disaster episode, encompassing onset, response, aftermath and recovery phases. Different sets of 'elements at risk' will emerge in the different phases of the disaster episode. *For eaxmple*, the threat to life and limb of the disaster prone residents is an issue during the response phase, while the rapid return of the water supply, sewerage and communication systems to serviceability is an issue during the recovery phase.

On the other hand vulnerability is a measure of the level of exposure of people and property to the various water-related hazards. Vulnerability can be measured as:

(a) Physical vulnerability, which relates to buildings, infrastructure and agriculture.

(b) Social vulnerability which relates to the impact the hazard will have on various social groups.

(c) Economic vulnerability, which is a measure of hazards causing losses to economic assets and processes.

These three items, taken collectively and combined with damage information, measure the probable damage for a given frequency of hazard. When the potential damage for a given disaster has been assessed, the disaster risk can be determined by the product of the damage and the probability of occurrence of the disaster.

Vulnerability is a measure of the degree of susceptibility and resilience of a disaster prone community. Vulnerability determines how well a community can cope with a disaster. This in turn depends upon the magnitude of the disaster, the disaster awareness of the community and the topographic, infrastructure, social and economic factors which determine the social and economic disruption caused by the hazard.

Risk Evaluation

By evaluating the risk of various hazards to which the country is liable or potentially liable, it becomes practicable to formulate strategies to mitigate the impact of hazards in a cost-effective way. If a community is especially vulnerable to a particular type of disaster severe risk treatment measures may be required to reduce the disaster risk to acceptable levels.

More recently, the definition of risk management has been expanded to include the notion of uncertainty. "Risk" is defined as the possibility that an expected outcome is not achieved or replaced by another, or that an unforeseen event occurs. This is a broad view of risk that includes both uncertainty due to future events and the consequences of limited knowledge, information and experience.

Disaster mitigation projects, as currently undertaken, are formulated to provide economical protection to disaster prone areas. Projects are determined by analyzing disaster potential, together with damage performance and cost, for a range of project sizes and configurations. The disaster mitigation plan selected is based on maximizing net economic benefits consistent with acceptable risk and functional performance. This approach treats the input variables as deterministic functions.

The trend is now towards the use of a combined risk model which incorporates "uncertainty" into the input variables as a probability density function representing possible statistical error in each of the input variable relationships. This risk management approach acknowledges that there is not a specific, unequivocal performance level.

Initially, the evaluation of risk, or the evaluation of disaster potential, is based on the analysis of available meteorological and hydrological records of the individual country, augmented by data available from other countries in the region, depending on the nature of the disaster. Meteorological data for hazard assessment need to be based on a comprehensive, nation-wide system of meteorological recording stations. It is also highly desirable that this system is closely associated with and compatible with, the national meteorological recording systems operated by neighbouring countries. The main categories of meteorological data needed for effective water-based natural disaster identification are:

(a) Precipitation data.

(b) Wind and atmospheric pressure.

(c) Synoptic observations of relevant weather elements.

Hydrological data for hazard assessment should also be based on a comprehensive, nation-wide system of stream gauging stations. There are three major components of hydrological data required for hazard assessment, namely, flood discharges, water levels and flow velocities. Long-term streamflow data are also required to predict and quantify drought behaviour.

Over the past decade, remote sensing techniques have become an essential feature of data collection systems for monitoring watershed conditions. These techniques are invaluable for the rapid collection of data and for the study of extensive areas, particularly in developing countries for which conventional resource mapping sources are limited. Under favourable conditions, they are well suited for reconnaissance studies of water-related disasters affecting large areas, such as flooding.

Normal aerial photography has proved to be a useful technique for watershed monitoring, because of the high degree of resolution obtainable and the ability of this technique to show the spatial distribution of ground characteristics.

Over the past twenty years, the enormously increased amount of resource evaluation and assessment data available from the various types of remote sensing systems, much of it available directly in computer accessible format and increasingly widespread availability of low-cost computer equipment, has greatly encouraged the development of techniques for the archiving, analysis, mapping and presentation of such data, using GIS methodology. These techniques are supported by a wide-range of commercial software packages and systems which allow the ready manipulation of vast amounts of data. Available computer models have been developed to predict the flood behaviour of river flow, such as rates of rise and fall, duration, frequency and magnitude of floods and periods of low flow.

INTEGRATION OF DISASTER MANAGEMENT MEASURES

In the light of the many major disasters experienced throughout the Region during the past decade, it would be desirable to review the disaster management practices of the member countries. The experiences gained should be used as a basis to assist further evolution of disaster management practices, especially in those areas where implementation practices could be improved.

Wholesale changes do not appear warranted but adjustments to the existing approach would achieve:

(a) Further mitigation of disaster damage to existing development.

(b) Control over the future growth of potential disaster losses.

To achieve these objectives, there appears to be a case for the adoption of a system which could be effectively implemented as part of the member's disaster strategies.

After examining the available information on the status of disaster management in the ESCAP region, it is apparent that many of the member countries are yet to adopt an integrated approach for disaster management. The preferred disaster management system should integrate the following elements:

(a) The disaster management plan and the disaster emergency plan.

(*b*) The individual management measures.

(*c*) The roles and responsibilities of all stakeholders.

(*d*) The resource management considerations and programmes.

(*e*) Where applicable, the concept of comprehensive land-use planning based on total watershed management principles.

The objectives of the overall management system should ensure that:

(*a*) Disaster management matters are dealt with having regard to community safety, health and welfare requirements.

(*b*) Public information is freely available on the likely extent and nature of possible future hazards.

(*c*) All reasonable measures are taken to alleviate the hazard and damage potential to existing properties at risk and there is no significant growth in future hazard and damage potential resulting from new developments.

(*d*) Appropriate forecasting and warning systems exist and emergency services and Government assistance are available in the event of future disasters.

(*e*) The disaster management system is managed having regard to social and economic costs and benefits to individuals as well as the community at large.

An integrated approach is required to bring together these diverse issues, which are usually fragmented over a number of different authorities. This can be achieved through greater co-operation amongst the agencies, authorities and individuals involved in all aspects of disaster prevention and pre-paredness.

The extent to which the integrated approach can be achieved relies on a number of factors, including the management of natural resources and the strength of existing legislation. As a general principle however, the overall co-ordination of disaster management plans should be vested in a single organization, preferably operating at the national level, which assumes responsibility for legal, administrative and financial matters relating to the management of natural disasters.

INFORMATION SHARING

The adoption of such a system could however, pose a problem for some countries, which may lack the specialist technical skills needed to develop a comprehensive management plan and the capacity to implement the resulting prevention and preparedness measures. These problems could be addressed by the provision of specialist professional support and training for their agencies and institutions and financial subsidies from national Governments and donor countries.

The disaster management process requires an ongoing commitment to the education and training of disaster managers by the various tiers of Government and professional bodies. The exchange of information regarding difficulties, problems and solutions and the results of research is essential for improved disaster management. This can be fostered by the free flow of information at the local and international levels through formal agreement, workshops and conferences.

There is a number of significant advantages to be gained by adopting a national and international approach to water-related disaster management. This approach would lead to a better and more efficient use of the resources of each nation and the region. Disaster management principles have developed to a different degree and in different ways in the various ESCAP countries. Considerable cost savings and efficiencies could be achieved through the sharing of information and experiences in the co-ordination of disaster management research activities among the various countries. This form of co-operation would promote a consistent approach to disaster management policies and techniques, leading to better disaster management practices and would help to reduce each country's exposure to the risk of future disasters. Moreover, wider co-operation amongst neighbouring countries would facilitate the development of a regional data base of disaster related information throughout the region.

DISASTER PREPAREDNESS IN ESCAP REGION

Mitigation Strategies

To date, the principal thrust of the water-related disaster mitigation strategies employed in the ESCAP Region has concentrated on disaster preparedness, rather than on disaster prevention. Whilst this approach has in many countries been successful in reducing the overall death toll associated with these hazards, the amount of physical damage has continued to mount.

The prevention measures which can be directed towards the reduction of the effects of the hazard prior to its occurrence and the preparedness measures which may be implemented during and after the disaster.

In summary, these mitigation measures attempt to lessen the impact of the hazard by adopting both structural and non-structural approaches. The objective of the structural approach is to control the effects of the hazard by using specific engineering works as the best means of protecting life and property. On the other hand, the objective of the non-structural approach is to modify susceptibility to the hazard through a range of controls and other non-engineering devices.

The most successful preventive measures employed to curb the destructive and injurious effects of tropical cyclones are building design and construction standards, established to assist buildings and other structures to resist wind and water damage. The range of measures available for protection against the effects of flooding is much wider than that available to reduce the impact of tropical cyclones. It includes civil engineering-oriented structural measures, such as channel modifications, flood storages and levees, as well as non-structural measures such as planning controls and flood proofing of buildings.

The selection of the best mix of measures for application at a given location to prevent the occurrence of future water-related disasters should be based on a consideration of all the available structural and non-structural options. The optimal mix of measures should be based on risk analysis and the economic performance of the overall scheme. Consideration of social and environmental factors in addition to the legislative and legal constraints should form part of the planning process.

Disaster preparedness covers those actions that are taken when a potentially hazardous event threatens to become a disaster. Preparedness activities are designed to reduce social disruption and losses to existing property and are an essential component of overall disaster planning. Although these activities can serve, in the absence of more permanent mitigation measures, to reduce the threat to loss of life and property, they are more effective when employed as a component of a comprehensive, overall disaster management plan.

PROGRAMME DEVELOPMENT

Overview

As part of its contribution to the mid-term review of the IDNDR Programme, the Water Resources Section Secretariat of ESCAP prepared an overview of the status of the natural disaster mitigation efforts of its members. It found that there has been a growing recognition in the region of the significant benefits of disaster prevention and mitigation, rather than ad hoc relief reduction activities. Some countries had a long-established framework for responding to the disaster mitigation requirements of the country. Others had either strengthened their institutional mechanisms or were in the process of overhauling them.

Substantial progress had been achieved in meteorological forecasting and warning of tropical cyclones and the capability to forecast floods had improved considerably through the individual efforts of various countries, with assistance from the support given by ESCAP, the World Meteorological Organization (WMO), UNDP and other organizations. Useful programmes and the capability to forecast tropical cyclones and floods had improved considerably through the establishment of the Typhoon Committee and the Panel on Tropical Cyclones. These two bodies had co-operated in the forecasting and warning of cyclones, information exchange, provision of training and other forms of activity relating to the reduction of the impact of water-related natural disasters.

The development and use of radar for forecasting and measuring rainfall events and the increased number of telemetric rainfall stations in some countries had increased their capability for the rapid collection and processing of precipitation data and the forecasting of floods. There was still considerable variation among countries of the region with regard to the availability and reliability of equipment needed for effective cyclone and flood forecasting and warning.

It was determined that each country needed to improve the quality of forecasts and warnings in relation to water-related natural hazards and to increase the lead time of warnings, to enable areas likely to be affected to make adequate advance preparations. The need for emphasis to be given to the improvement of communication links for the transmission of basic data and providing related warning information about natural hazards was seen to be a priority issue.

Risk assessment and mapping had not been undertaken by most of the countries of the region. There was a need for comprehensive vulnerability analysis to be undertaken for disaster-prone areas, incorporating information about past disaster events, the socio-economic conditions of the population living in the affected area and inventories of major structures liable to damage. Risk assessment and hazard mapping would then be used to delineate areas vulnerable to natural hazards and determine the frequency, intensity, impact, return period and other data in relation to each category of hazard.

Almost all countries in the Asian and Pacific region experienced severe flood problems at comparatively frequent intervals. Their traditional approach to the reduction of flood losses relied upon the use of structural flood mitigation measures such as the construction of dams, levees and channel improvements. Most of the earlier flood mitigation programmes adopted by individual countries had been specific to a city or to a discrete agricultural area and had employed a narrow range of engineering works to provide solutions to the flooding problem.

Although some projects were successful, some of them have actually exacerbated flood damage. In recent years, most countries have recognized the inadequacy of programmes based solely on structural measures. Numerous attempts had been made to employ non-structural flood loss prevention measures to assist in minimizing losses, principally through exercising control over development in flood-prone areas. These measures were usually associated with a mix of structural measures and, in some circumstances, provided a comprehensive means of coping with a flood problem.

Bangladesh

Bangladesh is pre-dominantly a rural country, relying heavily upon agricultural production for its existence. Unfortunately, its topographic and climatic systems make it one of the most water-related disaster prone countries in the Asian region. It is frequently struck by destructive cyclones, devastating floods and crippling droughts. These hazards cause severe agricultural losses and place great strains on country's economy and its ability to achieve sustainable development.

Cyclones frequently sweep out of the Bay of Bengal and impact on the coastline with devastating effects. These cyclones generate dangerous floods, which are exacerbated by storm tides and wreak havoc along the entire coastal belt. Further upstream, in the delta formed by the three great rivers, the Padma, the Jamuna and the Meghna, frequent major flooding can inundate up to 70 percent of the entire country. The effects of these floods in terms of loss of life and property, ecological damage and lost production have crippled the country's economy and set back development programmes by years. In addition to the loss of production caused by cyclones and floods, Bangladesh has also experienced severe drought conditions which have resulted in disastrous crop failures.

In order to combat the many major disasters which have afflicted Bangladesh in recent years, the Government has pursued a vigorous programme of disaster management. This programme gave the initial priority to improvement in the forecasting and early warning systems for cyclones and floods, alongwith emphasis on emergency response and relief. Subsequent initiatives have involved prevention and preparedness measures with a bias towards infrastructure development, such as the construction of coastal dykes and river embankments. More recently, multi-level initiatives are being pursued which include: awareness and education programmes; decentralized planning and community participation in disaster mitigation and response; involvement of NGOs in disaster mitigation and response; and incorporation of disaster management and reduction component in development projects.

Bangladesh is aware that although the comprehensive control of water-related natural hazards is not entirely possible and the population will have to continue to live with the associated disasters which they bring, continuing effort is required in the development of a national disaster management plan to ameliorate their future impact.

Adequately constructed and equipped cyclone shelters had considerably reduced the number of lives lost to typhoons and tropical cyclones. As a preventive measure, cyclone-resistant designs for dwellings had helped reduce the number of casualties and reduce serious damage to buildings.

Progress had been achieved in developing mitigation measures to improve the safety of non-engineered structures such as ordinary dwellings and simple public buildings constructed with local materials in the traditional manner. In some countries of the region there was a need for preparation or review of cyclone resistant design codes for buildings and other engineering structures and for their enforcement, as well as the undertaking of proper arrangements for the infrastructure to be able to deal with natural hazards.

Republic of Korea

The Republic of Korea frequently suffers disasters resulting from tropical cyclones, storms and floods. Over the last 20 years, these hazards have caused considerable loss of life, disruption to the economy and massive property damage. Occasional droughts also affect the agricultural and industrial sectors and impact upon rural communities.

A review of the available damage statistics discloses that the Government's efforts in natural disaster reduction has resulted in a dramatic reduction in the death toll. During the IDNDR the average annual loss of life has been reduced from 280 to less than 80. However, the average annual damages have remained substantially constant over the same period.

These achievements can be attributed to improved disaster management planning and the initiatives associated with the plan. The most significant initiatives have involved the following: a strengthening of the institutional framework for natural disaster prevention and pre-paredness by concentrating the overall responsibility for the task into a single agency; a comprehensive revision of the Natural Disaster Countermeasures Act to incorporate comprehensive disaster prevention measures, provision of adequate funding for operational aspects and the encouragement of private participation in disaster mitigation; the placing of greater emphasis on scientific research in the field of disaster prevention; and the formulation of a 5-year Disaster Prevention Plan directed towards the implementation of measures covering afforestation, flood control, disaster prevention and technology development.

To cope with the fact that disasters are becoming more varied and larger in scale, the Korean Government is continuing its efforts in the field of disaster reduction by concentrating on such aspects as: Streamlining land development regulations; availability of flood insurance; greater investment in flood control; systematic scientific research for disaster prevention; development of a national disaster management system; and active international co-operation.

Most countries of the region had enacted legislation to provide for the controls and responsibilities necessary to cope with disaster situations. This legislation has permitted the relevant authorities to govern the long-term requirements of disaster prevention and the short-term needs of disaster preparedness. Although statutory controls were available to govern the relevant aspects of community planning and development, including zoning, sub-division controls and environmental issues pertaining to disaster prevention, many Governments were reluctant to invoke them. Many Governments had appointed a central organization to co-ordinate the disaster mitigation activities of the various Government bodies and other interested groups, so that a comprehensive approach was adopted. In certain countries, some of these organizations were established on an *ad hoc* basis only when a natural disaster had occurred or was expected to happen. It was only the more developed countries of the region that had cohesive institutional arrangements in place.

Most countries had upgraded their civil defence capability for the rescue of people from endangered areas, through the mobilization of armed forces or the organization of the local community in response to threats of disaster through co-operative activities involving volunteers.

The Typhoon Committee

The Typhoon Committee was established by the participating countries under the auspices of ESCAP and WMO and has been functioning and holding annual sessions since 1968. The Typhoon Committee covered a wide range of activities on typhoon-related disaster reduction for which several important initiatives were launched under its framework, particularly those aiming at improving typhoon and flood forecasts.

Among the initiatives undertaken, the two most important ones were the Typhoon Operational Experiment (TOPEX) programme and the SPECTRUM (Special Experiment

Concerning Typhoon Recurvature and Unusual Movement) which laid down important infrastructure and established human resources and facilities for subsequent contribution to disaster prevention and preparedness.

It may be noted that the objective of TOPEX was to carry out, through international co-operation in the prompt and reliable collection and exchange of observational data, an operational test of the functioning of the various systems used for typhoon analysis, forecasting and warning. TOPEX consisted of three components the meteorological hydrological and warning dissemination and information exchange components. TOPEX was an exercise that tested the effectiveness of the totality of the system built up over more than a decade for flood warnings, typhoon warnings and dissemination of information to the public. For flood loss prevention, the Committee had carried out the following activities:

(i) Evaluation of the established system for forecasting and warning of the hydrological effects of floods and/or storm surges by comparison of their outputs with actual observed data in the fields.

(ii) Identification of simple deterministic forecasting models used by, or available to services in the typhoon area, selection of specific models for application to each designated area and comparison of the models' results in real-time forecasting operational mode.

(iii) Evaluation of separate and/or combined hydrological effects of typhoons, particularly river and storm surge flooding and thereby determination of associated flood risk.

In parallel, other regular activities have been in operation include:

(i) Operation, maintenance and improvement of existing flood forecasting and warning systems.

(ii) Establishment of flood forecasting and warning systems in other river basins.

(iii) Establishment of pilot areas for comprehensive flood loss prevention and management which included investigation, survey and study of the pilot areas, preparation of comprehensive plans for flood loss prevention and management within the context of overall water resources development of the pilot areas and implementation of selected aspects of the comprehensive plans by stages, if necessary.

In terms of activities for disaster preparedness, the Committee provided assistance in establishment of appropriate national organizations at all levels and in formulation of plans; improvement of facilities and services for emergency communications; improvement of effectiveness of warnings and community reaction; training in disaster preparedness; improvement of techniques for assessment and reporting of damage and consequent needs; preparation and implementation of pilot projects for pre-disaster planning, including analysis of hazards and resources at all levels and case studies on such plans and their effectiveness in practice; and development of measures to reduce damage associated with storm surge.

The advent of IDNDR has strengthened the co-operation among the Committee members and also helped enhance awareness on the importance of natural disaster reduction. The membership of the Committee continued to increase from 7 to lately 15, consisting of the Governments of Cambodia, China, Democratic People's Republic of Korea, Indonesia, Japan, Lao People's Democratic Republic, Malaysia, Macau, Philippines, Republic of Korea, Singapore, Thailand, United States, Viet Nam and Hong Kong, China.

Example of the WMO/ESCAP Panel on Tropical Cyclones

In parallel with the operations of the Typhoon Committee, the Panel on Tropical Cyclones was also established under the auspices of WMO and ESCAP to promote measures to improve tropical cyclone warning systems in the Bay of Bengal and the Arabian Sea. The Panel aims to direct their common endeavours towards successful implementation of a comprehensive cyclone operational plan to facilitate the most effective tropical cyclone warning system for the region with existing facilities.

As part of the common endeavour, the Panel adopted a comprehensive cyclone operational plan for this subregion. The basic purpose of the operational plan was to facilitate the most effective tropical cyclone warning system for the region with existing facilities.

In doing so the plan defined the sharing of responsibilities among Panel countries for the various segments of the system and records the co-ordination and co-operation achieved. The plan recorded the agreed arrangements for standardization of operational procedures, efficient exchange of various data related to tropical cyclone warnings, issue of cyclone advisories from a central location having the required facilities for this purpose, archival of data and issue of a tropical weather outlook for the benefit of the region.

The operational plan contains an explicit formulation of the procedures adopted in the Bay of Bengal and Arabian Sea region for the preparation, distribution and exchange of information and warnings pertaining to tropical cyclones. Experience has shown that it is of great advantage to have an explicit statement of the regional procedures to be followed in the event of a cyclone and this document is designed to serve as a valuable source of information always available for reference by the forecaster and other users, particularly under operational conditions.

A technical plan aiming at the development and improvement of the cyclone warning system of the region has been drawn up by the Panel. Implementation of some items under the technical plan would lead to a strengthening of the operational plan. The operational plan is evolutionary in nature. It is intended that the text of the plan be updated or revised from time to time by the Panel and that each item of information given in the annexes to the plan be kept up to date by the member country concerned. The plan included a hydrological programme comprising two main components:

(i) Hydrological network and flood forecasting systems.

(ii) Storm surge project.

Co-operation among the members continues to be strengthened with the implementation of these components in addition to work on meteorology. An important point to note in this respect is that through the implementation of the plan, the exchange of hydrological data among the member countries for flood warnings has been greatly improved.

Community Awareness

In many countries of the region it was recognized that the initial and most vital response to a disaster must be at the local level and that the community must be well informed about disaster-preparedness measures and be alert in the time of disaster. It was considered essential that the building of disaster awareness in the general population, starting with the individual, was essential in reducing casualties. In order to promote community involvement in disaster prevention and preparedness, community awareness programmes and educational programmes relating to warning systems and other aspects of disaster preparedness were developed and implemented and committees that included representatives of non-governmental organizations and the public were established at the local level to monitor and guide disaster-relief operations.

India

The main water-related disasters affecting India are tropical cyclones, floods and droughts. Although the incidence of cyclone strikes in the coastal belt is not high, India is regarded as one of the most flood prone countries in the region, with 40 million hectares, or 12 percent of the whole country, being affected. India is also often subject to drought when the monsoon rains fail to occur.

India is a union of 25 States and 7 Union Territories. The Union Territories are subject to the direct rule-making powers of the National Parliament and the administrative control of the Central Government. The States are fully autonomous in relation to their activities under the Constitution. The responsibility for natural disaster management is spread over the various tiers of Government, with State Governments assuming a primary role in disaster rescue and relief measures.

In recent times many advances have been made in disaster mitigation, response and preparedness. Major advances have been achieved in the field of disaster response at both the Central and State Government level through closer collaboration among the various agencies. Overall co-ordination has been assumed by the Ministry of Agriculture with support from other relevant ministries. Streamlining the disbursement of relief funds following a disaster has substantially improved the relief operations and reduced hardship.

Improvement in cyclone forecasting and warning has been made possible by the use of remote sensing systems, including satellite and weather radars. Timely warnings and quick response has permitted the early evacuation of threatened populations. As a consequence, the number of cyclone related deaths has been reduced by a factor of 10.

Flood modification strategies include both structural and non-structural measures. The construction of numerous dams, drainage channels and protective embankments along rivers has helped to mitigate the intensity of floods and reduce damage in many areas. The non-structural measures include risk mapping, flood plain zoning and forecasting and warning. The flood forecasting and warning functions are the responsibility of the Central Government, which has established a comprehensive network throughout the country. Watershed management has been elevated in importance to further reduce run-off and promote sustainable development.

Drought monitoring and alleviation is also afforded a high priority in disaster management. The construction of water storages, monitoring of crop situations and the implementation of drought management strategies has helped to ameliorate the effect of drought and to reduce the amount of associated damage.

In an effort to further its achievements in water-related disaster reduction, India is directing its efforts towards the linking of disaster mitigation with development planning, the establishment of more effective communication systems, the use of the latest information technology, the introduction of disaster insurance, the employment of extensive public awareness and education campaigns, particularly in rural areas, the greater involvement of the private sector and the strengthening of institutional mechanisms and international co-operation.

***

9

Emergency Management and Preparedness

Emergency management is the continuous process by which all individuals, groups and communities manage hazards in an effort to avoid or ameliorate the impact of disasters resulting from the hazards. Actions taken depend in part on perceptions of risk of those exposed. Effective emergency management relies on thorough integration of emergency plans at all levels of Government and non-government involvement. Activities at each level (individual, group, community) affect the other levels. It is common to place the responsibility for Governmental emergency management with the institutions for civil defense or within the conventional structure of the emergency services. In the private sector, emergency management is sometimes referred to as business continuity planning.

Emergency Management is one of a number of terms which, since the end of the Cold War, have largely replaced Civil defense, whose original focus was protecting civilians from military attack. Modern thinking focuses on a more general intent to protect the civilian population in times of peace as well as in times of war. Another current term, Civil Protection is widely used within the European Union and refers to Government-approved systems and resources whose task is to protect the civilian population, primarily in the event of natural and human-made disasters. Within EU countries the term Crisis Management emphasises the political and security dimension rather than measures to satisfy the immediate needs of the civilian population. The academic trend is towards using the more comprehensive term disaster risk reduction, particularly for emergency management in a development management context.

Phases and Professional Activities

The nature of emergency management is highly dependent on economic and social conditions local to the emergency, or disaster. This is true to the extent that some disaster relief experts such as Fred Cuny have noted that in a sense the only real disasters are economic. Experts, such as Cuny, have long noted that the cycle of emergency management must include long-term work on infrastructure, public awareness and even human justice issues. This is particularly important in developing nations. The process of emergency management involves four phases: mitigation, preparedness, response and recovery.

Mitigation

Mitigation efforts attempt to prevent hazards from developing into disasters altogether, or to reduce the effects of disasters when they occur. The mitigation phase differs from the other phases because it focuses on long-term measures for reducing or eliminating risk. The implementation of mitigation strategies can be considered a part of the recovery process if applied after a disaster occurs.

Mitigative measures can be structural or non-structural. Structural measures use technological solutions, like flood levees. Non-structural measures include legislation, land-use planning (*e.g.*, the designation of non-essential land like parks to be used as flood zones) and insurance. Mitigation is the most cost-efficient method for reducing the impact of hazards.

However, mitigation is not always suitable and structural mitigation in particular may have adverse effects on the ecosystem.

A precursor activity to the mitigation is the identification of risks. Physical risk assessment refers to the process of identifying and evaluating hazards. In risk assessment, various hazards (*e.g.*, earthquakes, floods, riots) within a certain area are identified. Each hazard poses a risk to the population within the area assessed. The hazard-specific risk (Rh) combines both the probability and the level of impact of a specific hazard. The equation below gives that the hazard times the populations' vulnerability to that hazard produce a risk. Catastrophe modeling tools are used to support the calculation. The higher the risk, the more urgent that the hazard specific vulnerabilities are targeted by mitigation and preparedness efforts.

Preparedness

In the preparedness phase, emergency managers develop plans of action for when the disaster strikes. Common preparedness measures include :

- Communication plans with easily understandable terminology and chain of command.
- Proper maintenance and training of emergency services.
- Development and practice of multi-agency co-ordination and incident command.
- Development and exercise of emergency population warning methods combined with emergency shelters and evacuation plans.
- Stockpiling, inventory and maintenance of supplies and equipment.

An efficient preparedness measure is an Emergency Operations Center (EOC) combined with a practiced region-wide doctrine for managing emergencies. Another preparedness measure is to develop a volunteer response capability among civilian populations. Since, volunteer response is not as predictable and plannable as professional response, volunteers are most effectively deployed on the periphery of an emergency.

Response

The response phase includes the mobilization of the necessary emergency services and first responders in the disaster area. This is likely to include a first wave of core emergency services, such as firefighters, police and ambulance crews. They may be supported by a number of secondary emergency services, such as specialist rescue teams.

In addition volunteers and Non-Governmental Organizations (NGOs) such as the local Red Cross branch or St. John Ambulance may provide immediate practical assistance, from first aid provision to providing tea and coffee. A well rehearsed emergency plan developed as part of the preparedness phase enables efficient co-ordination of rescue efforts. Emergency plan rehearsal is essential to achieve optimal output with limited resources.

Where required, search and rescue efforts commence at an early stage. Depending on injuries sustained by the victim, outside temperature and victim access to air and water, the vast majority of those affected by a disaster will die within 72 hours after impact. Individuals are often compelled to volunteer directly after a disaster. Volunteers can be both a help and a hindrance to emergency management and other relief agencies.

Recovery

The aim of the recovery phase is to restore the affected area to its previous state. It differs from the response phase in its focus; recovery efforts are concerned with issues and decisions that must be made after immediate needs are addressed. Recovery efforts are primarily concerned with actions that involve rebuilding destroyed property, re-employment and the repair of other essential infrastructure. An important aspect of effective recovery efforts is taking advantage of a 'window of opportunity' for the implementation of mitigative measures that might otherwise be unpopular. Citizens of the affected area are more likely to accept more mitigative changes when a recent disaster is in fresh memory.

PHASES AND PERSONAL ACTIVITIES

Mitigation

Personal mitigation is mainly about knowing and avoiding unnecessary risks. This includes an assessment of possible risks to personal/family health and to personal property.

One example of mitigation would be to avoid buying property that is exposed to hazards, *e.g.*, in a flood plain, in areas of subsidence or landslides. Homeowners may not be aware of a property being exposed to a hazard until it strikes. However, specialists can be hired to conduct risk identification and assessment surveys. Purchase of insurance covering the most prominent identified risks is a common measure.

Personal structural mitigation in earthquake prone areas includes installation of an Earthquake Valve to instantly shut off the natural gas supply to a property, seismic retrofits of property and the securing of items inside a building to enhance household seismic safety. The latter may include the mounting of furniture, refrigerators, water heaters and breakables to the walls and the addition of cabinet latches. In flood prone areas houses can be built on poles, as in much of southern Asia. In areas prone to prolonged electricity black-outs installation of a generator would be an example of an optimal structural mitigation measure.

Preparedness

Unlike mitigation activities, which are aimed at preventing a disaster from occurring, personal preparedness focuses on preparing equipment and procedures for use when a disaster occurs, *i.e.,* planning. Preparedness measures can take many forms including the construction of shelters, installation of warning devices, creation of back-up life-line services (*e.g.,* power, water, sewage) and rehearsing evacuation plans. Two simple measures can help prepare the individual for sitting out the event or evacuating, as necessary. For evacuation, a disaster supplies kit may be prepared and for sheltering purposes a stockpile of supplies may be created. The preparation of a survival kit, commonly referred to as a "72-hour kit", is often advocated by authorities. These kits may include food, medicine, flashlights, candles and money.

Response

The response phase of an emergency may commence with search and rescue but in all cases the focus will quickly turn to fulfilling the basic humanitarian needs of the affected population. This assistance may be provided by national or international agencies and organizations. Effective co-ordination of disaster assistance is often crucial, particularly when many organizations respond and Local Emergency Management Agency (LEMA) capacity has been exceeded by the demand or diminished by the disaster itself.

On a personal level the response can take the shape either of a home confinement or an evacuation. In a home confinement a family would be prepared to fend for themselves in their home for many days without any form of outside support. In an evacuation, a family leaves the area by automobile (or other mode of transportation) taking with them the maximum amount of supplies they can carry, possibly including a tent for shelter.

Recovery

The recovery phase starts after the immediate threat to human life has subsided. During reconstruction it is recommended to consider the location or construction material of the property.

The most extreme home confinement scenarios include war, famine and severe epidemics and may last a year or more. Then recovery will take place inside the home. Planners for these events usually buy bulk foods and appropriate storage and preparation equipment and eat the food as part of normal life. A simple balanced diet can be constructed from vitamin pills, whole-meal wheat, beans, dried milk, corn and cooking oil. One should add vegetables, fruits, spices and meats, both prepared and fresh-gardened, when possible.

As a Profession

Emergency managers are trained in a wide variety of disciplines that support them through out the emergency life-cycle. Professional emergency managers can focus on Government and community preparedness (Continuity of Operations/Continuity of Government Planning), or private business preparedness (Business Continuity Management Planning). Training is provided by local, state, federal and private organizations and ranges from public information and media relations to high-level incident command and tactical skills such as studying a terrorist bombing site or controlling an emergency scene.

In the past, the field of emergency management has been populated mostly by people with a military or first responder background. Currently, the population in the field has become more diverse, with many experts coming from a variety of backgrounds and having no military or first responder history at all. Educational opportunities are increasing for those seeking undergraduate and graduate degrees in emergency management or a related field.

Professional certifications such as Certified Emergency Manager (CEM) and Certified Business Continuity Professional (CBCP) are becoming more common as the need for high professional standards is recognized by the emergency management community, especially in the United States.

Tools

In recent years the continuity feature of emergency management has resulted in a new concept, Emergency Management Information Systems (EMIS). For continuity and interoperability between emergency management stakeholders, EMIS supports the emergency management process by providing an infrastructure that integrates emergency plans at all levels of Government and non-government involvement and by utilizing the management of all related resources (including human and other resources) for all four phases of emergencies.

Within Other Professions

Practitioners emergency management (disaster preparedness) come from an increasing variety of backgrounds as the field matures. Professionals from memory institutions (*e.g.*, museums, historical societies, libraries and archives) are dedicated to preserving cultural heritage-objects and records contained in their collections. This has been a major component within these fields, but now there is a heightened awareness following the events on 9/11 and the hurricanes in 2005.

To increase the opportunity for a successful recovery of valuable records, a well-established and thoroughly tested plan must be developed. This task requires the co-operation of a well-organized committee led by an experienced chairperson. Professional associations schedule regular workshops and hold focus sessions at annual conferences to keep individuals up to date with tools and resources in practice.

Tools

The joint efforts of professional associations and cultural heritage institutions have resulted in the development of tools to assist professionals in preparing disaster and recovery plans. The tools are available to users as well as templates created by existing libraries and archives that can be helpful to a committee preparing a disaster plan or updating an existing plan.

dPlan™, The Online Disaster Planning Tool, developed in partnership between the Northeast Document Conservation Center (NEDCC) and Massachusetts Board of Library Commissioners (MBLC) is free and fairly simple to use. Users log-in to complete the comprehensive interactive form, the information is saved and stored, then, a hardcopy (PDF file) can be printed. The hardcopy should be readily available in case of emergency.

With dPlan™, there are seven sections including: Institutional Information; Prevention; Response and Recovery; Supplies and Services; Scope and Goals; Staff Training; Distribution, Review and Updating. It does not have to be completed in one sitting. The Data Collection Form can be printed in advance and the template can be filled in by hand before entering the data online. Or, it is possible to enter the data online and save it along the way. The 129-pages document may seem daunting, but will prove to be invaluable. To reduce the amount of time needed to complete the form, check boxes and pull-down menus are provided. A scale of 1 to 4 is (one being serious risk and four not a risk at all) is used to measure conditions. The scale forces the user to make a choice resulting in a more effective reading. dPlan™ offers consistency in plans through vocabulary and format, yet an upload file feature allows for flexibility-necessary attachments and/or appendices may be added to supplement the plan.

The Emergency Response and Salvage Wheel is another useful tool. It was produced by the Heritage Emergency National Task Force on Emergency Response. The design of the waterproof, hand-held tool provides essential information in an easy to read format. The two-sided disc outlines action steps and salvage steps for emergency situations, including a section on electronic records. It is also available in Spanish.

The Disaster Mitigation Planning Assistance Website. is a Website created by Michigan State University Libraries, the Center for Great Lakes Culture and the California Preservation Program. It is possible to search resources based on individual needs. Pull down menus filter results and an export feature makes it possible to download the data to an (CSV) Excel document. The document may contain company names, addresses, phone numbers, email addresses and URL addresses for the corresponding service, supplier, or expert on file. It is also possible to submit resource as well as view sample plans from this Website.

There are workbooks from libraries and archives with published disaster plans. Many can be found online, but only two will be named at this time. The first one is New York University Library's Disaster Plan Workbook. A committee of ten works in partnership with the Library's Preservation Department to administer the plan. It contains seven chapters with forms, priorities and procedures alongwith a table of contents, appendices-divided into six sections-and index. "Instructions in the workbook provide undamaging salvage methods for all types of library materials, including a list of supplies needed for each. Consultants, specialists, hardware stores and staff telephone trees are listed."

The workbook is displayed using HTML for navigation between the pages by clicking. It is not possible to type into the pages of the Workbook, but the pages may be printed and customized with pertinent information of the library or archive using this format.

Western New York Disaster Preparedness and Recovery Manual for Libraries and Archives is available for download as a PDF document. This manual provides a number of worksheets to be completed by the user. It contains a glossary of terms to ensure those involved in the planning and executing process are speaking the same language. A section on "Protection" lists emergency supplies; decisions to make when assembling in-house disaster response teams; and types of alarms and systems to warn against smoke and fire. Salvaging techniques and rehabilitation are also covered extensively. It is not limited to paper materials but also includes film, magnetic and digital media.

✹✹✹

10

Disaster Management and Policy Framework

Over the past couple of years, the Government of India have brought about a paradigm shift in the approach to disaster management. The new approach proceeds from the conviction that development cannot be sustainable unless disaster mitigation is built into the development process. Another corner stone of the approach is that mitigation has to be multi-disciplinary spanning across all sectors of development. The new policy also emanates from the belief that investments in mitigation are much more cost effective than expenditure on relief and rehabilitation.

Disaster management occupies an important place in this country's policy framework as it is the poor and the under-privileged who are worst affected on account of calamities/disasters.

The steps being taken by the Government emanate from the approach outlined above. The approach has been translated into a National Disaster Framework [a roadmap] covering institutional mechanisms, disaster prevention strategy, early warning system, disaster mitigation, preparedness and response and human resource development. The expected inputs, areas of intervention and agencies to be involved at the National, State and district levels have been identified and listed in the roadmap. This roadmap has been shared with all the State Governments and Union Territory Administrations. Ministries and Departments of Government of India and the State Governments/UT Administrations have been advised to develop their respective roadmaps taking the national roadmap as a broad guideline. There is, therefore, now a common strategy underpinning the action being taken by all the participating organizations/ stakeholders.

The changed approach is being put into effect through:

(a) Institutional changes.

(b) Enunciation of policy.

(c) Legal and techno-legal framework.

(d) Mainstreaming Mitigation into Development process.

(e) Funding mechanism.

(f) Specific schemes addressing mitigation.

(g) Preparedness measures.

(h) Capacity building.

(i) Human Resource Development and, above all, community participation. These are detailed in the following chapters.

INSTITUTIONAL AND POLICY FRAMEWORK

The institutional and policy mechanisms for carrying out response, relief and rehabilitation have been well-established since Independence. These mechanisms have proved to be robust and effective insofar as response, relief and rehabilitation are concerned. The changed policy/approach, however, mandates a priority to pre-disaster aspects of mitigation, prevention and preparedness and new institutional mechanisms are being put in place to address the policy change.

Mitigation, preparedness and response are multi-disciplinary functions, involving a number of Ministries/ Departments. Institutional mechanisms which would facilitate this inter-disciplinary approach are being put in place. It is proposed to create Disaster Management Authorities, both at the National and State levels, with representatives from the relevant Ministries/Departments to bring about this co-ordinated and multi-disciplinary with experts covering a large number of branches.

The National Emergency Management Authority is proposed to be constituted. The organization will be multi-disciplinary with experts covering a large number of branches. The National Emergency Management Authority is proposed as a combined Secretariat/Directorate structure—a structure which will be an integral part of the Government while, at the same time, retaining the flexibility of a filed organization.

The Authority will be headed by an officer of the rank of Secretary/Special Secretary to the Government in the Ministry of Home Affairs with representatives from the Ministries/Departments of Health, Water Resources, Environment and Forest, Agriculture, Railways, Atomic Energy, Defence, Chemicals, Science and Technology, Telecommunication, Urban Employment and Poverty alleviation, Rural Development and Indian Meteorological Department as Members. The authority would meet as often as required and review the Status of warning systems, mitigation measure and disaster preparedness. When a disaster strikes, the Authority will co-ordinate disaster management activities. The Authority will be responsible for:

- Providing necessary support and assistance to State Governments by way of resource data, macro-management of emergency response, specialized emergency response teams, sharing of disaster related database etc.

- Ensuring adequate preparedness at all levels.
- Co-ordinating/mandating Government's policies for disaster reduction/mitigation.
- Co-ordinating response to a disaster when it strikes.
- Co-ordinating resources of all National Government Department/agencies involved.
- Assisting the Provincial Government in co-ordinating post disaster relief and rehabilitation.
- Monitor and introduce a culture of building requisite features of disaster mitigation in all development plans and programmes.
- Any other issues of work, which may be entrusted to it by the Government. The States have also been asked to set-up Disaster Management Authorities under the Chief Minister with Ministers of relevant Departments [Water Resources, Agriculture, Drinking Water Supply, Environment and Forests, Urban Development, Home, Rural Development etc.] as members. 10 States and UTs—Tamil Nadu, Arunachal Pradesh, Uttaranchal, Orissa, Gujarat, Kerala, Nagaland, Delhi, Andaman Nicobar Administration and Chandigarh Administration have notified the authority. The other States are in the process of setting-up similar authorities.

Re-structuring of the Relief Department in the States: At the State level, the work of post calamity relief was being handled by the Departments of Relief and Rehabilitation. The Government of India is working with the State Governments to restructure the Departments of Relief and Rehabilitation into Departments of Disaster Management with an enhanced area of responsibility to include mitigation and preparedness apart from their present responsibilities of relief and rehabilitation.

The changeover has already happened in 11 States/ UTs—Andhra Pradesh, Arunachal Pradesh, Bihar, Himachal Pradesh, Rajasthan Tamil Nadu, Uttaranchal, Nagaland Andaman and Nicobar Administration, Sikkim and Lakshadweep. The change is under process in other States. The States have been advised to restructure/re-group the officers/staff within the Department of Disaster Management with definite functions to pursue the holistic approach to disaster management. The four functional groups to be assigned with specific tasks within the departments are as indicted below:

- Functional Group 1 : Hazard Mitigation.
- Functional Group 2 : Preparedness and Capacity Building.
- Functional Group 3 : Relief and Response.
- Functional Group 4 : Administration and Finance.

At the district level, the District Magistrate who is the chief co-ordinator will be the focal point for co-ordinating all activities relating to prevention, mitigation and preparedness apart from his existing responsibilities pertaining to response and relief. The District Co-ordination and Relief Committee is being reconstituted/re-designated into Disaster Management Committees with officers from relevant departments being added as members. Because of its enhanced mandate of mitigation and prevention, the district heads of the departments engaged in development are now being included in the Committee so that mitigation and prevention is mainstreamed into the district plan. The existing system of drawing up preparedness and response plans will continue. There will, however, also be a long-term mitigation plan.

Similarly, sub-divisional and Block/Taluka level Disaster Management Committees are also being constituted. At the village level Disaster Management Committees and Disaster

Management Teams are being constituted. Each village in multi-hazard prone district will have a Disaster Management Plan. The process of drafting the plans at all levels has already begun. The Disaster Management Committee which draws up the plans consists of elected representatives at the village level, local authorities; Government functionaries including doctors/paramedics of primary health centres located in the village, primary school teachers etc.

The plan encompasses prevention, mitigation and preparedness measures. The Disaster Management Teams at the village level will consist of members of youth organizations like Nehru Yuvak Kendra and other non-governmental organizations as well as able bodied volunteers from the village. The teams are provided basic training in evacuation, evacuation, search and rescue, first aid trauma counseling etc. The Disaster Management Committee will review the disaster management plan at least once in a year. It would also generate awareness among the people in the village about dos' and don'ts for specific hazards depending on the vulnerability of the village.

Disaster Management Policy

Disaster management is a multi-disciplinary activity involving a number of a number of Departments/agencies spanning across all sectors of development. Where a number of Departments/agencies are involved, it is essential to have a policy in place, as it serves as a framework for action by all the relevant departments/agencies.

A National Policy on disaster management has been drafted and is in the process of consultations. In the line with the changed focus, the policy proposes to integrate disaster mitigation into development planning. The policy shall inform all spheres of Central Government activity and shall enjoin upon all existing sectoral policies. The broad objective of the policy are to minimize the loss of lives and social, private and community assets because of natural or man-made disasters and contribute to sustainable development and better standards of living for all, more specifically for the poor and vulnerable section by ensuring that the developments gains are not lost through natural calamities/disaster.

The policy notes that State Governments are primarily responsible for disaster management including prevention and mitigation, while the Government of India provides assistance where necessary as per the norms laid down from time to time and proposes that this overall framework may continue. However, since response to a disaster requires co-ordination of resources available across all the Departments of the Government, the policy mandates that the Central Government will, in conjunction with the State Governments, seek to ensure that such a co-ordination mechanism is laid down through an appropriate chain of command so that mobilization of resources is facilitated.

The broad features of the draft national policy on disaster management are enunciated below:

(i) A holistic and proactive approach towards prevention, mitigation and preparedness will be adopted for disaster management.

(ii) Where there is a shelf of projects, projects addressing mitigation will be given priority. Mitigation measures shall be built into the on-going schemes/programmes

(iii) Each Ministry/Department of the Central/State Government will set apart an appropriate quantum of funds under the Plan for specific schemes/projects addressing vulnerability reduction and preparedness.

(iv) Each project in a hazard prone area will have mitigation as an essential term of reference. The project report will include a statement as to how the project addresses vulnerability reduction.

(*v*) There will be close interaction with the corporate sector, non-governmental organizations and the media in the national efforts for disaster prevention/ vulnerability reduction.

(*vi*) Community involvement and awareness generation, particularly that of the vulnerable segments of population and women has been emphasized as necessary for sustainable disaster risk reduction. This is a critical component of the policy since communities are the first responders to disasters and, therefore, unless they are empowered and made capable of managing disasters, any amount of external support cannot lead to optimal results.

(*vii*) A culture of planning and preparedness is to be inculcated at all levels for capacity building measures.

(*viii*) Standard operating procedures and disaster management plans at state and district levels as well as by relevant Central Government departments for handling specific disasters will be laid down.

(*viii*) Institutional structures/appropriate chain of command will be built up and appropriate training imparted to disaster managers at various levels to ensure co-ordinated and quick response at all levels; and development of inter-State arrangements for sharing of resources during emergencies.

(*x*) Construction designs must correspond to the requirements as laid down in relevant Indian Standards.

(*xi*) The existing relief codes in the States will be revised to develop them into disaster management codes/ manuals for institutionalizing the planning process with particular attention to mitigation and preparedness.

(xii) To promote international co-operation in the area of disaster response, preparedness and mitigation in tune with national strategic goals and objectives.

The States have also been advised to formulate State DM Policies with the broad objective to minimize the loss of lives and social, private and community assets and contribute to sustainable development. The States of Gujarat and Madhya Pradesh have States Policies for Disaster Management in place while other States are in process.

LEGAL AND TECHNO-LEGAL FRAMEWORK

Disaster Management Act. The States have been advised to enact Disaster Management Acts. These Acts provide for adequate powers for authorities co-ordinating mitigation, preparedness and response as well as for mitigation/ prevention measures required to be undertaken. Two States Gujarat and Bihar, have already enacted such a law. Other States are in the process.

Disaster Management Code. In line with the changed approach, the State Governments have also been advised to convert their Relief Codes into Disaster Management Codes by building into it the process necessary for drawing up disaster management and mitigation plans as well as elements of preparedness apart from response and relief. A Committee constituted under the Executive Director, National institute of Disaster Management has drafted a Model Disaster Management Code which is being circulated to the States so as to assist them in this process. Some States have constituted committees to revise the codes as per Government of India guidelines.

DISASTER PREVENTION AND MITIGATION

The Yokohama message emanating from the international decade for natural disaster reduction in May, 1994 underlined the need for an emphatic shift in the strategy for disaster mitigation. It was *inter alia* stressed that disaster prevention, mitigation, preparedness and relief are four elements which contribute to and gain, from the implementation of the sustainable development policies.

These elements alongwith environmental protection and sustainable development, are closely inter related and it was therefore, recommended that Nations should incorporate them in their development plans and ensure efficient follow up measures at the community, sub-regional, regional, national and international levels. The Yokohama Strategy also emphasized that disaster prevention, mitigation and preparedness are better than disaster response in achieving the goals and objectives of vulnerability reduction. Disaster response alone is not sufficient as it yields only temporary results at a very high cost.

Mainstreaming Disaster Management into Development. The Government of India have adopted mitigation and prevention as essential components of their development strategy. The Tenth Five Year Plan document has a detailed chapter on Disaster Management. The plan emphasizes the fact that development cannot be sustainable without mitigation being built into developmental process. Each State is supposed to prepare a plan scheme for disaster mitigation in accordance with the approach outlined in the plan. In brief, mitigation is being mainstreamed into developmental planning.

Financial Arrangement. As indicated in the earlier chapter, the Finance Commission makes recommendations with regard to devolution of funds between the Central Government and State Governments as also outlays for relief and rehabilitation. The earlier Finance Commissions were mandated to look at relief and rehabilitation.

The Terms of Reference of the Twelfth Finance Commission have been changed and the Finance Commission has been mandated to look at the requirements for mitigation and prevention apart from its existing mandate of looking at relief and rehabilitation. A Memorandum has been submitted to the Twelfth Finance Commission after consultation with States.

The Government of India have issued guidelines that where there is a shelf of projects, projects addressing mitigation will be given a priority. It has also been mandated that each project in a hazard prone area will have disaster prevention/mitigation as a term of reference and the project document has to reflect as to how the project addresses that term of reference.

Flood Preparedness and Response. In order to respond effectively to floods, Ministry of Home Affairs have initiated National Disaster Risk Management Programme in all the flood-prone States. Assistance is being provided to the States to draw up disaster management plans at the State, District, Block/Taluka and Village levels. Awareness generation campaigns to sensitize the all the stakeholders on the need for flood preparedness and mitigation measures. Elected representatives and officials are being trained in flood disaster management under the programme. Bihar, Orissa, West Bengal, Assam and Uttar Pradesh are among the 17 multi-hazard prone States where this programme is being implemented with assistance from UNDP, USAID and European Commission.

Earthquake Risk Mitigation. A comprehensive programme has been taken up for earthquake risk mitigation. Although, the BIS has laid down the standards for construction in the seismic zones, these were not being followed. The building construction in urban and suburban areas is regulated by the Town and Country Planning Acts and Building Regulations. In many cases, the Building regulations do not incorporate the BIS codes. Even where they do, the lack of knowledge regarding seismically safe construction among the architects and engineers as well as lack of awareness regarding their vulnerability among the population led to most of the construction in the urban/sub-urban areas being without reference to BIS standards.

In the rural areas, the bulk of the housing is non-engineered construction. The mode of construction in the rural areas has also changed from mud and thatch to brick and concrete construction thereby increasing the vulnerability. The increasing population has led to settlements in vulnerable areas close to the river bed areas which are prone to liquefaction.

National Core Group for Earthquake Risk Mitigation. A National Core Group for Earthquake Risk Mitigation has been constituted consisting of experts in earthquake engineering and administrators. The Core Group has been assigned with the responsibility of drawing up a strategy and plan of action for mitigating the impact of earthquakes; providing advice and guidance to the States on various aspects of earthquake mitigation; developing/organizing the preparation of handbooks/pamphlets/type designs for earthquake resistant construction; working out systems for assisting the States in the seismically vulnerable zones to adopt/integrate appropriate Bureau of Indian Standards codes in their building bye-laws; evolving systems for training of municipal engineers as also practicing architects and engineers in the private sector in the salient features of Bureau of Indian Standards codes and the amended bye-laws; evolving a system of certification of architects/engineers for testing their knowledge of earthquake resistant construction; evolving systems for training of masons and carry out intensive awareness generation campaigns.

Review of Building Bye-laws and their Adoption. Most casualties during earthquakes are caused by the collapse of structures. Therefore, structural mitigation measures are the key to make a significant impact towards earthquake safety in our country. In view of this the States in earthquake prone zones have been requested to review and if necessary, amend their building bye-laws to incorporate the BIS seismic codes for construction in the concerned zones. Many States have initiated necessary action in this regard. An Expert Committee appointed by the Core Group on Earthquake Risk Mitigation has already submitted its report covering appropriate amendments to the existing Town and Country Planning Acts, Land Use Zoning Regulation, Development Control Regulations and Building Bye-laws, which could be used by the State Governments and the local bodies thereunder to upgrade the existing legal instruments.

The Model Building Bye-laws also cover the aspect of ensuring technical implementation of the safety aspects in all new constructions and upgrading the strength of existing structurally vulnerable constructions. To facilitate the review of existing building bye-laws and adoption of the proposed amendments by the State Governments and UT administrations, discussion workshops at regional level in the country are being organized. It is expected that all planning authorities and local bodies will soon have development control regulations and building bye-laws which would include multi-hazard safety provisions.

Development and Revision of Codes. There are Bureau of Indian Standard (BIS) codes which are relevant for multi-hazard resistant design and construction. Some of the codes need to be updated. There are some areas for which codes do not exist. An action plan has been drawn up for revision of existing codes, development of new codes and documents/ commentaries and making these codes and documents available all over the country including on-line access to these codes. An Apex committee consisting of representatives of Ministry of Consumer Affairs, BIS and MHA has been constituted to review the mechanism and process of development of codes relevant to earthquake risk mitigation and establish a protocol for revision by BIS.

National Programme for Capacity Building of Engineers and Architects in Earthquake Risk Mitigation. Two National Programmes for Capacity Building in Earthquake Risk Mitigation for Engineers and Architects respectively, have been approved to assist the State Governments in building up capacities for earthquake mitigation. Under these two programmes 10,000 engineers and 10,000 architects in the States will be given training in seismically safe building designs and related techno-legal requirements. Assistance is being provided to the State/UTs to build the capacities of more than 125 State Engineering Colleges and 110 Architecture Colleges to be able to provide advisory services to the State Governments to put in place appropriate techno-legal regime, assessment of building and infrastructures and their retrofitting. These institutions will function as State Resource Institutions. Twenty-one Engineering and Architecture Institutions have been designated as National Resource Institutes to train the faculty members of selected State Engineering and Architecture colleges. 450 engineering faculty members and 250 architecture faculty members of these State Resource Institutions will be trained during the current year.

Hazard Safety Cells in States. The States have been advised to constitute Hazard Safety Cells (HSC) headed by the Chief Engineer, State PWD with necessary engineering staff so as to establish mechanism for proper implementation of the building codes in all future Government. constructions and to ensures the safety of buildings and structures from various hazards. The HSCs will also be responsible for carrying out appropriate design review of all Government buildings to be constructed in the State, act as an advisory cell to the State Government on the different aspects of building safety against hazards and act as a consultant to the State Government for retrofitting of the lifeline buildings. Rajasthan, West Bengal,

Delhi and Chhattisgarh have already constituted these cells and other States are in the process.

Training of Rural Masons. A programme to assist the States/UTs in training and certification of 50000 masons has been formulated in conultation with Housing and Urban Development Corporation (HUDCO) and the Ministry of Rural Development. The training module for masons to include multi-hazard resistant construction has also been prepared by an expert committee and revised curriculum will be introduced in the vocational training programme of Ministry of Human Resource Development.

Retrofitting of Lifeline Buildings. While these mitigation measures will take care of the new constructions, the problem of unsafe existing building stock would still remain. It will not be possible to address the entire existing building stock, therefore, the life line buildings like hospitals, schools or buildings where people congregate like cinema halls, multi-storied apartments are being focussed on. The States have been advised to have these buildings assessed and where necessary retrofitted.

The Ministries of Civil Aviation, Railways, Telecommunication, Power and Health and Family Welfare have been advised to take necessary action for detailed evaluation and retrofitting of lifeline buildings located in seismically vulnerable zones so as to ensure that they comply with BIS norms, Action plan have been drawn up by these Ministries for detailed vulnerability analysis and retrofitting/strengthening of buildings and structures. The Ministry of Finance have been requested to advise the financial institutions to give loans for retrofitting on easy terms. Accordingly the Ministry of Finance had advised Reserve Bank of India to issue suitable instructions to all the Banks and Financial Institutions to see that BIS codes/bye laws are scrupulously followed while financing/refinancing construction activities in seismically vulnerable zones.

National Earthquake Risk Mitigation Project. An Earthquake Mitigation Project has been drawn up, with an estimated cost of ₹ 1132 crore. The project has been given in-principle clearance by the Planning Commission. The programme includes detailed evaluation and retrofitting of lifeline buildings such as hospitals, schools, water and power supply units, telecommunication buildings, airports/airport control towers, railway stations, bus stands and important administrative buildings in the States/UTs in seismic Zones IV and V. The programme also includes training of masons in earthquake resistant constructions, as well as, assistance to the State Governments to put in place an appropriate techno legal regime.

Mainstreaming Mitigation in Rural Development Schemes. Rural housing and community assets for vulnerable sections of the population are created on a fairly large scale by the Ministry of Rural Development under the Indira Awas Yojna (IAY) and Sampooran Grameen Rojgar Yojna (SGRY). About 250 thousand small but compact housing units are constructed every year, besides community assets such as community centres, recreation centres, anganwadi centres etc.

Technology support is provided by about two hundred rural housing centres spread over the entire country. The Ministry of Home Affairs is working with the Ministry of Rural Development for changing the guidelines so that the houses constructed under IAY or school buildings/community buildings constructed under SGRY are earthquake/cyclone/flood resistant; as also that the schemes addressing mitigation are given priority under SGRY. Ministry of Rural Development are carrying out an exercise for this purpose.

Core Group on Cyclone Mitigation. A National Core Group on Cyclone Monitoring and Mitigation has been constituted. Experts from Indian Meteorological Department, National Centre for Medium Range Weather Forecasting,

Central Water Commission, National Remote Sensing Agency and Indian Space Research Organization have been made the Members of the Core Group, besides administrators from the relevant Ministries/Departments and State Governments vulnerable to cyclones. The Group has been assigned the responsibility of looking at warning protocols for cyclones; co-ordination mechanism between different Central and State Ministries/Departments/Organizations; mechanism for dissemination of warning to the local people and; cyclone mitigation measures required to be taken for the coastal States. The Group will also suggest short-term and long-term measures on technology up-gradation. The cyclone warning formats have been revised to ensure that the warning is more meaningful to the community at risk.

National Cyclone Mitigation Project. A project for Cyclone Mitigation (estimated cost ₹ 1050 crore) has been drawn up in consultation with the cyclone prone States. This project envisages construction of cyclone shelters, coastal shelter belt plantation in areas which are prone to storm surges, strengthening of warning systems, training and education etc. This project has also been given inprinciple clearance by the Planning Commission and is being taken up with World Bank assistance.

Landslide Hazard Mitigation. A National Core Group has been constituted under the Chairmanship of Secretary, Border Management and comprising of Secretary, Department of Science and Technology, Secretary, Road Transport and Highways and the Heads of Geological Survey of India and National Remote Sensing Agency for drawing up a strategy and plan of action for mitigating the impact of landslides, provide advise and guidance to the State Governments on various aspects of landslide mitigation, monitor the activities relating to landslide mitigation including landslide hazard zonation and to evolve early warning systems and protocols for landslides/landslide risk reduction.

The Government have designated Geological Survey of India (GSI) as the nodal agency responsible for co-ordinating/ undertaking geological studies, landslides hazard zoantion, monitoring landslides/avalanches, studying the factors responsible and suggesting precautionary and preventing measures. The States/UTs have been requested to share the list of habitations close to landslide prone areas in order to supplement GSI's on going assessment of such areas based on the Survey of India's Toposheet and their existing database on landslide for the purpose of landslide hazard zonation being carried out by them.

Disaster Risk Management Programme. A Disaster Risk Management Programme has been taken up in 169 districts in 17 multi-hazard prone States with the assistance from UNDP, USAID and European Union. These States are Assam, Arunachal Pradesh, Bihar, Delhi, Gujarat, Maharashtra, Meghalaya, Mizoram, Manipur, Nalaland, Orissa, Sikkim, Tamil Nadu, Tripura, Uttar Pradesh, Uttaranchal and West Bengal, Under this project, the States are being assisted to draw up State, district and Block level disaster management plans; village disaster management plans are being developed in conjunction with the Panchayati Raj Institutions and disaster management teams consisting of village volunteers are being trained in preparedness and response functions such as search and rescue, first aid, relief co-ordination, shelter management etc. States and District level multi-hazard resistant Emergency Operation Centres (EOCs) are also being set-up under the programme. Equipment needs for district and State Emergency Operation Centres have been identified by the State nodal agencies and equipment is being provided to equip these EOCs. Orientation training of masons, engineers and architects in disaster resistant technologies have been initiated in these districts and construction of model demonstration buildings will be started soon.

Under this programme Disaster Management Plans have been prepared for 8643 villages, 1046 Gram Panchayat, 188 blocks and 82 districts. More than 29000 elected representatives of Panchayati Raj Institutions have already been trained, besides imparting training to members of voluntary organizations. About 18000 Government functionaries have been trained in disaster mitigation and preparedness at different levels. 865 engineers and 425 architects have been trained under this programme in vulnerability assessment and retrofitting of lifeline buildings.

Disaster Management Committees consisting of elected representatives, civil society members, Civil Defence volunteers and Government functionaries have been constituted at all levels including village/urban local body/ward levels. Disaster Management Teams have been constituted in villages and are being imparted training in basic functions of first aid, rescue, evacuation and related issues. The thrust of the programme is to build up capabilities of the community since the community is invariably the first responder. Capacity building of the community has been very helpful even in normal situations when isolated instances of drowning, burns etc., take place. With the creation of awareness generation on disaster mitigation, the community will be able to function as a well-knit unit in case of any emergency.

Mock drills are carried out from time to time under the close supervision of Disaster Management Committees. The Disaster Management Committees and Disaster Management Teams have been established by notifications issued by the State Governments which will ensure that the entire system is institutionalized and does not disintegrate after the conclusion of the programme. The key points being stressed under this programme are the need to ensure sustainability of the programme, development of training modules; manuals and codes, focused attention to awareness generation campaigns;

institutionalization of disaster management committees and disaster management teams, disaster management plans and mock-drills and establishment of techno-legal regimes.

Human Resource Development. Human Resource Development at all levels is critical to institutionalization of disaster mitigation strategy. The National Centre for Disaster Management at the national level has been upgraded and designated as the National Institute of Disaster Management. It is being developed as a Regional Centre of Excellence in Asia. The National Institute of Disaster Management will develop training modules at different levels, undertake training of trainers and organize training programmes for planners, administrators and command functionaries. Besides, the other functions assigned to the National Institute of Disaster Management include development of exhaustive National level information base on disaster management policies, prevention mechanisms, mitigation measures; and providing consultancy to various States in strengthening their disaster management systems and capacities as well as preparation of disaster management plans and strategies for hazard mitigation and disaster response.

NDM Cells in Administrative Training Institutes. Disaster Management faculties have already been created in 29 State level training institutes located in 28 States. These faculties are being directly supported by the Ministry of Home Affairs. The State Training Institutions take up several focused training programmes for different target groups within the State. The Disaster Management faculties in these Institutes are being further strengthened so as to enable them to develop as Institutes of Excellence for a specific disaster. Assistance to the State level training institutes will be provided by the National Institute of Disaster Management in the development of training/capsules training modules for different functionaries at different levels.

Awareness Generation. Recognizing that awareness about vulnerabilities is a *sine qua non* for inducing a mindset of disaster prevention, mitigation and preparedness, the Government has initiated a nation-wide awareness generation campaign as part of its overall disaster risk management strategy. In order to devise an effective and holistic campaign, a steering committee for mass media campaign has been constituted at the national level with due representation of experts from diverse streams of communication. The Committee has formulated a campaign strategy aimed at changing peoples' perception of natural hazards and has consulted the agencies and experts associated with advertising and media to instill a culture of safety against natural hazards.

Apart from the use of print and electronic media, it is proposed to utilize places with high public visibility *viz.*, hospitals, schools, railway stations and bus terminals, airports and post offices, commercial complexes and municipality offices etc., to make people aware of their vulnerabilities and promote creation of a safe living environment.

Disaster Awareness in School Curriculum. Disaster management as a subject in Social Sciences has been introduced in the school curriculum for Classes VIII and IX. The Central Board of Secondary Education (CBSE) which has introduced the curriculum runs a very large number of schools throughout the country and the course curriculum is invariably followed by the State Boards of Secondary Education. Teachers are being trained to teach disaster management Syllabus for Class X is being finalized and will be introduced in the course curriculum soon. The State Governments have been advised to take similar steps vis-à-vis their school boards. Several States Governments have already introduced the same curriculum in Class VIII. Ministry is working with the Council of Board of School Education (CBSE) to facilitate inclusion of disaster management in public education in all 39 School Boards in the country.

Information, Education and Communication. In order to assist the State Governments in capacity building and awareness generation activities and to learn from past experiences including sharing of best practices, the Ministry of Home Affairs has compiled/prepared a set of resource materials developed by various organizations/institutions to be replicated and disseminated by State Governments based on their vulnerabilities after translating it into the local languages. The voluminous material which runs into about 10000 pages has been divided into 4 broad sections in 7 volumes. These sections cover planning to cope with disasters; education and training; construction toolkit; and information, education and communication toolkit including multimedia resources on disaster mitigation and preparedness.

The Planning section contains material for analyzing a community's risk, development of Preparedness. Mitigation and disaster management plans, co-ordinating available resources and implementing measures for risk reduction. Model bye-laws, DM Policy, Act and model health sector plan have also been included. Education and Training includes material for capacity building and upgradation of skills of policy makers, administrators, trainers, engineers etc., in planning for and mitigating against natural disasters. Basic and detailed training modules in disaster preparedness have been incorporated alongwith training methodologies for trainers, for community preparedness and manuals for training at district, block, panchayat and village levels. For creating a disaster-resistant building environment, the Construction Toolkit addresses the issue of seismic resistant construction and retrofitting of existing buildings.

PREPAREDNESS

Mitigation and preparedness measures go hand in hand for vulnerability reduction and rapid professional response to disasters. The Bhuj earthquake in January, 2001 brought out several inadequacies in the system. Professionally trained search and rescue teams were not available; specialized dog squad to look for live bodies under the debris were not available; and there was no centralized resource inventory for emergency response. Although army played a pivotal role in search and rescue and also set-up their hospital after the collapse of Government hospital at Bhuj, the need for fully equipped mobile hospitals with trained personnel was felt acutely.

Despite these constraints, the response was fairly well organized. However, had these constraints been taken care of before hand, the response would have been even more professional and rapid which may have reduced the loss of lives. Specialist search and rescue teams from other countries did reach Bhuj. However, precious time was lost and even with these specialist teams it was not possible to cover all severely affected areas as quickly as the Government would have desired. It was, therefore, decided that we should remove these inadequacies and be in a stage of preparedness at all times.

Specialist Response Teams

The Central Government are now in the process of training and equipping eight battalions of CPMFs as specialist response teams. Each team consists of 45 personnel including doctors, paramedics, structural engineers etc., and thus, there will be 144 Specialist Search and Rescue Teams in the earmarked eight battalions. The process of training and equipping of the 144 specialist search and rescue teams etc has begun. 18 teams have been trained so far.

These teams are being trained in collapsed structure search and rescue, medical first response, rescue and evacuation in flood and cyclone, under water rescue etc. In effect they will have the capability to operate in all types of terrain in all contingencies/disasters. It is proposed to group together the eight battalions of CPMFs earmarked for specialized emergency response as "National Emergency Response Force". These specialist response teams are being provided modern equipments and also dog squads for search and rescue. They will be provided with special uniforms made of fire retardant materials with enhanced visibility in low light and having equipment carrying capacity.

Setting-up of Search and Rescue Teams in States

The States have been advised to set-up their own Specialist Teams for responding to disasters. Ministry of Home Affairs will provide assistance for the training of the State trainers. Many States/UTs have initiated action for setting-up of specialized SAR units. Ten States have identified the Training Centers for training in Search and Rescue in the States. They have also identified trainers who will be imparted training at CPMF training institutions. Some states *e.g.*, Maharashtra, Orissa, Gujarat and Delhi have trained search and rescue teams. It has been provided that 10% of the annual inflows into the CRF can be used for the procurement of search and rescue equipment and communication equipment. States have been advised to include training in search and rescue in the training of State Armed Police.

Regional Response Centres

Fourteen Regional Response Centres (RRCs) are being set-up across the country to enable immediate response to floods, cyclones, earthquakes, landslides etc. Standard cache of equipment and relief materials will be kept in these RRCs and Specialist Response Teams will be stationed during the flood/ cyclone seasons for immediate assistance to the State Governments. Caches of equipments are being procured and all RRCs will be operational soon.

A Steering Committee has been constituted in the Ministry to oversee the creation of capabilities for emergency response.

Health Preparedness

A 200 bedded mobile hospital, fully trained and equipped is being set-up and attached to a leading Government hospital in Delhi. Three additional mobile hospitals with all medical and emergency equipments are proposed to be located in different parts of the country. These mobile hospitals will also be attached to the leading Government hospitals in the country. This will enable the mobile hospitals to extend assistance to the hospitals with which they are attached in normal time. They will be airlifted during emergencies with additional doctors/paramedics taken from the hospitals with which the mobile hospitals are attached to the site of disaster.

Hospital Preparedness and Emergency Health Management

Hospital preparedness is crucial to any disaster response system. Each hospital need to have an emergency preparedness plan to deal with mass casualty incidents and the hospital administration/doctor trained for this emergency. The curriculum for medical doctors does not at present include Hospital Preparedness for emergencies. Therefore, capacity building through in-service training of the current heath managers and medical personnel in Hospital Preparedness for emergencies or mass causality incident management is essential. At the same time in order that, the future health managers acquire these skills it is proposed to include health emergency management in the undergraduate and post graduate medical curricula. In consultation with Medical Council of India (MCI), two committees have been constituted for preparation of curriculum for introduction of emergency health management in MBBS curriculum and preparation of in-service training of Hospital Managers and Professionals.

Emergency Support Function Plans

It is seen that the relevant departments start constituting teams/mobilizing resources only after the crisis/disaster has struck, leading to delays. The relevant departments/agencies have been asked to draw up Emergency Support Function (ESF) Plans and constitute response teams and designate resources in advance so that response is not delayed. Ministries/Departments have drawn up their ESF Plans and communicated it to MHA. States have also been asked to take similar steps. Similarly States have been advised to finalize pre-contract/agreement for all disaster relief items so as to avoid delays in procuring relief items after disaster situations.

Incident Command System

In order to professionalize emergency response management, it is proposed to introduce the Incident Command System in the country. This system provides for specialist incident command teams with an Incident Commander and officers trained in different aspects of incident management—logistics, operations, planning, safety, media management etc. The LBSNAA Mussoorrie has been designated as the nodal training institution. Three programmes for the training of trainers have so far been held at LBSNAA and 42 officers have been trained in Basic and Intermediate ICS course and 29 officers trained in Planning Sections module.

India Disaster Resource Network

A web-enabled centralised database for the India Disaster Resource Network has been operationalized. The IDRN is a nation-wide electronic inventory of essential and specialist resources for disaster response both specialist equipment and specialist manpower resources. The IDRN list out the equipments and the resources by type and by the functions it performs and it gives the contact address and telephone numbers of the controlling officers in-charge of the said resources. The IDRN is a live system providing for updating of inventory once in every quarter. Entries into the inventory are made at district and State level.

The network ensures quick access to resources to minimise response time in emergencies. The list of resources to be updated in the system has been finalized. It has 226 items. About 69,329 records in 545 districts throughout the country have already been uploaded since September 1, 2003 when the India Disaster Resource Network was formally inaugurated. The system will give, at the touch of the button, location of specific equipments/specialist resources as well as the Controlling authority for that resource so that it can be mobilized for response in the shortest possible time.

Emergency Operation Centres

The States are being assisted to set-up control rooms/ emergency operations centres at the State and district level. Assistance for this is being given under the GOI—UNDP project in the States covered by the project. Assistance under the Modernization of Police Scheme is also available for setting-up EOCs. The control rooms, which will function round the clock, will be composite control rooms to look after law and order issues as well as disaster management. Equipments are also being provided for these control rooms under the disaster risk management programme. Hazard zone-wise standard layout, structural design and construction drawings have been developed for State and District EOCs and shared with all the States. Construction work has stated for multi-hazard resistant EOCs in six States and 64 districts.

National Emergency Operation Centre

To co-ordinate the entire disaster/emergency operations effectively, the existing Control Room at the national level has been being upgraded as National Emergency Operations Center (NEOC). The National EOC is equipped with satellite phones, GPS, computers, emergency lights, GIS information system etc in five on-site emergency co-ordination kits in ready-to-use mode. Staffs in the NEOC have been trained. A State-of-the-art underground and all-hazard resistant, National

EOC with superior structural features and communication facilities is being set-up. A Committee of CPWD/BARC/ DRDO has been constituted to finalize the design parameters.

National Emergency Communication Network

The communication network between the national and the state EOCs and the site of the emergency/crises are currently based on the DOT network. It has been observed that in a calamity/hazard, communication is the first casualty. It has therefore, been decided to put in place multi-mode and multi-channel communication systems so that enough redundancy is available. It has been decided that the POLNET will also be used for disaster management; and for this the POLNET communication facility will be extended to SDMs and Collectors as well as the Emergency Operation Centers. For emergency communications, discussions have also been held with the Department of Space. They will be making available alternate satellite communication units to connect with State EOCs and mobile units which can be transported to the site of a disaster.

Development of a GIS-based National Database

The Geographical Information System (GIS) database is an effective tool for emergency responders to access information in terms of crucial parameters for the disaster affected areas. The crucial parameters include location of the public facilities, communication links and transportation network at national, state and district levels. The GIS database already available with different agencies of the Government is being upgraded and the gaps are proposed to be bridged. A project for this purpose is being drawn up with a view to institutionalize the arrangements.

The database will provide multi layered maps on district wise basis. These maps taken in conjunction with the satellite images available for a particular area will enable the district administration as well as State Governments to carry out hazard zonation and vulnerability assessment, as well as co-ordinate response after a disaster.

Strengthening of Fire Services

In order to further strengthen the capacity for response, the fire services are proposed to be developed into multi hazard response units as is the normal practice in several other countries A project for this (with an estimated cost of ₹ 2457 crores) has been drawn up. The Planning Commission has given in-principle clearance to the project. The exercise for mobilization of resources is being undertaken. It is proposed to provide rescue tenders in addition to fire tenders to each fire unit and fill up all gaps upto sub-divisional level. Hazmat vans will be provided to State capitals and metropolitan cities.

Strengthening of Civil Defence

India has a large network of Civil Defence and Home Guards volunteers. The existing strength is about 1.2 million. However, this organization has not so far been associated with disaster mitigation, preparedness and response functions. It is proposed to revamp the Civil Defence organization to enable them to discharge a key responsibility in all the facets of disaster management including preparedness. A proposal in this regard has been finalized and is under consideration of the Government.

Handling of Hazardous Materials

In the light of the experience of the Bhopal Gas Tragedy, the Ministry of Home Affairs has been interacting with Ministry of Environment and Forests and new guidelines have been sent to the States for industries handling hazardous materials. It has been prescribed that onsite and offsite disaster response plans for the industries dealing with hazardous material be updated in consultation with District Administration and that this may be rehearsed once every year. It has also been prescribed that these industries will carry out awareness campaign for the population in the vicinity regarding the dos/don'ts in case of any accident involving hazardous material

With the development of disaster management committees and disaster management teams at all levels including village/urban local body/ward level, the stage will be set for comprehensive preparedness measures to be taken with active participation of the community and non-governmental organizations.

We can conclusion Disaster Management requires multi-disciplinary and pro-active approach. Besides various measures for putting in place institutional and policy framework, disaster prevention, mitigation and preparedness enunciated in this paper and initiatives being taken by the Central and State Governments, the community, civil society organizations and media also have a key role to play in achieving our goal of moving together, towards a safer India. The message being put across is that, in order to move towards safer and sustainable national development, development projects should be sensitive towards disaster mitigation.

Our mission is vulnerability reduction to all types of hazards, be it natural or manmade. This is not an easy task to achieve, keeping in view the vast population and the multiple natural hazards to which this country is exposed. However, if we are firm in our conviction and resolve that the Government and the people of this country are not prepared to pay the price in terms of massive casualties and economic losses, the task, though difficult, is achievable and we shall achieve it.

We have taken the first few but significant steps towards vulnerability reduction, putting in place prevention and mitigation measures and preparedness for a rapid and professional response. With a massive awareness generation campaign and building up of capabilities as well as institutionalization of the entire mechanism through a techno-legal and techno financial framework, we are gradually moving in the direction of sustainable development.

The various prevention, mitigation measures outlined above are aimed at building up the capabilities of the communities, voluntary organizations and Government functionaries at all levels. Particular stress is being laid on ensuring that these measures are institutionalized considering the vast population and the geographical area of the country. This is a major task being undertaken by the Government to put in place mitigation measures for vulnerability reduction. This is just a beginning. The ultimate goal is to make prevention and mitigation a part of normal day-to-day life.. We have a firm conviction that with these measures in place, we could say with confidence that disasters like Orissa cyclone and Bhuj earthquake will not be allowed to recur in this country; at least not at the cost, which the country has paid in these two disasters in terms of human lives, livestock, loss of property and means of livelihood.

❋❋❋

11

Building Assessment and Strengthening

Assessment of an existing structure is much more difficult a task than evaluation of a design on paper. *Firstly,* the construction of the structure is never exactly as per designer's specifications and a number of defects and uncertainties crop up during the construction. *Secondly,* the quality of the material deteriorates with time and the assessment of an existing structure becomes a time dependent problem. The problem of the assessment involves not only the current status of the structure but also its extrapolation in the life of the structure with or without repairs. There are three sources of deficiencies in structures:

1. Defects arising from the original design, such as under estimation of loads as per old standards/ practices, inadequate section/reinforcement, inadequate reinforcement anchorage and detailing.

2. Defects arising from original construction, such as under strength concrete, poor compaction, poor construction joints, improper placing of reinforcement and honeycombing.

3. Deterioration since the completion of the construction due to reinforcement corrosion, alkali—aggregate reaction, etc.

In Indian conditions, it is generally a combination of all the three deficiencies and the retrofitting of the structure has to take care of all the three.

If the design documents are available, the first type of deficiencies can be assessed with a satisfactory level of confidence. However, if the design details are not available, it makes the task of assessment, next to impossible. Till date, no testing technique with sufficient reliability is available to completely outline the reinforcement detailing inside the concrete. A number of techniques have been developed to detect the other two types of deficiencies. However, almost all of them depend on indirect measurements and have a low reliability. Further, the variation of test results is large and interpretation of results requires experience and skill. This chapter gives a brief account of different techniques available for assessment of structures and in-situ properties of concrete.

Valnerability Assessment of Buildings

According to the Vulnerability Atlas of the country, more than 80 % houses are non-engineered construction, which are mainly load bearing masonry buildings in rubble or coursed stone or brick masonry in mud or cement mortar. However, there are many RC framed urban buildings which have been constructed without any consideration to resist earthquake forces or without using the current codal practices on Earthquake Resistant Design. For such a large number of seismically deficient buildings, a quick assessment method and guidelines have to be developed together with training and capacity building. To handle the mammoth task of seismic evaluation of existing buildings, three levels or Tiers have been suggested.

Rapid Visual Screening (RVS) Procedure (Level-1, Procedure)

In a city there is very large number of existing buildings, which need to be examined for assessing the Seismic vulnerability of the city and for making policies for mitigation and management of seismic risk. For this purpose two approaches have been developed:

(*i*) Based on Indexes/scores assigned by trained surveyors after visual inspection of the buildings.

(*ii*) Checklist method, based on the basic structural and earthquake resistant features of the building.

Based on the behaviour of buildings in the past earthquakes scores or types/classes of buildings have been assigned. These classes are consistent with the MSK or European Intensity scales. For this screening a team of at least two surveyors visits the building and try to collect the information in a specially designed format. Once the class or the score of the building is decided, the expected behaviour of the building or the expected damage during a future earthquake can be assessed. These methods are based on behaviour of the buildings during past earthquakes and have significant subjective component. The results of the evaluation depend to a large extent of the training and skill of the surveyors. The purpose of this screening is to identify the buildings which require further investigation using Level—2 or Level—3, procedure. Rapid visual screening of buildings is also required after a major earthquake which results in large scale damage of existing buildings. The purpose of such a screening is to identify buildings which are severely damaged and should be evaluated.

Simplified Vulnerability Assessment (SVA) Procedure (Level—2, Procedure)

The buildings which have identified as vulnerable in the Level—1 procedure need to be investigated further. The Level—2 procedure involves a more systematic inspection and a limited engineering analysis based on the available structural drawings or on site measurements. Simplified calculations are made for strength and drift of the building based on sizes and strength of critical members. This method is more complex than the Level -1 procedure and requires a qualified structural engineer, well experienced in earthquake resistant design of buildings. If should be emphasized that this procedure can be used only for normal and regular types of buildings.

Detailed Vulnerability Assessment (DVA) Procedure (Level—3, Procedure)

The detailed vulnerability assessment is used for those buildings, which are found vulnerable from Level—2 procedure, for buildings with abnormal or irregular structural configurations and for monumental or important buildings. This procedure is normally more complex than the design of a new building and requires comprehensive engineering analysis considering the expected earthquake motion and in-situ strength of materials.

FIXING OF GOALS

One important question in seismic strengthening/retrofitting of the buildings is "How much retrofitting?" or what is the level of performance expected from the building after retrofitting. Building performance level requirement depends on the usage and importance of Buildings.

Performance level of a building depends on both structural and non-structural components. FEMA—273 gives a detailed description of different performance levels for structural and non structural components. Here, four overall performance levels, which are compatible with the philosophy of Indian Code of Practice, are described.

Operational Performance Level

Some of the post earthquake importance buildings, such as major hospitals are expected to be fully operational after an earthquake. In these buildings, not only the safety of structural and non-structural components should be ensured, but the smooth functioning of services should also be ensured. The maximum drift should be within tolerance limits of services. There should be no permanent drift and structure should retain its original strength and stiffness. For this performance level, only minor cracking of facades, partitions and ceiling etc., is acceptable.

Immediate Occupancy Performance Level

Post earthquake importance buildings, which are expected to provide shelter to earthquake victims, are required to have immediate occupancy performance level. These buildings should have minimal or no damage to structural components and only minor damage to non-structural components. The building should have no permanent drift and only minor cracking of facades, partitions, ceiling and structural elements is acceptable. Elevators and fire protection system should be working after earthquake. However, equipment and component may not work due to mechanical failure and lack of utilities such as water and power supply.

In such buildings, immediate occupancy of the building after earthquake is possible, but some minor repair, restoration of supplies and cleanup may be necessary before normal usage of the building. All the buildings designed as per IS-1893 are expected to have this performance level for a minor or moderate earthquake.

Life Safety Performance Level

In normal buildings, the damage to structural and non-structural components, after a major earthquake, is extensive but the risk to life should be low. The damage level may sometimes be so extensive that the repair may be uneconomical. The structures have some residual strength left at all the storeys. The non-structural parts should not fall and pose risk to life but these may be extensively damaged.

Collapse Prevention Performance Level

In no case a building should be allowed to collapse after an earthquake, as collapse will result in severe risk to life. This performance level is related to only structural components without any consideration to non-structural components. The building will have very little residual lateral stiffness and columns should function against gravity action, even in damaged state. The building may have large permanent drifts, some of the exits may be blocked, in fills and parapets may fail and building may be in near collapse state. In a severe earthquake most of the buildings with this performance level may result in complete economic loss. This is the mandatory seismic performance level to be ensured in all the buildings.

HAZARD ASSESSMENT

The first step in detailed vulnerability assessment of an important structure is to estimate the likely intensity of the earthquake at the site. Earthquake intensity at a site can be estimated from the seismic zoning map of India. For better estimation site specific earthquake intensity studies are carried out. Seismic microzonation of major cities of India is on cards. Once the seismic microzonation maps are available more accurate estimation of earthquake intensities will be possible.

Levels of earthquakes which should be considered in the evaluation of an important structure are defined as:

1. Serviceability Earthquake. This is the level of ground shaking which has 50 % chance of being exceeded in the 50 years period (normal life time of a structure). This has a mean return period of 75 years. This is typically 0.5 times the level of ground shaking corresponding to Design Earthquake.

2. Design Earthquake. This level of ground shaking has a 10 % chance of being exceeded in 50 years, which corresponds to a return period of approximately 500 years. This is the same level of ground shaking, defined as Design Basis

Earthquake (DBE) by IS 1893: 2002. This represents an infrequent earthquake, which can occur during the life time of structure.

3. Maximum Earthquake. This is the maximum expected level of ground shaking at the site. This has a 5 % probability of being exceeded in 50 years, which corresponds to a return period of about 1000 years. This level of shaking is about 1.25 to 1.5 times the level of shaking corresponding to Design Basis Earthquake.

IS 1893 defines another level of ground shaking termed as Maximum Considered Earthquake (MCE). Although this term has not been defined by the IS 1893 in terms of probability of exceedance or return period, but the same term has been used and defined in UBC. This is much higher level of ground shaking, which has a return period of about 2,500 years. This corresponds to the upper bound on the expected ground shaking depending on the geological conditions at site. This has only 2 % probability of exceeding in 50 years. This level of level of ground shaking is typically 2 times the ground shaking corresponding to the Design Basis earthquake.

The hazard assessment at a site consists of followings steps:

1. Identification and characterization of all potential earthquake sources, *i.e.,* active faults within the influence zone of the site (normally within a radius of 200 km).
2. Identification of predictive (attenuation) relationships applicable to the area.
3. Assigning magnitudes to the identified sources, based on source characteristics and past records.
4. Consideration of local site effects (soil amplifications, ridge effect and basin effect).

5. Estimation of ground motion parameters and development of design response spectrum.

Vulnerability of building has to be assessed with respect to ground failure hazard, also. The ground failure hazard consists of soil liquefaction, proximity to slope failure/rock fall areas and proximately to surface fault rupture. These can be estimated by considering the expected level of shaking alongwith the local site conditions.

Visual Inspection and Study of Available Documents

A systematic visual inspection provides a fair idea about the irregularities in building configuration, construction, consideration defects and deterioration/distress of the structure. Extensive photography of the building is helpful in the study of the building in office. Visual inspection is helpful in deciding the extent of investigation and selection of tests. Visual inspection should start from the roof, which gives the best view of the building plan and configuration. It should concentrate on the irregularities in configuration, construction defects and most importantly, the signs of distress and deterioration. Different distress agents have characteristic cracking patterns and a close inspection of crack patterns may provide a good idea of the cause of distress.

Sketches showing the general plan and elevations of building and cracking patterns/crack locations are helpful in later reference in office. Removal of cover at some selected locations may be helpful in identifying extent of corrosion taken place in the building. In masonry buildings, vertical slits may be cut through the plaster to see whether earthquake bends have been provided.

In case of slopping and jack-arch roof buildings, false ceiling should be removed at a few locations to have a view of the trusses/girders. In the absence of proper maintenance, the girders and trusses corrode and should be properly investigated. In case of wooden trusses, the joints should be carefully examined and wooden members should be examined for attack of insects and rottening.

Pounding of adjacent buildings has been observed to cause damage in the past several earthquakes. Therefore, attention should also be given to adjacent buildings and the gap between the adjacent buildings. If separation joints have been provided within the building, these should be carefully observed. As these are a maintenance problem, it has been observed that in most of the cases the gap in the separation joints is filled and the desired action is not available during the earthquake.

Maintenance of building records in India is very poor. Generally, the structural drawings are either not available or these are incomplete and in poor condition Attempt should be made to get as much information as possible about the original design, construction, repairs and extensions of the building. Any change in usage of the building should also be recorded.

Planning and Interpretation of Results

In-situ testing of structures is a costly and time consuming affair. Lot of money and time can be saved by proper planning of the testing program. The visual inspection should be done in a systematic manner and extensive photography or video taping of the structure should be undertaken prior to testing and retrofitting.

Depending on the aim of testing and funds available the optimum number of various tests is to be decided. The number and type of test have to be decided keeping in view the reliability of the test and the accuracy desired.

Foundation Capability

Structures have to be assessed for their performance, settlement, depth of foundation, deterioration due to weathering or age, capacity of foundation, stability against overturning, ties between foundation elements, load path for transfer of seismic forces to soil and special requirements in sloping sites.

Non-structural Components

Parapets, sunshades, projections, fixtures, cladding, etc., have to be assessed for their capacity to withstand earthquake forces. Safety of non-structural components is particularly important in case of buildings such as hospitals, telephone exchanges, control buildings, etc. The failure of fixtures and connections may lead to not only the disruption of the function but also the loss of life due to disruption as well as due to direct injury from the falling component.

Partitions and infills are another component, which are usually considered as nonstructural in the design. Their safety is not ensured in design. Failure of masonry infills in out of plane bending may be fatal to the inmates. Safety of partitions and infills must be ensured by the retrofitting engineer.

MODELING AND ANALYSIS

A lot of research has taken place in the area of analysis of buildings for earthquake forces. The analysis methods can be broadly classified into Linear and Non-linear methods. Earthquake resistance design relies heavily on the ductility or post yielding behaviour of the structure and therefore, the non-linear methods appear to be more reliable. However, these methods also have inherent assumptions and require skill and computer software, as these are computationally intensive. Another classification is based on the type of load considered in the analysis. Static analysis procedures consider equivalent static force, while the dynamic analysis procedures take into account the time varying nature of the earthquake forces. The dynamic analysis is nearer to reality but require high degree of computation. On the other hand, the static analysis procedure is simple, easy to use and provide insight in to behaviour of structure.

Mathematical Modeling of Buildings

Development of a mathematical model of the building structure is the first step in its analysis. Depending on the torsional effects in the building, either 2D or 3D modeling of the building may be used. If the maximum horizontal displacement of a point on a floor is more than 120% of the average displacement of the floor, the building is considered to have a torsional irregularity and a 3D space frame model is to be used. For calculating the torsional displacement, both actual and accidental torsions are to be considered. A number of mathematical models are available with varying degrees of sophistication in the analysis. Earlier research was centered on developing hand calculation methods based on simplified assumptions and understanding of the overall behaviour of the structure.

Now-a-days, the computer hardware and software for analysis of structures is widely available and stress is on more sophisticated mathematical modeling. The actual structure and its behaviour at the micro level is always very complex. It is not possible to model each and every detail of the structure, what so ever being the sophistication of the computer software. The mathematical modeling of the structure is based on certain simplifying assumptions and the understanding of the overall behaviour of the structure. Therefore, caution is required to interpret the output of the computer software and the user should have a sound knowledge of the behaviour of the structure.

1. Linear Static Procedure (LSP) and Linear Dynamic Procedure (LDP) of Analysis. The LSP for evaluating an existing building is the same as described in IS-1893: 2002 for design of a new building with a pre-defined distribution of earthquake forces along height of the building.

In LDP also the modeling of the structure is same as in LSP, but in spite of using a pre-defined distribution of earthquake forces along the height of the building, the distribution is obtained by dynamic analysis of the building. The dynamic analysis can be performed either using a response spectrum (Modal Analysis) or using time histories of earthquake motion (Time History Analysis).

2. Non-linear Dynamic Procedure (NDP). NDP is the well-known Non-linear Time History Analysis based on step-by-step solution of the equation of motion. This method simulates the real behaviour of a structure during an earthquake and can be used, at least theoretically, to analyze any structure. The main difficulty in use of this procedure is that it requires design time histories, which are difficult to be specified, as the codes specify only design response spectrum. Further, it is computationally very extensive method. Both NSP and NDP require a comprehensive understanding of building components, their interconnections and their material properties. It is difficult to estimate realistically the non-linear load-deformation relationships for building components and therefore, the practical benefit of NSP and NDP is doubtful.

3. Non-linear Static Procedure (NSP) of Analysis. This recently developed method is a revolutionary idea to have a non-linear analysis based on response spectrum method. The method gives an iterative solution for the maximum non-linear displacement of the building. This non-linear displacement is checked for each component to determine its safety and damage state. Different performance levels put different restrictions on the maximum non-linear displacement components.

Seismic Strengthening of Buildings

After the vulnerability assessment of any existing building, the decision as to whether the building needs to be strengthened and to what degree, must be based on assessment that show if the levels of safety demanded by present codes and recommendations are met. As we have seen, difficulties in establishing actual strength arise from the considerable uncertainties related with material properties and with the amount of strength deterioration due to age or to damage suffered from previous earthquakes. The method of repair and strengthening would naturally depend very largely on the structural scheme and materials used for the construction of the building in the first instance, the technology that is feasible to adopt quickly and the amount of funds that can be assigned to the task which are usually very limited. The concepts of repair, restoration and strengthening are described in the following sections.

Repairs

The main purpose of repairs is to bring back the architectural shape of the building so that all services start working and the functioning of building is resumed quickly. Repair does not pretend to improve the structural strength of the building and can be very deceptive for meeting the strength requirements of the next earthquake. The actions will include the following:

1. Patching up of defects such as cracks and fall of plaster.
2. Repair doors, windows, replacement of glass panes.
3. Checking and repairing electrical wiring.
4. Rebuilding non-structural walls, smoke chimneys, boundary walls etc.
5. Checking and repairing gas pipes, water pipes and plumbing services.
6. Re-plastering of walls as required.
7. Relaying cracked floor at ground level.
8. Redecoration—white washing, painting etc.
9. Rearranging disturbed roofing tiles.

The architectural repairs as stated above do not restore the original structural strength of cracked walls or columns and may sometimes be very illusive, since the redecorated building will hide all the weaknesses and the building will suffer even more severe damage if shaken again by an equal shock since the original energy absorbing capacity will not be available.

Restoration

It is the restitution of the strength the building had before the damage occurred. This type of action must be undertaken when there is evidence that the structural damage can be attributed to exceptional phenomena that are not likely to happen again and that the original strength provides an adequate level of safety.

The main purpose of restoration is to carry out structural repairs to load bearing elements. It may involve cutting portions of the elements and rebuilding them or adding more structural material so that the original strength is more or less restored. The process may involve inserting temporary supports, underpinning etc. Some of the approaches are stated below.

1. Removal of portions of cracked masonry walls and piers and rebuilding them in richer mortar.

   Use of non-shrinking mortar will be preferable.

2. Addition of reinforcing mesh on both faces of the cracked wall, holding it to the wall through spikes or bolts and then covering it suitably. Several alternatives have been used for this purpose so far.

3. Injecting epoxy like material, which is strong in tension, into the cracks in walls, columns, beams etc.

Where structural repairs are considered necessary, these should be carried out prior to or simultaneously with the architectural repairs so that total planning of work could be done in co-ordinated manner and wastage is avoided.

Strengthening of Existing Buildings

The seismic behaviour of old existing buildings is affected by their original structural inadequacies, material degradation due to time and alterations carried out during use over the years such as making new openings, addition of new parts inducing unsymmetry in plan and elevation etc. The possibility of substituting them with new earthquake resistant buildings is generally neglected due to historical, artistic, social and economical reasons. The complete replacement of the buildings in a given area will also lead to destroying a number of social and human links. Therefore, seismic strengthening of existing damaged or undamaged buildings can be a definite requirement in same areas. Strengthening is an improvement over the original strength where the evaluation of building indicates that the strength available before the damage was insufficient and restoration alone will not be adequate in future quakes. The extent of the modifications must be determined by the general principals and design methods and should not be limited to increasing the strength of members that have been damaged, but should consider the overall behaviour of the structure. Commonly the strengthening procedures should aim at one or more of the following objectives:

1. Increasing the lateral strength in one or both directions, by reinforcement or by increasing wall areas or the number of walls and columns.

2. Giving unity to the structure by providing a proper connection between its resisting elements, in such a way that inertia forces generated by the vibration of the building can be transmitted to the members that have the ability to resist them. Typical important aspects are the connections between roofs and floors

and walls, between intersecting walls and between walls and foundations.

3. Avoiding the possibility of brittle modes of failure by proper reinforcement and connection of resisting members. Since its cost may go to as high as 50 to 60 % of the cost of rebuilding, the justification of such strengthening must be fully considered.

4. Eliminating features that are sources of weakness or that produce concentrations of stresses in some members. Asymmetrical plan distribution of resisting members, abrupt changes of stiffness from one floor the other, concentration of large masses, large openings in walls without a proper peripheral reinforcement are examples of defect of this kind.

STRENGTHENING MATERIALS

Considerable research has taken place in the field of repair and retrofitting materials and a large variety suitable to different applications and working conditions is available. Most of the materials are patented and available in brand names. We need to have information about these materials for designing the retrofit scheme.

The repair and retrofit materials can be broadly classified into three categories:

(i) Grouts for repair of cracks, strengthening of masonry and honeycombed concrete.

(ii) Replacement and jacketing materials for replacing the damaged portions, increasing the size of members, enhancing the confinement and external reinforcement of the members.

(iii) Bonding agents for enhanced bonding between old and new concrete and concrete and reinforcement.

A brief description of different materials available under these categories is given below.

Bonding Agents

Bond between existing concrete, new concrete and reinforcement is very important for effectiveness of repair/ retrofitting. There are three methods available for enhancing the bond:

(i) Application of adhesives at the interface.

(ii) Surface interlocking.

(iii) Mechanical bonding.

Polymers and epoxy are the adhesives used for bonding between old and new concrete and reinforcement. After removal of the concrete cover, the existing concrete surface and steel are cleaned by sand or water blasting.

After cleaning and drying, concrete and steel is painted by epoxy/polymer or polymer modified cement grout. If the new steel is to be welded, it is welded prior to coating of the concrete and steel. This coating provides enhanced bond between the old and new material and reduces the risk of corrosion in steel.

To improve the surface interlocking, the existing concrete surface is coated with epoxy/polymer and a layer of coarse sand is applied above the coating. Mechanical bonding consists of keys and anchors provided in the existing members at regular interval.

Replacement and Jacketing Materials

In case of damaged structures, material in some parts of members is to be replaced by new material. For strengthening existing members in deficient buildings, additional material including reinforcement is to be provided. The material used for replacement should have good bond with existing material and it should be non-shrinking. A variety of strengthening and replacement materials is available.

Shotcrete

Shotcrete or guniting has the same characteristics as ordinary concrete but it has smaller aggregate size and it is applied under pressure with low water content. It requires no framework and can be applied on any surface including inclined and vertical surfaces and even on ceilings.

This results in very good adhesion between old and new concrete and good compaction due to application under pressure. The low water cement ratio results in high strength and low shrinkage. The permeability of shotcrete is also lower than that of ordinary concrete and results in better protection of steel against corrosion.

Shotcrete requires special equipment. Two types of equipment are used depending on dry or wet mix type of application. In dry mix application, the proportioned or pre-pakaged cement aggregate mixture is transferred to nozzle using highly compressed air. Water is introduced at nozzle under pressure.

The mixture is impacted on the surface to be shotcreted. In wet mix type shotcrete, proportioned mixture of cement aggregate water and admixtures are discharge into a conventional concrete pump through a discharge nozzle. Compressed air is used to project the material from nozzle.

Before application of shotcrete, damaged concrete is removed and the surface is thoroughly cleaned by sand blasting to remove all dirt and to expose the aggregate. Steel is cleaned on full circumference of bar to bare metal. Usually a melded wire mesh is applied over the surface to be shotcreted and attached to the existing concrete through nailing. This wire mesh reduces the shrinkage and improves the bond between existing concrete and shotcrete.

Sometimes, to improve the bond between old and new material, surface coatings, such as epoxy bonding agents, latex modified cement slurries or neat cement slurries are also used. In case of dry mix shotcrete, the water/cement ratio cannot be controlled quantitatively as it is mixed at nozzle and controlled visually by the operator. Therefore, the skill of the crew is very important.

Polymer Modified Concrete and Mortar

Polymers are long molecule hydrocarbons, built by combination of single units called monomers. The process is called polymerization. Small diameter particles of polymers emulsified in water are called polymer latexes.

These latexes form continuous film at drying. Adding polymer latexes to ordinary mortar and concrete is the most common method of making Polymer Modified Mortar (PMM) and Polymer Modified Concrete (PMC). Cement hydration in PMM/PMC results in drying of latex and formation of the film of polymers.

This film binds the cement hydrates together to from a monolithic network in which the polymer phase interpenetrates throughout the cement hydrate phase. The resulting matrix binds the aggregate more strongly and enhances the properties of mortar/concrete.

The polymer can also be mixed in the form of re-dispersible powder in the dry cementaggregate mix. When water is added to this mixture, a process similar to that described above takes place. Some polymers are water soluble. When added to mortar/concrete, these result in enhanced workability but no increase in strength.

In some liquid thermosetting resins, polymerization is initiated by water. These are also added to concrete/mortar to result in enhancement similar to that resulting from latex. The PMM/PMC has better workability and water retention properties than ordinary concrete/mortar. This reduces the requirement of water curing considerably.

Polymer modification does not result in any appreciable increase in compressive strength of concrete, but it results significant increase in tensile and bending strength of concrete. The main advantage of PMM/PMC is its improved adhesion and bond with existing concrete and significantly reduced permeability. Reduced permeability results in reduced risk of corrosion of reinforcing steel.

Steel Plate Bonding

Steel plates can be bonded to concrete members as external reinforcement to increase their strength. The plates are glued to the member surface by epoxies. This requires a careful preparation of the member surface and application of epoxy layer.

Steel plates can also be provided in the form of jackets either by gluing to surface or by grouting. However, these jackets are not very effective as these try to separate out from the members due to Poisson's effect, loosing confinement.

Fibre Reinforced Plastics (FRP)

Fibre reinforced polymers/plastics is a recently developed material for strengthening of RC and masonry structure. This is an advanced material and most of the development in its application in structural retrofitting has taken place in the last two decades. It has been found to be a replacement of steel plate bonding and is very effective in strengthening of columns by exterior wrapping.

The main advantage of FRP is its high strength to weight ratio and high corrosion resistance. FRP plates can be 2 to 10 times stronger than steel plates, while their weight is just 20% of that of steel. However, at present, their cost is high. FRP composites are formed by embedding a continuous fibre matrix in a resin matrix.

The resin matrix binds the fibre together and also provides bond between concrete and FRP. The commonly used fibres are Carbon fibres, Glass fibres and Aramid fibres and the commonly used resins are polyester, vinyl ester and epoxy. FRP is named after the fibre used, *e.g.,* Carbon Fibre Reinforced Polymer (CFRP), Glass Fibre Reinforced Polymer (GFRP) and Aramid Fibre Reinforced Polymer (AFRP).

The fibres are available in two forms *(i)* Unidirectional tow sheet and *(ii)* Woven fabric. The application of resin can be in-situ or in the form of prefabrication of FRP plates and other shapes by pultrusion.

The in-situ application is by wet lay-up of a woven fabric or tow plate immersed in resin. This method is more versatile as it can be used on any shape. On the other hand, prefabrication results in better quality control.

The manufacturers supply these materials as a package and each brand has specific method of application, which is to be followed carefully. Specialized firms have developed in India also, which take up the complete execution work and supply of material.

Retrofitting and Load Bearing Wall Buildings

Buildings in which the roof and floor slabs are directly supported on the walls are called load bearing wall buildings. These walls serve as partitions and also bear the load from slabs. The lateral load resulting from earthquake and wind is also resisted by these walls and transferred to ground. Individual unreinforced masonry or mud walls are very weak in out-of-plane bending due to lack of tensile strength.

These are generally not capable of bearing out-of-plane bending moment, even resulting from their own inertia. These walls act as shear-walls in their in-plane action and possess sufficient in-plane strength, if not weakened by too many openings.

In a building, there are four or more than four walls, which act as a box under lateral load. The walls parallel to the lateral load, act as webs and the walls orthogonal to load act as flanges. The resistance of box is much higher than the resistance of individual walls.

The box action involves considerable interaction between webs and flanges at corners of building. It has been observed in past earthquakes that in many cases, the damage initiates at corners, resulting in loss of box action and walls start acting independently leading to collapse of building.

The basic principle of seismic safety of load bearing wall buildings lies in their integral box action during earthquake. In new buildings it can be ensured by providing seismic bands. In existing buildings, the integral box action is to be ensured by providing external bandage or pre-stressing.

Openings in walls are the source of weakness. Openings result in reduction of effective crosssectional area of wall resisting lateral loads. If the openings are very near to corners, these hamper the integral box action by weakening the joints. The piers between openings are subjected to higher stresses than the portion of the wall above and below the openings. It has been observed in the past earthquakes that diagonal X-shaped cracks in the piers originate from the corners of openings.

Retrofitting of RC Buildings

The retrofitting schemes for RC buildings are based on two principles:

(i) Reduction in earthquake demand by reducing mass, by base-isolation or by supplemental energy dissipation.

(ii) Enhancing the capacity of the structure to withstand the earthquake forces.

The capacity may be enhanced either by strengthening the deficient members or by improving the ductility and deformation capacity resulting in increased hysteretic damping. There is another important aspect of retrofitting—completion of load path and removal of configurational irregularities.

Completion of Load Path

A large number of buildings in India have incomplete load paths mainly to take advantage of the loopholes in the building by-laws and sometimes due to market compulsions and our quest for creating new shapes.

For example, floating column constructions are not uncommon in Indian cities to take maximum advantage of floor area with restrictions on ground area. The general seismic load path in a building is as follows- the inertial forces originating throughout the building are first transferred to horizontal floor diaphragms, the diaphragms transfer these forces to vertical framing system resisting lateral loads; the vertical framing system consisting of beam-column frames and shear walls, transfers the seismic force to foundation and supporting soil.

The common examples of such building are those in which shear walls or columns are not started from ground but started at first floor (or at a higher level). Such columns are commonly known as floating columns. This is done to increase the floor area at first floor level or to have large open spaces at ground floor for commercial purposes. In such buildings, the first floor beams are subjected to very high forces as the forces from floating columns/shear walls are transferred to other columns and walls through these beams.

The remedy to this deficiency is to complete the load path by providing the missing part of the column/shear wall. In case of a floating column, a new column is to be erected below the floating column. This column should have footing connected with the foundation of the existing building and the reinforcement of the new column should be welded with the reinforcement of existing column. Shrinkage compensating agents should be used in the new concrete to avoid shortening of the new column resulting in separation between new and old concrete. Similarly, a shear wall panel is to be provided below the existing shear wall. This panel should have rigid shear connections with adjacent columns, beam/slab above it and foundation.

Removal of Configurational Irregularity due to Soft/Weak Storey

In buildings having soft/weak storey, most of the ductility demand is concentrated in the soft/weak storey, resulting in excessive lateral displacement of the storey leading to failure of the building due to formation of unstable mechanism.

In Indian cities there is a lack of parking space. In multistory buildings, the ground storey is usually kept open (free of masonry in-fills) while the upper storeys have masonry infills for partitions. It has been seen that such a configuration results in the stiffness of the ground storey about one-third of the stiffness of the upper storeys.

IS: 1893-2002 has addressed this problem and suggests that either a non-linear analysis of such buildings should be performed or the ground storey beams and columns should be designed for a storey shear 2.5 times of that obtained from analysis of a bare frame without in-fills.

Strengthening by Addition of New Members

Addition of new members is perhaps the easiest option to strengthen an existing building. Addition of new members is possible externally, without disturbing the space inside the building. The main concerns in addition of new members are the connection of new and old members and foundation of the new members. It is possible to provide only a few stiff members to take most of the earthquake force of the existing structure, but the connections should be capable of transferring this load. Similarly, the foundations should be capable of transferring this load to the ground.

Several options, in the form of frames, shear walls and vertical trusses, are possible for strengthening an existing building. Addition of new members changes dynamic characteristics of the building. Sometimes, new members are also added to reduce eccentricity. Therefore, re-analysis of structure is required after addition of members.

Strengthening of Existing Members

In most of the cases, strengthening of at least a few of existing members will be required in seismic retrofitting of a building. A number of techniques based on steel/FRP plate bonding, RCC jacketing and FRP jacketing are available for strengthening of individual members. The choice of the technique depends on the specific weakness and demand on the member. Strengthening of individual members require good knowledge of the different materials available in the market for repair and retrofitting.

The load transfer mechanism between the old and new material is complex and proper bonding between the two is difficult to be ensured. Following points are to be considered in strengthening of individual members: A variety of materials, discussed above is available for strengthening of existing members.

A detailed study of manufacturer claimed properties of these materials is required before selecting a suitable material. Short-term as well as long-term properties are to be considered.

- The load transfer between old and new material can take place through several mechanisms, such as, compression against pre-cracked interfaces, adhesion between non-metallic materials, friction between non-metallic materials, load transfer through resin/ glue layers, clamping effect of steel, dowel effect of steel, etc. Modeling of this interaction is complex and not well understood, yet. It should be ensured that more than one mechanism of load transfer between new and old material are present.

- Anchorage lengths of reinforcement in new concrete should be as per codal specifications. However, in case of anchorage into old concrete, smaller anchorage lengths may be sufficient if special grouts are used to anchor the bars in drilled holes. This anchorage length should be in accordance with the manufacturer's specifications and should be verified by Pull-out tests.
- Anchoring of additional bars can also be accomplished by welding them with existing bars. For this purpose, spacers can be provided between old and new bars to provide a gap for intrusion of concrete. The weld is to be designed to develop full strength in the new bar.

Enhancing Deformation Capacity

Post yielding deformation capacity of a building plays a very important role in reducing the effective seismic force on the building. The members of a building are expected not to lose their vertical load carrying capacity, while undergoing large plastic deformations in lateral direction. Sometimes, a few poorly designed members can limit the capacity of the whole building to deform laterally.

These members may be modified to increase their deformation capacity and this will result in large reduction in effective seismic force on the building. If the number of the members to be modified is small, this strategy does not disrupt the functioning of the building.

Earthquake Demand Reduction

An alternative approach for retrofitting of existing buildings is to reduce the earthquake demand (forces and displacements). This can be achieved either by reducing the mass of the building or using base-isolation/energy dissipation devices.

Reduction of building mass is not always possible and it is mainly the use of base-isolation/supplemental energy dissipation devices, which is employed to reduce the earthquake demand on the buildings. Use of base-isolation/ supplemental energy dissipation devices is costly and it is recommended only for those building which are required to have operational performance level after an earthquake or which house sensitive equipment. Base-isolation has been found to be particularly useful for historic buildings, where it is not possible to modify the structure significantly. However, it is important to note that base-isolation and supplemental energy damping cannot be used in all buildings. In many cases, the structure is also to be strengthened in addition to base-isolation/energy dissipation.

Seismic Base-Isolation

Base-isolation is based on the principle of elongating the time period of the building by providing compliant bearings at the base of the building.

The bearings have sufficient stiffness and strength against vertical load, but relatively low stiffness and large deformation capacity in lateral direction. Sometimes, these bearings are also provided with enhanced energy dissipation characteristics or with additional dampers.

The base-isolation results in significant increase in fundamental time period of the structure and damping. Further, as the stiffness of the bearings is much smaller compared to structure, the lateral deformation gets concentrated into bearings, resulting in greatly reduced earthquake deformation demand in the portion of the structure above bearings.

Base-isolation is considered to be useful for buildings having a fundamental time period of one second or less, as it requires a relatively stiff building to have concentration of lateral deformation in bearings only.

Further, the building should remain elastic under the residual demand transmitted to the structure by the isolators. In order to achieve this, in many cases, the building structure is also required to be strengthened in addition to base-isolation. Base-isolation is considered to be very effective for historical buildings, believing that no intervention/ modification is required in the building, preserving its historical character.

Base-isolation provides an effective solution for retrofitting of buildings having enhanced performance objectives. Base-isolation results in significant reduction of displacement and force response of the building. This is a preferable condition for better performance of sensitive equipment, systems and other non-structural components.

Supplemental Energy Dissipation

Supplemental Energy Dissipation Systems dissipate the energy transmitted to the structure by the earthquake, in addition to the energy dissipated by the structure in normal course. This results in significant reduction in the displacement and acceleration response of structure. For this purpose, energy dissipation devices (EDDs) are installed in the lateral load resisting system of the building. These EDDs work either on viscous or on hysteretic damping.

Contrary to base-isolation, the energy dissipation system is more effective in flexible buildings with large lateral deformations, as the energy dissipated by EDUs is directly proportional to the force developed by EDUs and displacement across these EDUs.

For a rigid building, the small lateral displacement during earthquake will results in smaller energy dissipation and the reduction in effective earthquake forces will not be significant. Similar to base-isolation, supplemental energy dissipation system is also a costly method and is suitable for buildings with high post-earthquake importance.

The energy dissipation results in reduced seismic response of building and better performance of equipment, systems and non-structural components.

✸✸✸

12

Risk Transfer Mechanisms

Apart from disaster risk management measures to arrest the spiraling cost of disasters and their wider socio-economic import, a nascent beginning has also been made in India towards addressing them through risk transfer mechanisms.

One of the major mechanisms for risk transfer is the insurance sector and the proposed instrument is the insurance-linked savings-cumloan-cum-subsidy scheme. The logic behind cross-sectoral risk transfers being that the transferor takes on the risk as a part or consequence of its core business and his incentive being that the cost of transferring or hedging the risk is calculated to be lower than the cost of retaining it.

However, insurance in India is yet to receive due recognition as a socio-economic issue with the result that the insurance market in India, both life and non-life, has not been able to fulfill its potential and achieve higher penetration levels. The cover for natural disasters is today considered as part of the cover against the fire hazard. The need of the hour is to view disaster insurance as a step towards disaster preparedness. In some countries, a typical insurance strategy for catastrophic risk allows insurance against "layers" of risk up to 100 to 500 years with the underlying rationale being that losses up to certain limit can probably be sustained without major difficulties whereas for rarer but more catastrophic events risk transfer needs to be undertaken.

Under the sensitization programmes for the corporate sector, a capsule on risk transfer mechanisms is also included to familiarize them about these through a representative of one of the prominent insurance companies. It is well known that most industries would lose critical operational capability after an 'encounter' with a natural catastrophe. Each risk is evaluated and ranked according to its probability and severity and the strategy is to purchase insurance in order to transfer the financial risk. However, while going in for insurance, the company should make sure that the insurance company is financially stable with a long-term commitment; review risk financing options yearly; prepare early and be proactive for insurance renewals and underwriters and appraise the market realities *viz.,* higher deductibles, sizeable premium increases and limitations.

The overall benefit of the strategy being that the mechanism is an enabling instrument allowing for exchange of uncertainty of financial risk for the certainty of a premium. It indicates an acceptance of the risk and shows that the sector is aware of the hazards it is exposed to and is expected to protect itself against. In view of the same, it wishes to lower the impact and the probability of occurrence. The strategy helps in business continuity planning since it has taken care of the impact of risks and helps remove or reduce the cause or source of threat and exposure to a considerable extent.

Currently, there are two funding mechanisms in India for relief and rehabilitation efforts—the Calamity Relief Fund (CRF) and the National Calamity Contingency Fund (NCCF). This mechanism is reviewed by the Finance Commission every five years and makes recommendations regarding division of tax and non-tax revenues between the Central and the State Governments. The size of CRF is determined after taking into account the expenditure on relief and rehabilitation over the past ten years. The Central Government contributes

75% of the revenues while the States contribute the remaining 25% of the corpus.

However, where the calamity is of proportions beyond the capacity of the concerned State Government, they can seek assistance under the NCCF—a fund created at the Central level. For the period 2001-2005, the Finance Commission has allocated roughly Rupees ten thousand crores for the CRF.

In view of the increasing basic disaster frequency and the rapidly mounting disaster-related monetary losses, the insurance sector can provide the requisite risk transfer instruments. However, the private insurance market is struggling to meet the challenge due to low penetration levels.

India's general insurance market is at a nascent stage and is considerably underdeveloped in spite of the fact that it has a huge potential. Yet the catastrophe insurance purchasing is insufficient as major insurers do not have accurate up-to-date accumulation data. In the Bhuj earthquake, insurable losses were more than USD 2 million whereas the actual losses were around USD 16 million.

It is well known that natural disasters pose a threat to India's development and a formal risk management strategy incorporating risk transfer mechanisms is required. The States could be advised to prepare such strategies with fiscal incentives and technical support. The Government could also make insurance mandatory at least for those taking out mortgages. At the same time, disaster funding strategies need to be based on probabilistic determinations of loss potentials and funding gaps and where possible should use private risk financing markets.

The system of insurance should be accessible to all including the rural and the poor alike. It should compensate for catastrophic income losses to protect consumption and debt repayment capacity and the private sector should be able to extend the same with little or no Government subsidy. As long as the instrument is voluntary and unsubsidized, it will only be purchased when it is a less expensive and more effective alternative to existing risk management strategies.

Accordingly, adequate insurance protection must be made available especially in high-risk areas to low and moderate-income house owners. It is imperative that the cost of disasters is minimized through strong mitigation measures and these must include apart from Governments, the business sector and the insurance industry. Deductibles, co-insurance and surcharges are all ways of ensuring insurance protection. Moreover, any insurance programme must strategically aim to dissuade location of industries and buildings in high-risk areas and the pricing mechanism should be as per the level of risk and exposure.

In the Province (State) of Gujarat, the Gujarat State Disaster Management Authority (GSDMA) has launched a Housing Insurance Programme seeking to address monitoring and implementation of recovery programmes and long-term disaster management planning. Under it, more than two hundred thousand households, newly constructed after the earthquake, were insured for ten years against fourteen types of risks including natural hazards and humaninduced accidents. Over twenty one hundred thousand houses reconstructed were insured to mitigate the effects of disasters through risk sharing mechanisms. The Standard Fire and Special Perils Policy (SFSP) was launched with a one-time premium of ₹ 360/- (three hundred sixty rupees) to cover risks for a period of ten years up to a value of rupees one hundred thousand. It was made mandatory for all reconstruction programs.

Apart from the above-mentioned Government of Gujarat model of obtaining group insurance for the community, the

Municipalities and Development Corporations can add a small levy to the property tax to utilize the same for buying insurance against catastrophes. The Group Housing Co-operative Societies in urban areas can be authorized to recover insurance premiums alongwith maintenance charges. In addition, all lending financial institutions, banks and housing loan corporations must cause insurance to be obtained compulsorily against catastrophes. At the same time, all house building societies and organizations like Urban Development Authorities, City Development Authorities etc., associated with construction and development projects must be mandated to insure against catastrophes.

Taking a cue from the experience in community insurance in Gujarat, it would be in fitness of things to explore the possibility of group insurance for the corporate sector on the basis of a cluster of industries in an industrial estate or industrial zone. This will help generate awareness on the issue of securing the industrial assets and adopting a common approach to disasters.

In view of the imperative need to meet the gigantic challenge posed by natural hazards, the successes achieved, the experience garnered and the onerous task ahead to secure safety and disaster-free functioning of the corporate sector in the larger interests of the nation and the people, the Confederation of Indian Industry (CII) has decided to up scale and deepen its engagement with integration of disaster management agenda into the corporate sector functioning to minimize losses and prevent disruption of economic activity hampering achievement of developmental goals.

In this context, CII is expanding the scope of its activities in association with the Ministry of Home Affairs and the United Nations Development Programme (UNDP) to facilitate sustainable economic growth through disaster risk reduction and mitigation. This envisages an entire gamut of issues connected with mainstreaming disaster management concerns in the developmental efforts at all levels and across a spectrum of sectors. The main themes to be addressed are:

- Ensuring that existing and upcoming industrial assets and infrastructure are disaster-resistant.
- Ensuring proper citing of industrial establishments considering hazard parameters.
- Development of on-site and off-site DM plans by industries in association with the District Administration.
- Conducting mock-drills at regular intervals to determine the efficacy of the DM plans.
- Making industrial processes and procedures inherently safe.
- Ensuring that transportation, storage, handling and usage of chemicals and other hazardous raw materials does not pose a threat to the nearby areas and environment.
- Preparation of inventory of corporate resources and uploading them on the IDRN—India Disaster Resource Network.
- Assessment and retrofitting of existing industrial infrastructure.
- Training of a core team of Structural Engineers for advising member industries on requisite mitigation measures in association with the Ministry of Home Affairs.
- To move away from relief-centric approach to a pro-active assault on vulnerabilities through risk management measures and capacity building of industrial personnel.

- Large-scale association with awareness generation initiatives aimed at building the knowledge, attitude and skills of the common people for a safer habitat.
- Mainstreaming private sector participation in disaster management.
- Networking knowledge on best practices and tools for effective disaster management.
- Establishing linkages between private sector and the community.

Development and implementation of appropriate risk transfer mechanisms. In addition, it is also proposed to secure active participation of corporate sector in risk mapping of the area hosting the industry and in training and capacity building of the community in its disaster preparedness activities. It is also envisaged to create an industry-led voluntary force for search and rescue and first-aid etc. Given the destructive potential of man-made disasters, the activities will also aim at addressing the needs and concerns relating to management of man-made and industrial disasters. This envisages a regular interaction and involvement of the Ministry of Environment and Forests and other institutions associated with research and study of chemical and industrial hazards.

Development and enforcement of an appropriate technolegal regime is another dimension receiving greater attention. It involves examining and reviewing the existing building bye-laws and codes, the town and country planning acts and development control rules etc., to bring them in tune with disaster risk perceptions and mitigation needs. The enforcement of techno-legal regime and its application during the stages of building permit, supervision, completion certificate, occupancy permit and the annual renewal certificate is being done and efforts are being made to undertake training and capacity building of local bodies.

In addition, the techno-financial regime is also sought to be put into place with the provision that all building constructions by public, private, corporate, co-operative, community, joint and individual sectors receiving funds from any source must adopt techno-financial regime without exception. The financial institutions and banks must insist on disaster-resistant construction and incorporation cf disaster-resistant features as a precondition for providing loans or grants for projects. A provision is also proposed to be made for inspection and periodic audit and renewal certificate to move towards an enhanced and voluntary compliance. Even the fixation of insurance premium is also proposed to be linked to the incorporation of disaster-resistant features at the construction stage itself.

Sustainable Development

To many business executives, the concept of sustainable development and business remain abstract and quite simply do not go together. But the perception is being rapidly reversed and it is now being widely accepted with the recognition of linkages between protecting a corporates capital base and the natural resources. It is becoming an accepted practice to integrate sustainable development into the planning and measurement systems of business enterprises.

Sustainable development for corporates would entail adopting and implementing business approaches which meet the needs of the industry and its stakeholders while at the same time protecting, sustaining and enhancing the human and natural resources for the future. It means that economic development must while satisfying the needs of the enterprise protect the community by ensuring that the natural and human resources are not exploited to their detriment.

There is an umbilical bond between sustainable development and disaster risk management and the business organizations are recognizing it so. Integration of risk management measures has to be an all-pervasive activity by the corporates across the industrial spectrum and must not remain a one-off activity. It would seek minimization of expenditure on rehabilitation and reconstruction to obviate dissipation of precious developmental resources and help interweave a culture of safety and preparedness in every walk of national life and more so in the corporate sector so that the development efforts are both socially safe and commercially viable and sustainable. The need is to bring about a change in perceptions, attitudes, pre-conceived notions and mindsets among the corporate sector about the way the things are approached now. The challenge posed by the issue of sustainable development has been engaging the mind and thought of the international community and the need to achieve equitable and balanced socio-economic development has been acutely felt.

Sustainable development envisions integration of economic and social development with environment protection as interdependent and mutually reinforcing pillars. The overarching objective being to change the existing unsustainable patterns of production and consumption.

The World Summit on Sustainable Development (WSSD) defines sustainable development as "development that meets the needs of the present without compromising the ability of future generations to meet their own needs." The Johannesburg Plan of Implementation has made a fervent plea to the private sector to improve efficiency, alter existing production patterns and consciously move towards sustainable use of natural resources for all-round development.

The *sine qua non* for safe and sustainable development is promotion of corporate social responsibility and accountability, strengthening of public-private-partnerships and continuous attention to improvements in corporate sector practices and processes. For the corporate sector, it is imperative to usher into not only sustainable but also safer development for which harmonization of socio-economic and environment concerns is a must. A multi-hazard approach addressing the disaster management concerns in the corporate sector and the corporates in turn complementing the disaster management endeavors at all levels will ensure a strong and concerted attack on our vulnerabilities.

Green Business Centre

CII has launched a CII-Sohrabji Godrej Green Business Centre in association with the Government of Andhra Pradesh and the Godrej corporate house in March 2000 as a Centre of Excellence for energy efficiency, environment, water conservation and use of recycled products and renewable energy. In addition to making the business profitable, the activities seek to contribute towards sustainable development and a healthy economy. The objective being to make the world a better place to live in by providing world-class 'green' services. The Center is involved in promoting 'green' concepts leading to higher efficiency, equitable growth and sustainable development. In order to achieve the lowest specific energy consumption levels in the world, tools like benchmarking with international norms and identification of ways and means to achieve the same are promoted. It facilitates construction of 'green buildings' *viz.*, a place which is environmentally responsible, profitable and a healthy place to live and work in.

The 'Green Audit' presents an opportunity for better utilization of raw materials, consumables, water, energy at every stage of the manufacturing process. A Technology Centre provides a platform to showcase and demonstrate innovative 'green' products and technologies. The Green Business Incubation entails handholding of entrepreneurs to develop green products/technologies tillthey reach the stage of commercialization.

❋❋❋

13

National Disaster Management Framework

Expected Outputs Areas of intervention Agencies/sectors to be involved and resource linkages. Nodal agency for disaster management at the national level with appropriate systems

(i) Constitution of National Emergency Management Authority with appropriate legal, financial and administrative powers.

(ii) Roles and responsibilities of the NEMA:

- Co-ordinating multihazard mitigation, prevention, preparedness and response programmes.
- Policies for disaster risk reduction and mitigation.
- Preparedness at all levels.
- Co-ordination of response.
- Co-ordination of post-disaster relief and rehabilitation.
- Amendment of existing laws, procedures, instructions.

Ministries/Departments of Health, Water Resources, Environment and Forests, Agriculture, Railways, Atomic

Energy, Defence, Chemicals, Science and Technology, Rural Development, Road Transport and Highways etc.

Creation of State Departments of Disaster Management Departments of Relief and Rehabilitation to be redesignated as Department of Disaster Management with enhanced areas of responsibility to include mitigation, prevention and preparedness State Governments/UT Administration. Setting up State Disaster Management Authorities

(i) State Disaster Management Authority to be headed by the Chief Minister.

(ii) The Authority to lay down policies and monitor mitigation, prevention and preparedness as also oversee response. Ministers for Agriculture, Home, Disaster Management, Water Resources, Health, Road and Transport, Civil Supplies, Environment and Forests, Rural Development, Urban Development and Public Health Engineering Departments as Members.

Disaster Mitigation/Prevention

Disaster mitigation/prevention to be mainstreamed into the development process.

(i) Each Ministry/Department which has a role in mitigation/prevention will make appropriate outlays for schemes addressing mitigation/prevention.

(ii) Wherever possible Ministries/Department of Government. of India/State Governments/UT Administration schemes/projects in areas prone to natural hazards to be so designed as to contribute to mitigation and preparedness.

(iii) Where there is a shelf of projects/schemes, projects/schemes contributing to mitigation to be given a priority.

(iv) Projects in vulnerable areas/areas prone to natural hazards to be designed to withstand natural hazards. Techno-legal regime.

(i) Regular review of building codes and its dissemination.

(ii) Construction in seismic Zones III, IV and V to be as per BIS codes/National Building Codes.

(iii) Construction in areas vulnerable to cyclones to be so designed as to withstand the wind hazard as per BIS codes/National Building Codes.

(iv) Comprehensive review and compliance of :

- Town and Country Planning Acts.
- Development Control Regulations.
- Planning and Building Standards Regulations Bureau of Indian Standards/Ministry of urban Development State Urban Development Department/Urban Local Bodies State Urban Development Department/Urban Local Bodies State Urban Development Department/Urban Local Bodies.

(v) Put in place appropriate technofinancial regime.

(vi) Capacity enhancement of Urban Local Bodies to enforce compliance of technolegal regimes State Urban Development Department/Urban Local Bodies.

State Governments Land-use Planning and Zoning regulations :

(i) Zoning regulations to be enforced. Ministry of Urban Development Department of Land Resources (MORD) Ministry of Environment and Forests (GOI)

State Governments Plan schemes for vulnerability reduction and preparedness. State Governments to formulate Plan Schemes and submit to Planning Commission State Governments

(*ii*) Legal framework for Land-use planning and zoning regulations to be reviewed.

Legal/Policy Framework

Disaster Management to be listed in List—III—(Concurrent List) of Seventh Schedule to the Constitution:

(*i*) Bill to be drafted.

(*ii*) Bill to be brought

before Parliament Ministry of Home Affairs/Ministry of Law (Legislative Department) State Disaster Management Acts Model Act to be circulated to the States. Ministry of Home Affairs State Governments National Policy on Disaster Management :

(*i*) Mandate safe construction.

(*ii*) Mainstreaming disaster management into planning and development process. Ministry of Home Affairs, Ministry of Finance, Planning Commission, Ministry of.

(*iii*) Co-ordinated action by all relevant Departments as per policy.

Environment and Forests, Rural Development, Urban Development and other relevant Ministries to be consulted. States to enunciate Policy on Disaster Management.

(*i*) Mainstreaming disaster management into planning and development process.

(*ii*) Mandate safe construction.

(iii) Co-ordinated action by all relevant Departments as per policy.

State Governments State Disaster Management Codes Amendment of existing relief codes/scarcity codes/famine codes to incorporate mitigation, preparedness and planning measures at all levels from community to State, constitution of Emergency Support Teams/Disaster Management Teams/ Committees/State Disaster Management Authorities, delegation of administrative and financial powers to disaster incident managers etc, protocol to update the inventory of resources and plans, State Governments.

Preparedness and Response

National Emergency Response Force/Specialist Response teams:

(i) Designation of units for conversion into Specialist Response Teams.

(ii) Designation of training centres.

(iii) Training of trainers.

(iv) Procurement of equipment

(v) Training of teams. Ministry of Home Affairs

Central Industrial Security Force/Indo-Tibetan Boarder Police/Border Security Force/Central Reserve Police Force Specialized Response Teams at State level:

(i) Designation of units for conversion into Specialist Response Teams.

(ii) Designation of training centres.

(iii) Training of trainers.

(iv) Procurement of equipment using CRF resources.

(v) Training of teams.

State Department of Disaster Management/State Home Department State Police Training College/State Fire Training Institute.

National Network of Emergency Operation Centers [NNEOCs]

Setting up Emergency Operations Centre (EOC) at National level:

(i) Multi-hazard resistant construction.

(ii) Communication system linkages.

(iii) Mobile EOCs for onsite disaster information management

Central Public Works Department Department for Central Public Works Ministry of Home Affairs State level EOC :

(i) Multi-hazard resistant construction.

(ii) Communication system linkages.

(iii) Mobile EOC for onsite disaster management information

State Governments District level EOC :

(i) Multi-hazard resistant construction.

(ii) Communication system linkages.

State Governments Putting Incident Command System in Place :

(i) Designate nodal training centres.

(ii) Putting in place protocols/SOPs for Incident Command System.

Ministry of Home Affairs/Department of Personal and Training/Lal Bahadur Shastri National Academy of

Administration/State Governments/Administrative Training Institutes Emergency Support Function Plan *(i)* departments/agencies which perform emergency support functions to draw up ESF plans, constitute teams, Central Government Ministries/Departments State Governments and set apart resources in advance so that postdisaster response is prompt.

India Disaster Resource Network

(i) A web enabled GISbased resource inventory listing out all the necessary resources for emergency response available at the district and State level throughout the country so that resources can be mobilized at short notice.

(ii) Set-up servers, draw up and install programmes, input data.

(iii) Half yearly updating Ministry of Home Affairs State Governments.

Communication linkages which will be functional even post-disaster.

(i) Draw up communication plan.

(ii) Obtain sanctions.

(iii) Put communication network in place.

Ministry of Home Affairs Directorate Co-ordination of Police Wireless State Governments Regional Response Centres:

(i) Identify location of Regional Response Centres.

(ii) Obtain sanctions.

(iii) Identify caches of equipment required.

(iv) Put teams and caches of equipments in place.

Ministry of Home Affairs Border Security Force/Indo-Tibetan Border Police/Central Reserve Police Force/Central

Industrial Security Force Training in response to be made a part of training curriculum of CPMFs and State Police Forces.

(i) Draw up capsules.

(ii) Train trainers

Ministry of Home Affairs State Governments State Disaster Management Plans:

(i) Plan to be drafted under the supervision of the Chief Secretary.

(ii) The plan will be multi-disciplinary to be drawn up in conjunction/consultation with all relevant Departments concerned with mitigation, preparedness and response.

(iii) Plan will include mitigation, preparedness and response elements.

(iv) Plan to be updated once a year.

State Governments/State Disaster Management Authorities District Disaster Management Plans:

(i) To be drawn up under the supervision of District Magistrate/Collector and to include mitigation, preparedness and response.

(ii) To be drawn up in consultation with all State Governments/State Disaster Management Authorities relevant Departments.

(iii) Emergency Support Functions by various Departments to be included.

(iv) District inventory of resources to be maintained.

Block Disaster Management Plans:

(i) Emergency Support Functions by various Departments to be included.

(*ii*) To be drawn up under the supervision of District Magistrate/Collector and to include mitigation, preparedness and response.

(*iii*) To be drawn up in consultation with all relevant Departments.

(*iv*) District inventory of resources to be maintained.

State Governments/State Disaster Management Authorities/Block Development Administration Community based mitigation, preparedness and response plans:

(*i*) Enhance community capacity in multi-hazard prone States and districts to respond effectively to disasters-special attention to be given to empowering and capacity building of vulnerable communities and groups including women.

(*ii*) Set-up and train village/Panchayat (for rural areas) and wards/municipal council/corporations (for urban areas) disaster management committees and disaster management teams *e.g.*, Identification of safe shelters and management Stockpiling of relief materials etc., early warning dissemination first-aid and counselling assist in search and rescue.

(*iii*) Such plans to be made integral to annual development plan of local bodies

(*iv*) Mitigation plans of the community and Panchayats to receive priority under various rural development schemes administered by Panchayats and Urban local bodies State Governments/District Administration/ Panchayati Raj Institution/Urban Local Bodies.

Early Warning Systems

(*i*) State of the art sensors to be set-up.

(*ii*) Hazard monitoring, tracking and modelling.

(a) IMD/CWC to carry out a review of sensors available and draw up plans for strengthening the system.

(b) Models to be updated to improve prediction accuracy.

Indian Meteorological Department/Central Water Commission/National Centre for Medium Range Weather Forecasting Warning Protocols:

(i) Warning protocols to be user friendly.

(ii) Warning to be communicated as quickly as possible to the States/districts/community.

(iii) Districts to set-up protocols for communication of early warning to the community.

(iv) Protocols should be simple to understand.

(v) Panchayats/local bodies to be used for early warning communication.

(vi) Communication linkages for early warning.

Ministry of Home Affairs/State Governments/Indian Meteorological Department/Central Water Commission/ National Remote Sensing Agency/Information and Broadcasting/Doordarshan/All India Radio.

Human Resource Development and Capacity Building

Training for services/cadres/agencies involved in mitigation, preparedness or response.

(i) Training needs analysis/Human Resource Development Plan

(ii) Drawing up of capsule courses for Ministry of Home Affairs State Governments training.

(iii) Training of trainers.

(iv) Setting-up/strengthening training institutions in state faculties of Disaster Management in Administrative Training Institutes

(v) National Institute for Disaster Management to be strengthened.

Training of IAS/IPS, State Administrative Service Officers/State Police.

(i) Training curriculum for IAS/IPS and State Administrative Service Officers/State Police Officers to include capsules in disaster management.

(ii) Training of Block/Village level staff.

(iii) Training of PRIs.

Administrative Training Institutes/State Institutes of Rural Development and District Institutes of Education and Training to be used. Engineers/Architects Curriculum for undergraduate engineering and B.Arch courses to be amended to include mitigation technologies in general and elements of earthquake engineering in particular State Governments All India Council for Technical Education Indian Institute of Technologies Professional bodies Health Professionals Include crisis prevention, response and recovery and trauma management in the MBBS curriculum.

Ministry of Health and Family Welfare Medical Council of India Youth organization NCC, NSS, Scouts and Guides to include disaster response, search and rescue in their orientation/training programmes. Ministry of Youth and Sports Ministry of Defence Masons Mason training for safe construction Ministry of Rural Development/Department of Urban Development/State Governments School curriculum To include disaster awareness.

Central and State Boards of Education National mass media campaign for awareness generation Design and develop a communication strategy for awareness campaign Use audio, visual and print medium to implement awareness campaign Development of resource materials on mitigation, preparedness and response.

Ministry of Home Affairs/State Governments Ministry of Home Affairs/State Governments Ministry of Home Affairs Non-government community-based organizations involved in awareness generation and community participation in disaster preparedness and mitigation planning.

(i) Facilitate network of non-Government community based organizations at national/State/district levels.

(ii) Co-opted into the planning process and response mechanisms at all levels.

Corporate sectors involved in awareness generation and disaster preparedness and mitigation planning Sensitisation, training and co-opting corporate sector and their nodal bodies in planning process and response mechanisms

Ministry of Home Affairs/Federation of Indian Industries Inter-state arrangements for sharing of resources during emergencies and lessons learnt :

(i) Arrangements for inter-State sharing of resources to be incorporated in State.

(ii) Inter-state exposure visits to be facilitated for learning from the experiences of other States.

Research and Knowledge Management

Institutionalise knowledge and lessons learnt in the process of working on the national roadmap:

(i) Establish India Disaster Resource Network as knowledge portal to pool and exchange information and knowledge among all concerned institutions and organization.

(ii) Assessment and evaluation of ongoing programmes and activities regular documentation of key lessons.

Ministry of Home Affairs Develop national disasters database :

(i) Systematic inventorization of disasters.

(ii) Trend analysis and reporting.

National Institute for Disaster Management Promote research in national, state and regional institutions in the areas of disaster risk reduction:

(i) Mitigation technologies for housing, roads and bridges, water supply and sewerage systems, power utilities.

(ii) Cost-effective equipments for specialized rapid response and preparedness in-temporary and transition shelter in post-disaster situations Ministries/Departments of Central Government-search and rescue equipments post-trauma stress management and care.

(iii) Promote participation of corporate sector in finding out technological solutions for disaster risk reduction.

❋❋❋

14

Coalition Activities and Disaster

The 2005 hurricane season demonstrated the continued shortcomings of the federal, state and local disaster response efforts. Despite the wake-up call provided by the events of 9/11 and the development of the National Response Plan (NRP) and the National Incident Management System (NIMS) (DHS, 2004a, DHS, 2004b), response agencies from state to federal level were taken by surprise and were unprepared to respond effectively to a mass disaster. The failures of response efforts to hurricane Katrina point to a verity of systemic problems. In particular, the issue of co-ordinated state and local government integration with the US Military continues to prove particularly difficult. Lack of effective disaster management becomes magnified when coalitions made up of civil and military authorities form decoupled command structures, often amplifying co-ordination and communication difficulties rather than improving them.

Several contradictory, almost paradoxical, motivations exist among joint military-civilian coalition members in US disaster response efforts. *First,* complex legal and historical arguments about the involvement of federal troops on domestic soil give rise to conflict between state authorities and federal disaster managers. While the use of federal troops may assist in disaster relief by leveraging the effectiveness of military chain of command and resources, states often view federalization of a disaster as usurping regional control. However, a state's failure to allow military resources to be fully utilized at the outset of a major disaster may have secondary effects that reverberate for the rest of the relief effort, creating a cascade of sub-optimal responses that crippled overall performance.

Second, when joint coalitions are created, ambiguous authority relationships in these rapidly formed *ad hoc* teams disaster managers must follow many masters. They must accept the rules and political interests established by their parent agency, commit to the superordinate goals of the coalition, or struggle to find a balance between these objectives. Effective disaster managers must assert authority and transfer it to other agencies represented in the coalition, often overstepping the powers vested in them by their parent agency. A tense continuum exists, anchored by inaction at one end, modulated appropriate action in the center and overreaction at the other end of the spectrum. *For eaxmple,* overuse of authority assertions may cost the coalition in terms of overall operational awareness as actions begin to deviate too much from initial disaster plans. *Finally,* if the legal and social considerations are worked out, introducing the military into a coalition disaster response team is viewed as a slippery slope in which military command and control styles may dominate the coalition's deliberative process. No model of co-equal participation of civilian and military coalition representatives exists in which command is distributed among all parties, yet remains effective. Further, disaster managers from the various agencies are trained as experts within their fields and may have effective communication and decisioning skills within their respective teams. However, these communication strategies may not be enough to facilitate their work when they become representatives of their parent agency within a complex coalition. While the problem of coalition communication has been preliminarily addressed by Incident Command System/Unified Command (ICS/UC), typical large scale coalitions are made up of peer-to-peer relationships rather than formalized command structures.

DISASTER MANAGEMENT DIFFERS FROM OTHER COALITION ACTIVITIES

Communication Training

While the understanding of large-scale disaster management is based on findings derived from High Reliability Organizations (HROs) and military coalitions, joint civilian-military disaster management coalitions also differ substantially from these groups. *For eaxmple*, HRO organizations are usually made up of teams who have trained regularly together, who share some level of technical interoperability, operate using mutually understood and decisioning rules, employ communication approaches that enhance situational awareness and possess a fairly unified politico-cultural background that is implicitly understood by its team members. Other HROs, such as commercial aviation, cannot reliably put the same team members together for each flight because of operational needs, but have managed to overcome the loss in team cohesion by training all flight crew personnel in a shared approach to flight communication and decision making. In this way, individual pilots, co-pilots and flight attendants function fairly interchangeably across *ad hoc* flight crews.

In contrast, because of the fundamentally unpredictable nature of major disasters, the *ad hoc* teams that emerge during response and recovery often are comprised of individuals who have never trained together as a group, whose organizations use incompatible communication approaches, different decisioning rules, are not co-located and who come from organizations with widely differing (potentially competing) cultures and political interests. Even though individual disaster managers may be competent, overall response effectiveness may be profoundly impaired by communication problems that arise at the coalition level. Efforts to increase the ability of coalition members to communicate have lead to a wide range of technical efforts designed to allow greater information flow between response agencies. However, increasing inter-team communication through technology solutions alone has not improved response performance in disasters.

Time and Leadership

The privileges offered by time in *ad hoc* team development are afforded to even the most complex task environments-aviators, naval command teams and astronauts train until they are adequately prepared for the actual task. However, in disaster management the privilege of time is not available. Coalition members must quickly form teams to address a series of complex, low probability events that have not be adequately addressed by prior planning and training. As a result of not having sufficient time together as a group, problems with conflict, trust, establishing lines of authority, identifying resources and developing a shared mental model of the work often arise. The initial 72 hours following a major disaster is critical to re-establishing order and preventing secondary catastrophic events. Response teams do not have the luxury of getting to know one another socially or having repeated work experiences in which differences in their mental models can be ironed out.

Another factor is the ambiguity leadership relationships in disaster response coalitions. These networks are often comprised of peer-to-peer relationships between officials at fairly equivalent responsibility levels within their respective agencies. No one individual is in a position to establish and exert absolute authority over the group's interactions or the actions that are taken as a result of the group deliberation. This organizational structure has drawbacks that must be minimized (chaotic communication) and benefits that should be capitalized upon (*e.g.*, emergent leadership and flexibility).

Authority Hand-Offs

Because of over-reliance on military models of coalition management, strict authority relationships in coalition disaster management research are over-emphasized. *Ad hoc* teams are not governed by a single individual with vested authority from the outset. Instead, "emergent" leadership may occur, in which one or several people in the group begin to take on authority roles based on past experience, domain knowledge, or personal leadership characteristics.

However, emergent leaders in coalitions still face the problem of authorizing decisions. Typically, the authority to act is not completely vested in the individuals who have the content knowledge or the resources to solve a particular problem. Authority may be vested in several members of a coalition, or it may have to be obtained from other sources in their parent organizations. In these situations, disaster managers often attempt to "flatten" the bureaucratic hierarchy both within their parent organizations and in the coalition itself by asserting authority or "taking charge." These renegotiations of lines of authority are sometime times accomplished easily, *for eaxmple,* where an authority figure agrees that knowledge worker is best suited to make a decision and hands-off authority "gracefully"; or the transition of authority may be contested in "ungraceful" shifts of authority. While the co-location of authority, knowledge and resources is necessary for task execution, there is an inevitable performance trade-off when coalition members take charge. Transfer of authority leads to unplanned actions and allocation of resources that may occur outside the awareness of other members in the coalition. While operational efficiency on single tasks improves, eventually, as increasing numbers of authority hand-offs occur, the overall operational picture becomes blurred.

Problems in Rapidly Formed Disaster Response *ad hoc* Coalitions

A number of problems arise in rapidly formed, flexible *ad hoc* teams that may impede performance. These include socio-emotional factors, interoperability factors and team authority factors.

1. Dominance and Passivity. Socio-emotional problems may arise if team members exhibit high levels of dominance or passivity. In addition to drowning out important expert knowledge, dominance in communication systems results in low stakeholder acceptance of the team's decisions. In contrast, passivity of team members generally results in wider acceptance of decisions by all stakeholders, but the quality of decisioning is lower than in groups with either constructive or aggressive group styles.

2. Mistrust. It has been hypothesized that trust between team members is one of the central factors in developing constructive teams. Trust reduces information withholding, increases cohesion between members and eventually facilitates the development of shared mental models of the task environment. Factors that impede trust include lack of positive leadership, physical distance, unpredictable communication patterns and low-quality, low frequency feedback. Individual perceptions of others' integrity appears to be particularly important in the initial phases of team trust.

3. Interoperability Failure. Problems in technical interoperability factors include lack of uniform naming conventions for assets, resources and procedures that are central to disaster recovery. Additionally, lack of a common decisioning framework (non-technical interoperability) between coalition members necessarily impairs the development of shared mental models that are seen as central to effective co-ordination

4. Ambiguous Authority Relationships. Co-ordination difficulties in coalitions often occur because authority to act, expert knowledge and resources are not co-located in one individual or sub-team within a coalition. Further, attempts to remedy co-ordination problems are often compounded by the inefficient use of rich media communication systems (*e.g.*, teleconferencing and video conferencing) that encourage dominance, passivity and feed into the feeling of pressure to act, even if the ramifications of an action is not considered fully.

Factors Found in High Performance *ad hoc* Teams

While much of the literature on disaster management emphasizes the need for increased communication, more contact between disaster managers alone is not enough to ensure optimal performance. In fact, increasing, unmodulated communication can degrade overall co-ordination efforts. As team size and problem complexity increase, high performance teams must dynamically adapt their structure and communication norms to fit the demands of the task environment. These adaptations can appear to be counterintuitive, but they make sense once understood within the problem framework presented earlier.

- High performance teams engage in efficient communication, not more communication. Efficient communication involves "object oriented" team communication that focuses on semantic richness rather than media richness. Researchers in object oriented communication argue that, "The object-oriented team model shuns tight coupling in favor of a set of independent objects, which **(1)** have standardized or well-defined processes; **(2)** exchange information (inputs and outputs) with other objects through well-defined semantically rich interfaces; and **(3)** produce a decreased flow of information".

- While co-ordinating is important, effective teams also partition duties where possible by vesting authority, knowledge and resources necessary in one individual or small sub-teams thus, minimizing communication overhead. Rapidly establishing co-ordination norms is critical to ensuring effectiveness.

- High performance teams build trust rapidly. Although rich-media or face-to-face communication may be inefficient in many cases, there is convergent evidence supporting the utility of face-to-face interactions between virtual team members at the inception of the project. Initial face-to-face meetings may support the building of trust, conveyance of subtle non-verbal information and reduction in the perception of physical distance in virtual teams. Optimally, teams iterate through phases of rich media supported communication during the beginning phase of the task and equivocal situations (where meaning making based on a large number of alternative interpretations is necessary) and the use of semantically supported communication in uncertain situations (where there is agreement on course of action, but information is lacking) as semantically rich communication also reduces overhead and relieves cognitive load.

- Establishing norms for communication that simultaneously improve trust and decisioning accuracy may be facilitated by positive leadership and feedback. Team members and leaders should articulate short and long-term goals explicitly; expend effort in accurately identifying content knowledge experts within the team; establish and enforce communication and decisioning rules; encourage assertive, non-dominant communication from content knowledge experts and actively articulate and accept politico-cultural differences among team constituents at the outset of the task.

Semantically Rich, Cognitively Ergonomic Decision Communication

Decisioning problems that occur in coalition disaster management include impaired ability to discriminate between important and unimportant situational cues, pressure to make decisions results in reflexive rather than adaptive responses and increased likelihood of making risky decisions because of perceived pressure to act. However, even when explicitly taught, experts may not incorporate improved decisioning strategies into practice. It has been suggested this lack of adherence to new decisioning approaches occurs because innovative strategies do no take into consideration the information processing styles of the individual experts and the context in which actual decisions are made.. Recent efforts to improve decisioning performance focus on improving the cognitive ergonomics of supported decision making. One approach, the SHAPE decisioning model, encourages situational evaluation using simple rules empirically demonstrated to be readily accepted by decision-makers and to improve decisioning ability in complex, high consequence tasks. SHAPE stands for, "scrutinize symptoms, hypothesize solutions, perform modifications and corrections and evaluate results".. We suggest that some of the fundamental techniques of the SHAPE model embody the characteristics of semantically rich communication and that it is sufficiently ergonomic for rapidly formed *ad hoc* teams to adopt "on-the-fly" without prior training.

The SHAPE approach offers experts an iterative decisioning process that views the rejection of a decision and reexamination of the problem as forward movement toward a goal, where this process is generally viewed as time consuming and "moving backwards." Examined from a feedback control perspective, decision-makers not only want to reduce the discrepancy between the current situation and the desired outcome (disaster recovery), but they also monitor progress toward this outcome over time. Processes that are perceived as blocking progress (*e.g.*, reviewing problem symptoms and re-decisioning) lead to a desire to remove the block and reliance on reflexive responses unless the block is reframed and viewed as an important sub-goal associated with progress toward the valued outcome.

SHAPE offers two techniques that may be used by decision-makers across a variety of situations, but that can also be tailored to specific decisioning environments. The indication rule calls for team members to test the proposed decision to see that it meets all of the needs identified in the situation. The contraindication rule evaluates the decision for possible undesirable consequences. If both rules are adequately met, the decision is upheld as sound. If not, further reflection on the problem and possible alternative decisions are needed. These rules also serve as a basis for "object oriented" communication that standardizes communicative inputs and outputs to reduce overall cognitive load on team members.

Social Cognitive Theory Approach

We argue that modeling effective coalition communication and co-ordination techniques during a major disaster event may provide a powerful way of changing the behaviour of disaster managers over the course of the event.

The modeling approach overcomes problems associated with discrepancies in prior training, mental models and organizational biases. By embedding a human model that behaves and encourages others to behave using a core set of communication techniques that improve performance, social modeling may be able to bring order to co-ordination activities "on-the-fly"-in effect harmonizing the activities of all agents involved even though there is no official leader and the group has never trained together before.

Software based moderators for leaderless, *ad hoc* online teams have been suggested, however, some of the power that a human moderator possesses comes from his or her ability to model, provide corrective feedback across a wide range of situations and persuade others about their ability to perform in extreme conditions.

For eaxmple, such an agent might encourage the group to discuss individual expertise, lines of authority and available resources without actually assuming authority over the group. In situations in which the agent and other coalition members had to develop an action plan, the agent might press for alternative view points, simultaneously discouraging dominant and passive social patterns.

Finally, the agent would clearly articulate cognitively ergonomic, semantically rich decisioning rules and processes that are easily grasped by others (*e.g.,* indication and contra-indication rules in SHAPE, viewing the analysis of disconfirming information as forward rather than backward steps).

The goal of introducing a meta-communication agent to support coalition disaster response capitalizes on the emergent leadership paradigm found in *ad hoc* teams, but seeks to train emerging leaders with skills that specifically address the socio-emotional, interoperability and authority ambiguity problems that often cripple response.

DESIGN AND PROCEDURES

Participants

Students in a Homeland Security masters degree program at the US Naval Post-graduate School (NPS) will participate in the simulation as part of a Capstone Exercise requirement.

The participants are mid-career homeland security professionals in homeland defense related positions throughout federal and State Governments. The senior author in this proposal (LEB) is an instructor in the masters program and is funded through NPS to improve the training system.

Current Capstone Exercise

At present, participants are required to develop a disaster response plan for the city of San Luis del Rey, a fictional city in California. Several hazard scenarios are available and students' disaster plans are evaluated against these scenarios. However, a number of drawbacks have been identified with the current Capstone exercise. These include linear, pre-scripted scenarios that do not flexibly respond to students' input; undefined decision points; lack of ability to simulate coalition communication and performance; no automated, passive data collection for later assessment and after-action review; and comparatively low fidelity to actual coalition disaster management performance situations.

Coalition-Level Simulated Work Environment

The next logical step in improving the Capstone Exercise is to develop a Simulated Work Environment (SWE) that addresses the concerns that have been identified with the current table-top model. SWEs have been demonstrated to improve fidelity without the expense and overhead associated with high-fidelity simulators. A research simulation system, the Distributed Dynamic Decision-making simulator (DDD) a commercially available tool set that is used extensively in the US military for A2C2 (Adaptive Architectures for Command and Control) research will be modified for use in a coalition disaster management setting.

The simulator parameters will be changed so that the task environment presents a major disaster facing the city of San Luis del Rey rather than a military exercise. The linux-based simulator has been used in a range of military, commercial and medical studies involving team performance on complex tasks and has been made available to us through Aptima's DDDWeb group with support from the US Navy.

Experiment 1

A task environment in which team members must deal with primary tasks as well as a set of study specific meta-tasks will be presented to teams of 9 participants per trial. Participants will be instructed that they represent a large response agency and are responsible for co-ordinating the agency's efforts with other coalition members. Participants will be told about the political goals of their respective parent organizations and encouraged to both meet the internal goals of the organization and assist with the overall disaster response effort. Each trial will last 90 minutes.

Resources, knowledge and authority will be vested in different team members for several important meta-tasks, requiring team members to discuss lines of authority, identify the best expert in the team and gather information about available resources. Successful completion of meta-tasks will involve "graceful" transfer of authority, resources and expert knowledge to individuals or subgroups within the team. Authority assertions may take place, however, if they are not explicitly recognized by the team member originally vested with authority, the hand-off is considered to be "ungraceful" and results in team performance costs. In order to approximate the institutional politico-cultural pressures faced by disaster managers, individual performance scores which are sensitive to release of authority will be provided to participants during the simulation.

This approach recalls the co-operation vs. defection problem encountered in the prisoner's dilemma, but incorporates this design into a complex system with superordinate goals, allowing for the impact three important disaster management factors to be systematically varied in an ecologically valid context. These factors include the presence of a social model who acts as a moderator, the presence or absence of intra-organizational political costs for coalition members (*i.e.,* political needs of their parent organization) and effects of face-to-face meetings at the inception of the task.

In the "peer" moderated condition a confederate trained in the concepts of emergent leadership, coalition communication strategies, decision support and authority transfer models these behaviours while working as a coalition team member. The interactions of the moderator will change over the course of the experiment and are categorized into three communication modeling phases that take place over successive 30 minute segments while the simulation is running, embodying the social learning techniques suggested by Wood and Bandura. Finally, the third factor, involving a face-to-face team building exercise will be used to evaluate the relative merits of developing initial "swift trust" versus embedded "on-the-fly" communication modeling.

Experiment 2

The second experiment follows the same basic format as the first, but instead of a confederate, the design uses participants "infected" by the social model in prior trials with teams composed of new participants. Adoption and usage of modeled co-ordination skills will be evaluated by semantic analysis of communications coming from the "infected" agent.

Phased Modeling Intervention

A phased modeling intervention will be used in which a confederate moderator first displays and then begins to enforce communication, decisioning and authority rules that are hypothesized to improve coalition performance.

- Phase 1 (0-30 minutes). Moderator displays appropriate communication strategies (subtly discourages dominance and passivity, attempts to resolve conflict, suggests reductions in information broadcasting in favor of "selective push"), displays indication and contraindication rule strategies in communications with others and graceful authority hand-offs.
- Phase 2 (31-60 minutes). Moderator enforces appropriate communication strategies through correction of peer-to-peer communications directed toward the moderator if they are dominant or passive, enforces SHAPE decisioning rules when the moderator is impacted by the decision and punishes when peers fail to gracefully vest authority in the moderator when needed (*i.e.*, team member delays, does not recognize, or fails to confirm authority assertion).
- Phase 3 (61-90 minutes). Moderator monitors group communications and points out relationship between effective communication and improved team performance, using motivational techniques.

Coalition Performance Dependent Variables

Dependent variables include individual performance scores (*i.e.*, initial good standing with home organization minus costs associated with vesting authority in other team members) and overall team performance scores, based on three key coalition performance metrics: Assessment accuracy (time required to accurately identify locations of authority, content expertise and necessary resources); Adaptability (time required to vest authority, resources and knowledge in one person or sub-team); and Anticipation (anticipation ratio, implicit anticipation).

Psychological Performance Predictors

While much of the emphasis in optimal disaster response has been placed on creating increased technical interoperability, improving equipment available to first responders and formalizing procedures, it is clear that these are necessary but not sufficient efforts to improve performance. Effective management of large-scale, high-consequence events is also controlled by complex psychological, social and political phenomena. To date, individual psychosocial behaviour factors in organizational performance have focused largely on cognitive and emotion factors. We suggest that personality and integrative complexity factors may also play a significant role in optimal disaster management. Further, these characteristics may play a role in individual coalition members' willingness to adopt modeled co-ordination styles and predict the use of these styles in future un-moderated disaster management situations. Participants will complete the NEO-PI-R personality questionnaire and an integrative complexity task. These measures will be used on an exploratory basis to identify personality characteristics that are predictive of emergent leadership qualities and inclination toward accepting and integrating modeled communication strategies.

✸✸✸

Index

F

G

Other Books on

TEXT BOOKS

45. New Comparative Government **(Revised Edition)**	295/-
Advanced Study in the History of Modern India	
46. (Volume-1: 1707-1813)	225/-
47. (Volume-2: 1813-1920)	325/-
48. (Volume-3: 1920-1947)	175/-
49. Handbook of Nutrition & Dietetics	250/-
50. Development of Education in India	195/-
51. A Text Book of Environmental Studies	195/-
52. Teaching of History	175/-
53. Administrative Thinkers	195/-
54. Research Methodology	175/-
55. Curriculum Development	195/-
56. Teaching of Science	175/-
57. Teaching of Mathematics	175/-
58. Principles of Educational & Vocational Guidance	195/-
59. Child Psychology	175/-
60. Abnormal Psychology	175/-
61. Indian Education in Emerging Society	195/-
62. Human Resource Management	175/-
63. Higher Education and Global Challenges	175/-
64. Teaching of Geography	175/-
65. Teaching of Social Studies	175/-
66. Teaching of English	175/-
67. Education for All The Indian Saga	175/-
68. Value Education in Global Perspective	195/-
69. Teacher Training	175/-
70. Public Administration	175/-
71. Public Relations & Integrated Communications	195/-
72. Educational Psychology	175/-
73. Introduction to Educational Technology	175/-
74. Textbook of Food and Nutrition	175/-

Unit No. 220, Second Floor, 4735/22,
Prakash Deep Building, Ansari Road, Darya Ganj,
New Delhi - 110002, Ph.: 32903912, 23280047, 09811594448
E-mail: lotus_press@sify.com, www.lotuspress.co.in